FOUR PATTERNS OF REVOLUTION

FOUR
PATTERNS *of* REVOLUTION

COMMUNIST U.S.S.R.
FASCIST ITALY
NAZI GERMANY
NEW DEAL AMERICA

BY

ETHAN THEODORE COLTON

Essay Index Reprint Series

BOOKS FOR LIBRARIES PRESS
FREEPORT, NEW YORK

First Published 1935

Reprinted 1970

INTERNATIONAL STANDARD BOOK NUMBER:
0-8369-1747-2

LIBRARY OF CONGRESS CATALOG CARD NUMBER:
79-121456

PRINTED IN THE UNITED STATES OF AMERICA

"Civilization has struck its tents and
the caravan of humanity is on the
march."
—GENERAL JAN CHRISTIAN SMUTS.

CONTENTS

vii

FOREWORD

EVERYWHERE masses of common men move in the direction of securing for themselves a larger share of the material goods of life. Among informed people, few remain with doubts about their getting it. Those of good-will not only welcome the prospect of the plain man having a better chance at life: they are prepared to help him secure it. What concerns such men and women is how the result can best be reached.

The number multiplies, too, of those to whom it has become clear that they themselves have a stake in the outcome. These also wish to act upon knowledge. The total situation leaves room for none of us wisely to remain mere spectators of what is going on.

The questions I have met with in lecturing the past two years to all types of American audiences disclose lively and wholesome but generally unsatisfied interest as to how other nations are proceeding to make their political, economic, and social order better serve the peoples' needs. The stresses and changes being experienced in the United States in working relations and in living conditions lead to such inquiries as "Where are we going?" "What are we to do?"

We have been told by one group or another that America is or ought to be headed for Socialism; or is being steered at Washington by secret believers in the Soviet system; or is ripe for a Fascist dictatorship. The reactions have a range equally wide—from dark fears some entertain over this or that "menace" to ardent faith others have in one or another movement as the way of deliverance. There is eagerness to learn whether others may not be moving toward solutions of the issues that so press upon mankind universally in our time. The many who inquire are confused and want earnestly to know what the Russians, Italians, or Germans have to teach us to do or not to do.

Four Patterns of Revolution undertakes to present what Stalin, Mussolini, Hitler, and Roosevelt and their parties are doing for, with, and to the populations they govern; and in doing so to show wherein they are comparable and contrasting in objectives, principles, methods, and results. The studies present only the essentials of programs: those who wish to pursue them farther will find a bibliography directing them to the sources. The purpose has been to describe and interpret rather than to argue and pass judgment.

The accounts deal only with the more determining features of national policy and of public interest, and in this order: Origins and Objectives; Power and Party; Economic Theory and Structure; Labor; Agriculture; Education; Family, Women and Youth; Social Welfare and Protection; Religion; Nationalism and Militarization; International Relations.

Part IV presents the New Deal against the background of the Communist, Fascist, and Nationalist revolutionary types. The treatment should serve to make clearer the likenesses and differences in the four situations. It should further help in estimating the degree to which the New Deal is proceeding as revolution; and, finally, afford some factual basis for judging to what extent it may or may not be desirable for us to go in any of the directions pioneered by the others.

It is hoped that the study will render a service be-

yond the satisfaction of intellectual curiosity. No
preceding generation of Americans have found themselves caught in a comparable maze of issues. These
make up a political-economic-social complex bearing
upon every individual and upon all of life. Taken
together, they have most of us confused, yet they seem
inseparable. And in time, we shall have to choose
and act.

To name a few of the majors only in the system
in which we work to live: How much do we want, or
must we have, of the profit motive; of competition;
of trustification; of price fixing; of government ownership, operation, or control? Shall we take the way
of labor unionization, collective bargaining, the decent living-wage level, protection of women and children, full industrial democracy and social insurance?
What are the proper shares of Industry, Agriculture,
Exchange, Finance, and the Professions in the national income? What place in our foreign trade
policy shall we give to tariffs, quotas, embargoes, diplomacy, cruisers, planes, tanks, and guns? By whom
shall our lives be channeled—by ourselves, by a majority, by an armed minority, by blocs, by a bureaucracy, or by a dictator?

In the nature of our cultural inheritance, the presumption is that the new paths should be charted collectively either by common action or consent. Net
results, even in the most radical of undertakings,
point to the wisdom of that way for us. A few leaders
may seize the flag in a crisis to dash out impetuously
in advance of the social body, only to be drawn back
to reality to advance at the more glacierlike pace of
the masses.

It remains to the individual, none the less, to
choose, at the present stage, his own approach and

method of procedure. He will not know where he
is going, nor how, until both are determined. The
reader, then, faces two personal decisions as he threads
his way through these patterns of action. First, is
he to think and act only in the interest of himself
and his own, or of his class, or of his nation strictly
delimited, or of the world of mankind? Second, is
he committed to having others *led* to go his way, or
will he consent to have them taken by force if necessary? It is ventured that the American people have
more at stake in the answers to those two questions
than to all others put together: they will be deciding
whether or not to go on with faith in themselves and
in democratic processes.

The Honorable Frederick M. Davenport, in addressing the United States Chamber of Commerce
in May, 1934, on the issue of democratic self-govern-
ment before us today, recalled a saying of Fisher
Ames, a staunch old Yankee Federalist of one hundred years ago.

"Autocracy," said Ames, "is like a merchantman.
She sails out of the harbor with pennants flying, in
security and elation. But by and by she strikes a
reef and down she goes. Democracy is like a raft.
You never sink, but, damn it, your feet are always in
the water."

One result of the contacts, studies and experiences,
of which the pages to follow are a report, has been
to leave this observer a more contented occupant of
the raft.

Very material indebtednesses are gratefully acknowledged to a wide circle who have given assistance. Essential aid came through access to private
and public libraries, newspaper offices and files, and

government archives in the countries concerned. Many home and foreign friends have supplemented my personal observations and experiences by their insight and faithful correctives. The publishers of other authors quoted uniformly extended the courtesy of permission to use the portions desired. Especially liberal debts were incurred in respect to the following works, outstanding in their field: *Leninism,* by Stalin (International Publishers Company, New York); *Universal Aspects of Fascism,* by Barnes (Williams and Norgate, London); *Through Fascism to World Power,* by Munro (Alexander Maclehose and Company, London); *My Battle,* by Hitler (Houghton Mifflin and Company, Boston).

There remain to be cited for greatly appreciated service the devoted secretarial assistants without whose interest and cheerful toil the work could not have been completed. Finally, the form and style of the volume owe much to the editorial criticism of my faithful friend and one-time colleague, S. M. Keeny.

PART I
COMMUNIST U.S.S.R.

SUCCESSORS OF THE CZARS

REVOLUTION overtook and destroyed the imperial régime in Russia because that régime was too little concerned with the well-being of the masses of its subjects. A record of failures generation by generation left the old order with diminished justification for its existence, and with fewer friends for its support. The strains of the World War racked the weakened structure to ruin.

Undermining work had been going on for decades at the hands of growing parties. Strongest numerically were the Socialist Revolutionaries, with Right and Left wings. They were led mainly by intellectuals. They won their largest following on a "land to the peasants" policy. The rest of the program read moderately Socialist. An election that clearly showed their popular strength was the one held in 1918 for members of the ill-fated Constituent Assembly, which returned them almost exclusively. They were the principal support of the Provisional Government, which took over power from the Czar in March, 1917. After they took power they continued their former policy of supporting Russia's part in the war. Indeed, fidelity to the Allies hastened, if it did not bring about, the downfall of their government in October, 1917 (Old Style), when the Revolution passed into the Bolshevik phase.

Parallel with the Socialist Revolutionary process among the peasants, the much smaller Social Democratic Party of Labor was leading the industrial centers to revolt. They made their popular issue "the factories to the workers."

All this was dangerous business for all who took part. Like the Socialist Revolutionaries out among the peasants, they paid for their temerity with floggings, imprisonment, exile, and death. In 1903, this party of the workers had split apart in a division forced by Nicolai Ulianov (Lenin) at a party meeting of exiles in London. The two factions by usage came to be known as Bolsheviks and Mensheviks. They were equally against the Autocracy, and for the general program of Socialism. They differed on method. The Bolsheviks, under Lenin's lead, stood for a small, trusted body, steeled to more than military discipline. They scorned all democratic processes as futile. They agitated for violent seizure of the governing power, the smashing of the existing apparatus of the State, and the establishment in its place of completely dictatorial power in the name of the proletariat for the stern ends that have been pursued since they came to power in October, 1917.

The fall of Nicholas II and the Throne brought on an immediate contest for power, with the Bolsheviks and Left Socialist Revolutionary allies against the Socialist Revolutionaries of the Right and the Mensheviks. Represented in the first Provisional Government Cabinet and making common cause against the Bolsheviks were the Constitutional Democrats (the non-Socialist élite of Russian intellectuals). Their revolutionary program had never extended beyond demand for political reforms. Many of them would have preferred a limited monarchy to a straight republic.

The struggle was a short one as great events run. Lenin's better knowledge of the Russian masses and the resulting superior strategy quite confounded his opponents. He announced a platform that, in its appeal, went far beyond his original working class constituency. His promise of immediate "Peace, Bread, and Land" cut the ground from under the feet of the Socialist Revolutionaries. The Russian peasant masses had never grasped what the war was about. They only knew it took the boys away. On occasions, out-bound troop trains were delayed in the home stations by women throwing themselves on the tracks ahead. Later, sale of the family's one horse might be enforced for the Army and often the cow. The seasoned Russian armies by 1917 were in graves, hospitals, or prison camps. The lines were held by untrained ill-equipped recruits who knew they were helpless before the enemy whenever he chose to move forward. And this the enemy knew.

The great cities had known breadlines for two years. Waiting outdoors in Russian winters for food had made the winning of Constantinople lose any lure it ever had for simple folks. Lenin told them the railroads could not transport men for the front and at the same time feed and clothe the population in the cities. This was the truth.

Then there was the land. For centuries hunger for it had been the peasants' passion. They had been told that they would have all the land when the Revolution came. The Revolution had come but their Socialist Revolutionary leaders, now in control of the Provisional Government, were saying, "Wait. You shall have the land, only the distribution must be orderly after we make a Constitution, have an Assembly, and legislate about it." Lenin said, "Those are the same old promises. They are fooling you. There is the land. Take it." Once the peasants had the land, who held the power and what they would do with it were secondary matters. So by consent or default, Lenin and the Bolsheviks had their way. The rule of the moderate, democratic, Socialist forces came to an end after striving with scant success from March to October, 1917, to save the substance of Russian society from dissolution. Lenin's demand for "All power to the Soviets" (of Workers', Peasants', and Soldiers' Deputies) prevailed.

The Lenin Bolsheviks who thus seized power will be denoted from this point on as Communists—members of the All-Union Communist Party of Bolsheviks (V.K.P. according to the Russian initialing).

The beginning of understanding them is not to confuse them with buccaneers run amuck, and out simply to despoil the rest of society of their rights and property. They have a complete philosophy of life and of human society. Their technique of procedure is definite and detailed. They are sincere—the real ones—beyond question. It is inconceivable that men and women will go through what they endure, and enforce what they do upon a whole population except by complete faith in their cause and in the soundness of their method.

Sincere about what? Sincere in the purpose to give the masses of the people a better chance at life, beginning with the industrial workers as a matter of tactics. Dying for the cause and causing millions to perish for its realization are details that have no deterrent influence. In fact, the entire Communist strategy is cast in the terms of war. Nor is paper war meant, but literal fighting—guns and killing. Basic in their forthright thinking and action are these passages from the authoritative *A B C of Communism:*

"The class war arises out of the conflict of interests between the bourgeoisie and the proletariat. These interests are as essentially irreconcilable as are the respective interests of wolves and sheep."[1]

"Sooner or later, notwithstanding all the wiles of the bourgeoisie, the workers will come into violent collision with the master class, will dethrone it, will destroy its robber government, and will create for themselves a new order, a Communist order of labor."[2]

The bourgeois "wolves" of the Communists are the owning and managing people in the system for carrying on the production and distribution of goods. Men and women engaged as factory hands and manual laborers are the proletarian "sheep." The professional lawyers, journalists, educators, and clergy in capitalist society are classed along with the bourgeoisie. Supported by the system, the professionals will support it, runs the theory of economic determinism. Well-to-do peasants also are warred against; the others are left rather on the side lines in the early stages in the hope they will at least remain neutral. In Russia, Lenin managed them well. The petty bourgeoisie—shopkeepers, small office holders, and crafts-people—are pigeonholed as "a motley crowd," really held in contempt for adhering generally to the big bourgeoisie, and afraid to fight in their own supposed interest.

In contradistinction to the organized parties of Labor and of other interests in the world at large, the

[1] P. 63.　　　[2] P. 65.

Communist Party in Russia, as elsewhere, refused to work within the framework of the new democratic State they found being established. The Communist position is that the parliamentary form of State lends itself to domination by the owning class, and that in experience it actually becomes so. In such a case, the State no longer serves as the just arbiter between conflicting social and economic interests but is the tool of the exploiting class. Accordingly, the first march of the embattled workers must be against any government in power not exclusively their own.

Lenin called on his Party not to make over the old apparatus of government but to break it up "until not one stone is left standing upon another." In his work, *Leninism*,[3] Stalin has made clear the application of the principle:

"The bourgeois revolution, being no more than the replacement of one group of exploiters by another in the seat of power, has no need to destroy the old State machine; but the proletarian revolution means that the groups of exploiters one and all have been excluded from power, and that the leaders of all the workers, the leaders of all the exploited, the leaders of the proletarian class, have come to occupy the seat of power, and they therefore have no option but to destroy the old State machine and to replace it by a new one." In Soviet Russia the Communist Party has achieved just that.

WHERE POWER RESIDES

The Communist State is a pyramid erected upon a foundation of local occupational soviets (councils).

[3] International Publishers Company, New York, p. 21.

The voter is recognized where he works, not where he lives. The franchise is granted broadly to both sexes at the age of eighteen. Specifically, it was denied to several classes, regarded either as beneath citizenship or dangerous if given the exercise of it. Politically outcast until 1934 were all persons engaged in private trade (except peasants with their produce under fixed conditions); employers of other persons for private profit; survivors of the aggressive "enemy" classes; the clergy and other professional religious workers; those who forfeited citizenship by crime; and the usual categories of mental incompetents. Peasants resisting farm collectivization later came into the discard. By recent action, members of certain of the disfranchised groups can be reinstated if for five years preceding they have done "socially useful work."

To see the elective scheme in action, let us imagine it to be election time in Leningrad, with its population of 2,500,000. Let it be assumed that for the soviet which legislates for Leningrad locally, the unit of representation will be about 5,000 voters. If the Red Putilov Iron Works of the city employs 20,000 adults, four seats in the local soviet go to that plant. A Leningrad garrison of 15,000 soldiers will elect members to three seats. The faculties of the teeming higher schools and universities will belong to a union of their own with thousands of members and have their share of seats. Likewise the cab-drivers, plumbers, and cooks will be represented through their respective unions. In contrast to their pickings in an American legislative body, this system of soviets leaves lawyers a mere crust.

Communist partisans thrive on the system. When the Red Putilov ironworkers assemble in mass meeting to elect their members, a chairman from the Party presents a slate made up by the Party Committee of the plant. He reads the four names and asks all opposed to raise their hands. None are raised. The slate carries through. Opposition would put a worker's job in jeopardy.

The individual voter has finished now with choosing his governors, for the local soviet elects the members of the soviet of the next higher political unit. This higher soviet elects the members to its superior body. So the pyramid of power rises. On the bottom level will be non-party people, a majority possibly; but as the structure rises they become fewer in proportion. Before the high places of power are reached, they will have become negligible.

In any case a Party minority rules as completely as if it were a majority. The Party "fraction" is always right. They know "the Party line" on every item and lay it down. The others assent whether with or without inward consent. Not one of the political bodies from local soviet to the All-Union Congress is in any real sense deliberative. They do not even approach that description. They simply rubber stamp measures framed by the executive machine, which is still more strictly hand-picked out of the Party. It is the Party's will always in action on the spot. The "dictatorship of the proletariat" then has been set up, to be used "as a lever for the transformation of the old economy and for the organization of a new one." [4]   To check the peasants' numerical strength in national affairs, the Party has provided that it should take five times as many of them as of proletarians to make up a unit of representation.

When it seized the Russian Government, the Com-

[4] *Leninism,* p. 20.

munist Party numbered about 100,000. On the fall
of the Czarist power in March, 1917, the members
of this body emerged and foregathered from the se-
crecy of their haunts, and from the exile spaces of
Siberia and the four corners of the earth. The liberal Kerensky, practicing political idealism in the
name of free Russia, put up no barriers until the authority of the Provisional Government had been well
undermined. Then resistance was too late. To help
bedevil an enemy power in wartime, Germany provided the services of Lenin by giving him safe conduct in a locked railroad car between the Swiss and
Russian borders. Trotzky emerged from New York.
Together, they and the other comrades rocked the
army, the factories, and the populace with agitation that the inexperienced moderates in the Government could not withstand. The Cabinet stood
by helpless as the resourceful revolutionary extremists dug the grave of Russian democratic hopes.

The Party now has over 2,000,000 members including candidates. To join is difficult. Exit is
easier. Periodic "cleanings" cast out disappointing
material by tens of thousands. The winter of 1932-3
saw one of them that reduced the roster 15 to 25 per
cent, varying with the sections of the country. The
most thorough winnowing was in the Ukraine and
North Caucasus (for leniency toward the peasants
instead of enforcing on them good collective farming and grain deliveries).

No other Party can have legal existence in the
Soviet Union. A Party Congress, that meets every
two or three years for a few days, elects and con-
fers full powers on a Central Committee of about
seventy persons and a smaller number of alternates.
Within the Central Committee is set up the Political

Bureau of ten men and some alternates. This inner
circle is the throttle that starts or stops the actions of
168,000,000 people under Soviet jurisdiction spread
across one-sixth of the world's land surface.

If it be asked how less than 2 per cent in a land
rules with hand of iron the other 98 per cent, answers
are at hand. It is a people with a heavy strain of pas-
sivity in the masses. They are without political experience—used to obeying. They dwell over wide
spaces with all the mechanical means of communication in the hands of the rulers—railroads, the relatively little motor transport, the mails, telegraph,
telephone, and air services, the radio and press. An
espionage system so penetrates society that little assurance remains even to family confidences. This
has headed up in a State Political Administration
(O.G.P.U.), the skill and ruthlessness of which are
surpassed in degree only by its omnipresence. Long
ago it broke the heart of all resistance. Under the
guise of being dissolved and superseded the force has
been reshuffled and absorbed into the People's Commissariat of Internal Affairs. Its power to execute
without trial has been suspended. The summary
executions that followed the assassination of the powerful Kirov in December, 1934, demonstrated that the
ability to get wide and speedy punitive results has not
been impaired.

A network of civil organizations, directed by the
Party, stretches lengthwise and across the land. One
or more strands reach every community. The Trade
Unions, 21,000,000 strong, leave no industry discon-
nected. An Aviation, Chemical, and Defence League
has 12,000,000 members in local units planted over
the map. A Society of the Militant Godless enlists
4,500,000 in thousands of groups, bent on putting re-

ligion out of business in every city, town, village, collective farm, and home.   Not far from 7,500,000
League of Communist Youth members (*Comso-
mols*) and Pioneers constitute the shock-troops of
Youth and Childhood near and far.   From the center out to the smallest unit on the remotest frontier,
Party members are in command and on guard.   One
is a majority over any odds.

The significance of all this for power lies first in
the intelligence system the network affords.   No unfriendly act or word in any unit need escape registry
and transmittal down the line to headquarters.   No
suggestion of revolt can get on foot.   Punishments
for "unconscious counter-revolution" are on the records.   More constructively, here is a nerve system to
communicate and execute the will of the Political
Bureau brain out to the last cell of the Nation's
body.   It is absolutely masterful—a demonstration in
the science of centralized power that has never been
surpassed.

Stalin, as Party General Secretary, virtual dictator
of the Soviet Union, made no idle profession in declaring to the Party Conference of January, 1933:

"When it is a question of the responsibility and
the degree of blame, the responsibility falls wholly
and entirely upon the Communists, and we are to
blame for everything—we Communists alone. . . .
There is not and never was in all the world such a
strong authoritative power as the Soviet Power.
There is not and never has been such a powerful and
authoritative Party as our Party, the Communist
Party."   In *Leninism,*[5] Stalin states what he says may
be considered "the supreme expression of the guiding function of our Party": "In the Soviet Union, in

[5] P. 33.

the land where the dictatorship of the proletariat is in force, no important political or organization problem is ever decided by our soviets and other mass organizations without directives from the Party."

Usually the Party lets the Government go through the motions of legislation. In matters of special moment, the Central Committee of the Party associates itself with the Central Executive Committee of the State in proclaiming the law to give it the maximum of sanction. But again, the Party may take the short cut and alone lay down regulations of prime importance carrying full authority. It is immaterial through which organ the Power speaks. In either case the same men act and with them is lodged not only the lawmaking mandate but the executive and judicial as well.

A particularly effective way to get the Party will carried out is that of paralleling the Government's machinery with a piece of Party apparatus. This has worked so well in the army that a "political section" has been built into the Agricultural Administration based on the machine tractor stations, reporting directly to the Party. An organization of 23,000 Communists was set up for the job. More recently, with a persistent lag in transportation slowing down the whole economic development, such a Party section has been attached to that Administration as accelerator. In no small degree, these sections present the new face of the O.G.P.U.

The two crowning instruments of control for the whole of Soviet life were devised and installed by the Party Congress of January, 1934. Stalin called it "tightening up supervision of fulfilment of decisions." One is a Commission of Soviet Control of the Council of People's Commissars (Federal Cabi-

net) of the U.S.S.R. This Commission works under
the instructions of the Cabinet and has its direct representatives in the districts. They are independent of
the local authorities. The Party Congress nominates
the members of the Commission. The Cabinet and
Central Executive Committee of the Government
"endorse" them. They are empowered "to take proceedings against any responsible worker."

The other and superior organ is a Commission of
Party Control of the Central Committee of the All-
Union Communist Party. It works on the instructions of the Party and of its Central Committee, having also its direct agents in the districts, independent
of the local Party organizations. The General Secretary commented on it significantly: "It goes without saying that such a responsible organization must
wield great authority. And in order that it may
wield sufficient authority, and in order that it may be
able to proceed against any responsible worker, including members of the Central Committee, . . .
the members of this Commission must be elected and
dismissed only by the supreme organ of the Party,
namely, the Party Congress." This means that no
human being in the Soviet Union is beyond its reach.

REALISTIC PLANNED ECONOMY

The Communist economic order begins with "nationalization" of all properties related to production
and distribution. This sweeps into State ownership
all land, mines, forests, major industries, banks, railroads, and shipping. With so much momentum, the
nationalizing process in the U.S.S.R. went on to take
over all substantial urban housing, personal bank

accounts and safety deposit box contents. Declaring invalid all existing securities whether commercial or governmental—those held abroad as well as at home —practically finished the institution of private property.

The "factories-to-the-workers" stage of production soon came to grief and abandonment. It brought the output of the industries down almost to nil and the people to destitution. As an escape, Lenin laid down the New Economic Policy (NEP) in 1921. It was meant to administer oxygen to what had survived of the private system, and to use it to sustain the city population until another Socialistic approach could be devised and executed.

The NEP released private trade and small manufacturers from the prohibitions of militant Communism. Also, and more important for the people, the peasants with their products were given direct access to the consumer market. Life in the cities slowly recovered to a more tolerable level. But it was not sufficiently after the pattern of the collective society of Communism to be safe. Credit withdrawals and death-dealing taxation were therefore applied to any private industry or trade making real headway. Progressively, purely State enterprises and State-controlled Coöperatives occupied the field. Policies touching the peasants vacillated between measured freedom of market and grain requisitioning by force.

The year 1927 saw the Party launch the notable Five Year Plan. Several purposes were behind it. One aim reached well up toward full economic collectivism. Fully realized, this would mean directing the productive capacity and energies of all Soviet subjects, gathering all they produced under social control and redistributing it to them under conditions that determine in effect how much each can receive and what he can do with his portion. It took a long step forward along Lenin's pathway of "all citizens becoming hired employes of the State."

Great emphasis was placed upon industrialization of the country. Enormous sums have gone into new giant State-owned and operated enterprises to multiply production in iron and other metals, coal, oil, electric power, chemicals, textiles, machinery of all types, processed foods, and many other goods essential to a population's existence. The high goals set called not only for industrial construction and the rehabilitation of old plants but also for production within the period of the Plan.

The five years originally set for accomplishment were later shortened to four years and three months. In that time the construction program was substantially carried out, and the planned quantity of goods produced. There were arrears in the heavy metals, coal, and transport, but with offsetting overages in oil, lumber, and other products. The measure of performance in volume was placed officially at 93.7 per cent. The list of achievements in construction is impressive. Most satisfaction appears to be taken in the hydro-electric power station on the Dnieper; the Turkestan-Siberian railroad; the four automotive plants in Stalingrad, Moscow, Gorkii (Nizhni Novgorod) and Cheliabinsk; the iron and steel mills of the Magnitogorsk and Kusnetz regions; and now the Moscow subway under construction on an initial plan for 80.3 kilometers.

The following table of mounting industrial production in the U.S.S.R., in contrast to declines in the United States, England, Germany, and France since 1929, was shown to the 1933 Party Congress. It con-

notes impressive gains in volume over the low levels
from which the rise began.

VOLUME OF INDUSTRIAL PRODUCTION
(Per cent of pre-war level)

	1913	1929	1930	1931	1932	1933
U.S.S.R.	100	194.3	252.1	314.7	359.0	391.9
U.S.A.	100	170.2	137.3	115.9	91.4	110.2
England	100	99.1	91.5	83.0	82.5	85.2
Germany	100	113.0	99.8	81.0	67.6	75.4
France	100	139.0	140.0	124.0	96.1	107.6

Grave defects in quality and high costs of production marred the achievement in part—conditions inevitable with a tempo of expansion and technical advance far beyond the experience and training of ad-
ministrators, engineers, or mechanics at hand. Literally millions of the rawest recruits had to be taken
from their flocks and primitive plows to man the new
industry—often in some of the largest modern mills
of the machine age.

The progressive record of the great Stalingrad
Tractor plant may be cited both for difficulties met
and a successful attack on them. In May, 1931, this
plan had upwards of 15,000 on the payroll. Of
these, 80% had less than one year's experience
in any form of industrial production, nearly one-half
less than six months of it. Wastes of wartime magnitude prevailed. Early in 1931 according to the
official Party paper,[6] there were 1,196 tons of grey
castings spoiled and only 1,586 that passed inspection.
Spoiled malleable iron castings amounted to two and
a half times the good ones. In July of the same year,
90% of the fly-wheels produced were defective. Yet

6 *Pravda*, April 18-19, 1931.

before three years had passed, enough will power and intelligence had been exerted to bring production up to capacity and to turn out the 100,000th tractor at a unit cost reduced from 20,000 rubles to 3,150.

The mechanics of production, then, do not appear to be beyond solution. There is a vast amount of training on the job. During the years of the first Five Year Plan, the number of industrial workmen in night schools increased ninefold and factory apprentices five times. Technicians and engineers to the number of 580,000 passed through the higher educational institutions of the Union—a threefold increase. This brought the number of engineers per hundred workmen up from fewer than four to seven.

To be sure troubles are not done with, even at Stalingrad. In August of 1933, *Economic Life* deplored the conditions there that kept costs from being lowered. The foundry had 10¾% of rejects. Machine stoppage in the forging shop accounted for 30% of the time. In the repair shop the cost of a common bolt ran up to twenty rubles; an ordinary wood turning to twenty-six. The organ of industry [7] reported excesses of wastage well into the year 1934, and implied much left to be desired before there should be produced "a satisfactory, long-lived machine." The present one is guaranteed for nine months in one agricultural season, all defective parts to be replaced.

There is, however, no tendency to despair or to rest after partial gains. In reporting to the XVII Party Congress (1934), Stalin listed as still among the principal defects to be corrected in industry "a totally intolerable attitude toward the question of improving the quality of production"; and "continued lag in the increase of the productivity of labor,

[7] *For Industrialization*, April 11, 1934.

in the reduction of cost of production, and the establishment of cost accounting." He was moved to this language no doubt by such bad performance as that of the cotton mills in the first eight months of the year before. They had met their quota by putting out 1,600,000,000 meters of cloth, but 350,000,-000 meters of it were worthless and another 100,000,-000 meters were lost through bad handling of materials and other causes. Instead of the cost being lowered 1.2% it went up 4.9%. The country still could not produce the goods urgently needed by the population.

Poor dyes and dyeing led to colors that faded and ran.[8] The humorous periodical *Crocodile* earlier had described "a rainbow of breeches" after a workman at a conference to consider consumers' problems demonstrated one by exhibiting pants with one leg grey, the other dark blue. The reporter went on: "To make their beauty greater the firm had stamped them with oil paint 'spoilt.' Yet this does not prevent them being sent to Rostov workmen." Finally, "the Labor artel managed to pack 1,200 such suits into boxes that had contained lime." *Pravda,*[9] at the end of 1933, declared "no mercy for the spoilers" at the head of a report giving cotton spoilage running at the average of 23%, glass 20%, porcelain 15%, boots and shoes "seconds" from 15 to 40% (in the Ukraine over 50%).

A third area of shortcoming pointed out in the Stalin report deserves attention—"the bad organization of labor and wages, depersonalization in work, and equalitarianism in the wages system." Late in 1933, two leading newspapers wrote up the organi-

[8] *Economic Life,* October 15, 1933; *Izvestia,* October 18, 1934.
[9] December 25, 1933.

zational state in the machine-building industry. It
was based on large factory studies made in Leningrad and Moscow, where, out of the seven-hour day,
only five to five and one-half hours were going into
productive work.

The chief onus was placed on management in this
summary: "Hundreds of plants suffer from this weakness in planning and organizing the work, and the
loss of time from these causes is one of the greatest.
They are part of the greater problem of proper preparation for mass production—a field that in Soviet
Russia has not been covered anywhere, although attention has frequently been called to the necessity of
improvement here. The trouble is that in the past it
was the individual worker who was responsible from
start to finish, whereas with the new equipment now
in use, preparing the work, setting the machine, and
keeping up a continuous supply of material are the
important things, and many managers can not or will
not understand the difference between the old and
the new. At present the machine-building industry
has a surplus of equipment, if it were properly used,
and many a third shift is entirely unnecessary." [10]

The form of the wage has passed through successive
changes since 1917. In the first flush of naïve Communism, a wage as such was abolished. It was replaced by the "ration," measured according to the
social category into which the individual fell—
whether Red Army, industrial worker, clerical employe, or *déclassé*. The quantity had no relation to
what the recipient might be producing. Too many,
in the absence of any compelling necessity, brought
forth less than they consumed. The maladjustment

[10] *For Industrialization*, September 6; *Pravda*, September 3-6,
1933.

so contributed to the systemic decline in production that in four years the cities became reduced to unrelieved misery. The NEP compelled restoration of the wage system on a basis of equality of pay.

This failed in turn to furnish incentive enough to speed up production to the scale of the Five Year Plan. At a conference of economic workers in June, 1931, Stalin roundly berated the practice, which he said "makes the unskilled workman have no interest in becoming a qualified workman, gives him no prospect of promotion and advance, in consequence of which, so to speak, he considers himself a 'summer camper' at his place of work, remaining there only temporarily in order 'to make a little money' and then going away to some other place 'in search of luck.'" The "piece work" method of capitalism, reborn of necessity several years before, then and there received Communist baptism and performs orthodox service in the land of Soviets. In the great electrical factory of Kharkov, the manager reports a spread from 150 rubles to 500 between the earnings of the less skilled machine operators and the best.

But let no one have the illusion that the master pattern changes materially. It will remain Communist, notwithstanding the use of many of Capitalism's gadgets, so long as it is impossible for an individual either to employ another for profit, to trade for profit, or to live by other capitalistic returns. Nor is Capitalism in the offing when "national planned economy" rests upon complete State ownership of all the means of production and distribution, upon the State as sole employer of labor, upon disappearance of the independent farmer, and upon the State doing or controlling almost all of the retail selling of goods and services to the population.

LABOR DISCIPLINE

The change in wage systems is but one of many turns in the road along which Labor in the Soviet Union has been led since 1917. An industrial labor constituency as the base of power is central in the Communist scheme of things, although it can scarcely be said to have originated with the man in overalls and calloused hands. The framers have been intellectuals. Karl Marx, its theoretician of the middle nineteenth century, was a philosopher; Lenin of the Russian intelligentsia made a going concern of it in the beginning of the twentieth. In the grand strategy, the workers are handled by the Party leaders rather than march under their own orders. This statement implies no denial of the movement as one meant to be whole-heartedly for the workers. Nor does it do violence to Party theory. It does condition and determine tactics.

Nothing is clearer in Communist theory and practice than the necessity and the existence of a hierarchy of control and direction *of* the workers more than *by* them. Stalin's exposition of this in *Leninism* [11] gives chapter and verse: "The working class without a revolutionary party is an army without a general staff. Our Party is the war staff of the proletarian army." "The dictatorship of the proletariat is the issuing of directives by the Party, plus the carrying of these directives into effect on the part of the mass organizations of the proletariat, plus their being made actual by the population at large." "The Party constitutes a unity of wills which is incompatible with any setting up of fractions and any division

[11] Pp. 163, 35, 172, 166.

of power." And this quoted from Lenin, "Today we have become an organized Party: and organization . . . signifies the subordination of the lower constituents of the Party to the higher."

The mass strength of the Russian workmen, organized and directed by the Party, placed the Party in power in 1917, and kept it there through the critical years that immediately followed. With the bankruptcy of the "factories-to-the-workers" idea when tested in practice, the Party leaders had a task of great delicacy. Under the imperative necessity of getting industrial production, they had to get the operating power out of the factory committees which they had themselves created and empowered. The risk of disaffecting their sole supporting bulwark, at that time a very small minority, was real and imminent.

The first step was to insure Party control of the trade unions. This called for a contest with the rank and file Mensheviks in the unions. The Party won hands down by "administratively" suppressing opposition and adding to the Menshevik population in exile camps. Then followed for the Party and the workers a trying period of several years. During this time, discipline was progressively the order of the day in the factories. Improvement came by slow stages. It has yet a long course to run. It began by installing a three-sided control in the plant, shared equally by the factory committee of the workers, the Party committee in the plant, and management. Gradually the once absolute powers of the workers' committee were shorn down to little more than consultative. For a time, the Party committee of the plant dominated management.

Later, as the Five Year Plan put on its further

pressure for results, management was made supreme. The Party now exercises its operating control by a direct line from the Center. This short circuits its plant committee as factory control, yet leaves it there for the control of the plant trade union, and to be a moral check on management. This supremacy of the manager holds, although he be not of the Party. One measure enacted and now in force indicates the severity of the disciplinary purpose. It sets a minimum quota of production for each worker as to quantity and quality. For falling short, a commensurate reduction of pay is imposed. If the failure be his own fault, there is no limit to the penalty; if he be not personally to blame, the deduction cannot be more than one-third of the wage.

The total achievement is an industrial control of Labor by the State difficult to distinguish in degree from that exercised by the hated Capitalism, unless by the relative leniency of the latter. A discontented body of workers, if venturing upon action, would go with their grievances to their union—a union controlled by its fraction of Party members, whose higher-ups prescribed the conditions, the redress of which is sought.

The Party's unquestioned power over the unions was strikingly shown at the very top when Tomsky in 1929, as the head of the All-Russian Central Council of Trade Unions, held back from going the disciplinary pace prescribed by his Party. Tomsky and his colleagues were lifted from their seats by the Party. Men replaced them who asked no questions. Its Central Committee acted without resort to the trade union body itself. The manner of action was about as dignified as the old saloon bouncer commanded in throwing out a collection of bums. The powerful organ of the League of Communist Youth characterized the ejected chiefs as "rust and pus entrenched behind the walls of the Palace of Labor." [12]

This discipline of Labor in no sense signifies disregard of the interests of the workers. Throughout, they have been and continue to be the favorites of the system. With the Party basing its strength on them, industrial works are deliberately established in territory not hitherto industrialized. Admission to the Party is gained with least difficulty by workers. The Party's numerical strength is thus kept weighted on that side. More trust is bestowed on them in the army and in the other bodies for defence. Their youth enjoy marked advantages in entrance to the higher educational institutions. They are not without influence in arriving at the schedule of wages and the working conditions. The trade union organization and the People's Commissariat of Labor have been combined into a single unit of Government Administration.

The trade unions serve important ends in the social, educational, cultural, and recreational life of the workers. The standard working day above ground has become seven hours, below ground less. Vacations on pay are given, varying in length according to the more or less exacting nature of the work. Free hospitalization is a part of the protection afforded against accidents and sickness. Beyond doubt the industrial workers recognize the régime on the whole to be on their side. They will defend it from any domestic or foreign attack.

Soviet Russia has not yet won, however, a contented body of labor. The turnover rate in employment Stalin has called "a scourge" threatening the

[12] *Comsomolskaia Pravda,* June 1, 1930.

disorganization of industry. "Scourge" was not too
severe a term to describe the situation shown in the
turnover figures for 1929-30. These follow, reckoning those who came and those who left against the
average numerical staff strength of 100%: in coal
mining 275.9 and 282.6 respectively; in wood working 291.7 and 264.9; in ore mining 306.2 and 293.4;
in the food industry 319.7 and 294.5; for industry as
a whole 172.3 and 150.6.[13] From such peaks there
have been substantial recessions. By 1933, the
Donetz coal mining rate had fallen to 200%. The
fluidity continues most pronounced in the newer industrial centers, where expansion of population has
much exceeded facilities for meeting even all their
elementary needs. According to the central administration of the national economic accounting of the
Gosplan, the large-scale industries began 1933 with
5,135,000 workers. That year they took on 6,347,000
new ones and lost 6,286,000. On the railways, the
fluctuation in the power, maintenance, and traffic divisions was 42%.

Housing shortage prevails in all the cities. Despite
much building of new and better workers' quarters,
pace has not been kept with the demand induced by
the natural growth of population and the pull of
workers to the cities by the new industries and by
the lure of an easier and better life in them than on
the collective farms. The average cubic feet of living space per person for the country at large is less
now than in 1913. The valid claims which can be
made on behalf of the workers' housing are that the
new construction for them is superior to the old,
and that of the older houses and apartments they
have the best. In the latter, they have largely dis-

13 *International Labor Review,* p. 362.

placed the former bourgeoisie, landowners, and professional people, or have been crowded in with them.
The result for very many is the sharing of a single
apartment, including kitchen, by three to five families and sometimes more. One well-known professional gentleman, once prosperous, had ten other
families moved into his premises. There still remained to him, though, the rare privilege of being
allowed to stay there himself.

The small margin, if any, by which living conditions have improved for the workers, apart from
social protection features presented elsewhere, must
be charged against the financial demands of the Five
Year Plans. For the 1929-1933 period, a capital outlay of 60,000,000,000 rubles is officially reported.
Whence could come such a sum? Not from foreign
borrowings. At the close of 1934 the total of Soviet
credit abroad did not much exceed $216,750,000.
No private capital wealth inside had outlived nationalization. The aggregate balance of foreign
trade during the years of Soviet rule has been adverse, and required advances instead of yielding
funds.

There remained a single principal resource—the
earnings of the people. These were garnered in part
through loans. *Economic Life* [14] regards "one of the
most remarkable accomplishments of the Soviet
financial system" to be "the success in mobilizing the
public's funds." The public means industrial workers, employes, and collective farmers. Ten per cent
has been the prevailing interest rate on the domestic
issues and has been paid. Older issues are generally
funded into new ones. To several of them lottery
devices are attached. The total of internal bond

[14] January 29, 1933.

issues as of January 1, 1935, stood around 14,000,000,-000 rubles.

For "attracting the means of the population," the workers of a typical establishment have been called together. The Party Committee has been told from Moscow what part of the monthly wage will be required of the Soviet citizen for this particular bond issue. A corresponding resolution is proposed at the meeting. The whole month's wages may be the prescribed figure. "All who are opposed will so signify." It carries unanimously. Then the individuals sign up for the deduction from pay. The names of any who over-subscribe are posted on a red board. The "welchers," if any, get publicized as yellow dogs on a black board.

Taxation which falls finally on consumers and holds down their standard of living has ridden this population with no less severity. Budgets abound with such phrases as "heavier taxation on industry," "forcing the income of the State," "pressure exerted on the capitalistic elements in the villages and cities," and "higher excises" on vodka. Most of the national income (reported to be 50,000,000,000 rubles in 1933) never reaches the people as consumers. The completeness of economic control enables the State to hold back as much or little as the national plan calls for.

A large return results from the combination of "rationing" and a system of "dual prices." Each employed person receives monthly a book. Its possession entitles the holder to purchase with his wages certain limited amounts of necessary food and other goods at the low-priced store of the State or the Co-operative to which he is assigned. Often the outlet is his factory or other place of employment. The

store enters in his book all purchases up to the limit
of the rationed amount.

The ration level has been fixed at what may be
called the minimal line for living and being able to
do the day's work.   All he may have earned above
that line accrues to the State.   Some of it returns to
the workers through the State's social protection and
welfare agencies and mitigates the otherwise low return for his labor.

Also there is an escape for the skilled worker
whose earnings are above the average.   If he has left
of his wages a margin above what he is permitted to
spend by the control at the low-price store, he has
free access to high-price stores of the State.   In them
no limit to buying exists except the purchaser's supply of money.   But the price elevation is mountainous.   A retail unit of butter, which, if it were in the
low-price store, would cost fifty cents' worth of Russian money, will sell in the other store for from three
to five dollars.   Some genius devised that artifice.
Either a population must live on the marginal line
of tolerable existence, or at an expense enormously
profitable to the State.   Under Capitalism such a
system would be "exploitation of the masses."   Communism tells the workers they are "building up their
own new collective society."

The denials in living conditions, whether self-
imposed or enjoined from above, have been deep-
ened by a forcing of exports to pay for purchases
abroad essential to the great construction program
for industry and agriculture.   Quantities of essential
foods have been taken out of the domestic market
with which to acquire foreign exchange.   When
Pravda [15] reported daily receipts of 5,500 cans of milk

15 August 4, 1931.

in Moscow against a need of 14,000 cans, hundreds of tons of Russian butter were going into foreign-bound cargoes. Large quantities continue to sell in the British market for less than in the low-price Moscow stores. At the same time that Soviet sugar production was declining and the low-price rationing shops were often destitute of their meager allowances, the export of sugar rose 200 per cent in a year. Of the experiences of this period, the authorities had given the people notice at the outset of the first Five Year Plan. "A steel hoop to be placed around consumption" read one of the announcements of the rationing system just described. It brought the wheat allocation to the cities down 25 per cent at once.

The precedence given to heavy industry over the light or consumers' industry keeps down the living level. The first Plan majored on expansion of the former, with the result that a long-time and careful observer like W. H. Chamberlin in *The Soviet Planned Economy* named among its debits an actual lowering of the living standards, notably in the towns. Promise was given that the second Five Year program would restore the balance. The figures given out by Stalin in January of 1934 do not reflect any rapid change of emphasis. From 1931 to 1933, the annual output of consumers' goods rose in value 2,500,000,000 rubles while "implements and means of production" increased by 5,500,000,000. The percentage of consumer goods in the total actually fell 2.6 per cent. The new construction investments continue to be placed predominantly in other than consumer-goods industries.

The dearth of ordinary commodities became vividly real to a foreign visitor who offered to buy some of them in one of the Torgsin stores for a city family. (In Torgsin shops only foreign currencies or their equivalent can be used.) From Russians, these shops have drained the last articles of gold they had. Now diamonds and emeralds are accepted (at prices below the world market), and the treasured icons are being stripped. Torgsin selling prices are international—on a level with Berlin, London, or Paris markings—much below those of the State's high-price ruble places. They cater especially to foreigners and for that reason, probably, are the more completely stocked. The family mentioned above, which was not large, had the income of two employed members. They were asked to submit a list of articles difficult to keep on hand either because they were too expensive, or were often out of stock in their low-price store. This was the list in order: soap, sugar, hairpins, writing tablet, lead-pencils, electric light bulbs, scissors. That day Torgsin was out of sugar.

The Government speaks sympathetically to the population: "Your life is hard, but it is sacrificial for the future. We want to make it better. We shall do it. When the new mills are built and come to fully successful production, and as the peasants become contented and efficient, there will be abundance. It will all be yours just as the new enterprises are."

The words are sincere. The purposes are not less so. When they will be realized measurably does not yet appear. The results after seventeen years provide no final criteria. For what they promise, one or more generations may not be too long to wait. The leaders expect to be judged finally by this standard of performance. They are acquainted, Trotzky once wrote, "with the fundamental laws of history: victory belongs to that system which provides society with the higher economic plans."

COMMUNIZING RURAL "CAPITALISTS"

Much depends on the success that attends finally the revolutionary designs for agriculture. There have been three general phases of the greatest task the Communists undertook in Russia—socialization of the peasants. The "land to the peasants" slogan of the Socialist Revolutionary Party promised them the increase of their holdings. This involved adding to the 82 per cent they already held by villages, or in their individual right, from the holdings in possession of landlords, the Crown, and the Church. The Communist formula was of quite another order. It called for wiping out all private and village land ownership. The peasant possessions passed out of their hands and over into the nationalized status along with the big estates. Peasant chattel properties and buildings remained their own. The text of the land law contained no reservations. It read:

"The right of private property in land is to be abolished for all time. The land shall not be bought, sold, leased, or otherwise alienated. All lands, whether belonging to the State, the former imperial family, the ex-Czar, the monasteries, or the church, whether copyhold, entailed, private, public, or peasant, shall be taken over without compensation, turned into the property of the entire people, and placed at the disposal of all who till them for use."

The first terms offered the peasants gave them the use of the land by villages, to be apportioned for purposes of cultivation to the families according to the number of working members and the mouths to feed. The family could reserve to itself from the crop their year's food supply, the feed for their animals, seed for the next sowings, and a margin for purchasable necessities. The surplus was to be delivered to the State without return. The second year there were few surpluses visible. The towns went hungry. Nothing for export remained. Forced requisitions brought killings of officials and uprisings here and there. With these multiplying and the cities starving, the practical Lenin reversed gears.

His New Economic Policy levied on the peasants a not severe tax in kind. Upon payment, they were left free to market the rest in the ways most favorable to themselves. The relief to the towns was immediate. Flour, butter, eggs, meat, and wood flowed in. The peasants tended to prosper. Government, though, was unhappy over inability to acquire the needed large stocks for the army and for export, and the reserves needful for emergencies. The political pain suffered hurt worse. The peasants were becoming so many petty capitalists. At this rate, Socialism would never come.

Resort was had to laws requiring delivery and sales to State collection stations at fixed prices. The "Nepmen" (private traders) and consumers outbid the Government and continued to get the grain. Requisitions by armed State forces followed, and more village rioting. Then the peasants sowed less. Proclamations easing up on demands would appear at sowing time, and be ignored when the crop was grown. The grain levies were made lighter for small usufruct units—so the peasants split up the parcels. By 1928, the number of these had risen from the pre-Revolution seventeen to eighteen millions to 25,-

585,900. The total situation baffled the Government and embittered the peasants. With the Russian Communist Party's penchant for having the will and finding the way, some major stroke to break the deadlock was due.

That stroke came to be known as collectivization of the farms. Two main objectives were in view. One was practical—to get firm grip on the whole of agricultural production. Doctrine and broad policy dictated the other. Individual peasant cultivation and appropriation of the products were not of Socialism. Voluntary collectivizing had been encouraged throughout the years of Soviet rule without any appreciable result. The time had come for true Bolshevik action. The issue within the Party was fiercely contested, but the strong-arm wing won.

The existing system of "strip farming" that was in for uprooting was pitifully uneconomic. The lands attached to a large village would encircle it for miles. They were not all equally arable and fertile. In order to make allotments equitable among some hundreds of families, a peasant would be assigned for his workings strips A, B, C and so on, each a few rods wide running off over the landscape. A and C might be miles apart. Each boundary between strips was either waste or worse—a paradise for weeds.

Collectivization throws down all borders and works the entire village tract as a single economy. Beyond that the lands of several villages may be united. All draft animals and machinery go into the pool. It was the intention to permit one cow to be retained by a family, but on a wide scale overzealous organizers swept her in too, and not seldom sheep, pigs, and chickens. On an almost country-wide scale, the peasants in panic and rage took to the slaughter of

their livestock for food. Before the pressure was relaxed, Chamberlin estimates, they destroyed a tenth
of the horses, a fourth of the cattle, a third of the
sheep, and half the swine. The *Economic Review of
the Soviet Union* [16] gave generally corresponding
figures.

The violence of the pressures put on the peasants
to join "voluntarily" by the Party underlings concerned with making good with their superiors went
beyond the intention at the top. Certainly the re-
sistances exceeded expectations. Lives were taken
on both sides—probably some thousands in all. The
progress in collectivizing also ran high. The violent
onset was made in the autumn-winter of 1929-30.
When in April of 1930 Stalin called a halt on the
excesses of pressure, he gave 50% as the achievement. With the pressure relaxed, there was a reces-
sion back to slightly over 24%.

More persuasive policies have followed the stormy
period, and with larger and more permanent effect.
The official figures given to the Party Congress in
January, 1934, were 65% of the households collec-
tivized. Their allotments equalled 73.9% of the
total grain-growing area. The later inducements and
compulsions toward joining have been economic.
Billions of rubles have been laid out on the purchase
and manufacture of farm tractors, drills, combine
harvesters, and other machinery. Credits for seed
and fertilizers are advanced. Drivers for the tractors
and new machines have been trained to the number
of 1,900,000. One hundred and eleven thousand ag-
riculturalists, moderately to badly prepared, have
been supplied. These farm services are organized
and directed through machine tractor stations. Two

[16] October 1, 1930.

thousand eight hundred and sixty of them had been established up to the end of 1933. They will be built up to 6,000. Each one serves several collectives.

The peasant outside the collective system is handi-capped by having allocated to his use the poorest land. He does not have access to the services of the tractor station. He is denied all credit. His taxes are higher. The more independent and prosperous peasants who offered opposition to collectivization, beyond merely not joining up, were uprooted from the land and completely dispossessed. Stalin esti-mated over 400,000,000 rubles as the amount realized from these expropriations and turned over to the collectives. The victims numbered about 1,000,000 families. Very large numbers of them landed in the extreme northern forests, where they could work or starve under conditions removed little if any from forced labor. The Baltic-White Sea Canal has been dug, thanks to their toil chiefly, under O.G.P.U. direction. Siberia received hosts of them and buried tragic numbers.

Collectivization continues to struggle against an immense amount of peasant ill will. It took away even the illusion of owning land. The new organiza-tion of the farm labor by brigades took away per-sonal initiative of action. All work under direction. A contest between the Government and the peasants drags on over the principle of compensation accord-ing to the size of family, which the latter favor. The authorities insist on reward for the actual days of work done, the skill required for the work assigned, and the quality of the work. The scarcity of con-sumers' goods to be won by good work has made them further withhold good-will and energies. The chief deterrent is the Government's greed. According to *Izvestia,* official State organ, the amount of grain annually collected from the peasants at the Government's price since collectivization had risen more than 200%—with production increased scarcely at all. The peasants ask, "What's the use?"

The peak of passive resistance, or at any rate of its consequences, arrived with the harvests of 1932. A bumper crop in 1930 had given the new order the appearance of success. For the first time since the Revolution the cereal grain produced that year passed the 1913 level. The overage was 7%. The next two crops revealed much going wrong. In 1931, in some of the Ukraine districts, 30 to 40% of the crop remained unharvested. The following year, again great quantities of grain went to waste in the fields. With average weather conditions both years, the cereal yield each year was over 11,000,000 metric tons less than on the same territory in 1913. Since that year population had increased 20%.

Affairs at this pass aroused the Party fighting spirit. Throughout the regions where there had been neglect, the maximum of grain collections for 1932 were enforced, if not more. Hunger became widespread in such granary sections as the Ukraine and the North Caucasus. The estimates observers have made of those who died of hunger or diseases induced by malnutrition range from one to ten millions. Chamberlin writes that in the villages and collective farms of the Ukraine "10% of the population perished of famine and related causes during the winter and spring of 1932-33." [17]   He calls the famine "State organized." The export of grain that year was 1,500,000 tons.

Further punishment was meted out to some of the

[17] *Christian Science Monitor,* June 15, 1934.

worst offending peasants by way of example. In the
North Caucasus, where thousands of tons of grain
went unharvested by deliberation or could not be
reaped because of the weeds and lack of horses, the
populations of entire villages were exiled to the number of several tens of thousands. A Party "cleaning"
of members, whom Stalin called "milk-sops," took
place because in the collectives they had permitted
poor sowing, bad cultivation, the neglect of the harvest, and delinquencies in delivery of the grain. A
new political machine was set up, directed by the
O.G.P.U. and manned by thousands of trusted Communists sent from the cities. Their functions are a
combination of policing and constructive guidance.

An important new regulation seemed to give the
peasants a sporting chance to have a margin of their
products left to them unmolested. The Government
assesses against every collective farm a stated quantity
of grain, meat, milk, eggs, etc., to be delivered re-
gardless of the much or little produced. When this
service has been performed, the rest of the farm returns belong to the community to be kept for its several uses, or to be sold to the best advantage possible. A superior crop in 1933 topped the 1913 yields
for the second year during the Soviet period, this time
by 12%. Adoption of the new quota-collection system brought a more willing spirit into the collectives.
The Government's figures for grain collections fail,
however, to show any more of the bumper crop left
with the peasants than in the two years preceding.
Out of 200,000,000 centners more produced, the State
gathered in 199,300,000 centners.[18] (A centner equals
220 lbs.)

[18] *Izvestia,* January 8, 1934.

Economic Life,[19] in treating on "obstacles in the road to peasant prosperity," names among them exaggerated cost of administration of the collectives, carelessness and extravagance with the funds, and surplus personnel. Overhead costs are to be pegged upward at 8%. The net return of half a ton of grain to a family is remarked encouragingly as "not unusual." This equals less than seventeen bushels of wheat or potatoes. There must be continued education of the peasants in Socialistic theories and practice, the writer thinks, "to guard against greediness, relaxation of labor discipline and control by hostile elements." A more liberal goods supply reaching the villages, if attained, will serve to stimulate good work. Time also works for the new order. Usage somewhat reduces friction on the bearings throughout the vast machine.

The XVII Party Congress (1934) was the first one to hear a report on agriculture with what could pass for optimism. The year before, Stalin had recognized as yet no return to the State from this source for the large capital outlay. Molotov, the Premier, called the progress in yield of harvests "insignificant." The later improvement noted by Stalin was not so much in "the rapid rise and powerful upswing of agriculture" as from having created "the prerequisites for the rise and upswing in the near future." He saw the Soviet peasantry "put off from the shores of Capitalism for good . . . sailing forward in alliance with the working class toward Socialism." Success with such a technical crop as cotton has been undeniably heartening. Independence of the foreign-grown product is at hand.

He did not conceal grave facts about the livestock

19 September 9, 1933.

situation, but, with that certain savage self-criticism characteristic of Bolsheviks, he submitted the table below, showing decline in every item each year since collectivization began except for an upturn for pigs in 1931 and 1933.

Livestock in the U.S.S.R.[20]
(In millions of head)

	1916	1929	1930	1931	1932	1933
Horses	35.1	34.0	30.2	26.2	19.6	16.6
Large horned cattle	58.9	68.1	52.5	47.9	40.7	38.6
Sheep and goats	115.2	147.2	108.8	77.7	52.1	50.6
Pigs	20.3	20.9	13.6	14.4	11.6	12.2

This answers the question, Why an acute meat shortage throughout the Union? For practical consequences, the loss of more than one-half the horses between 1929 and 1933 has more significance. The cutting down of the motive power by 17,400,000 fewer horses was restored by tractors to the extent of only 3,100,000 h.p. This disparity counted heavily in the failures of peasants to reach goals set for their performance. And scant room for claiming great good-will exists when they let 3,000,000 horses perish in the last year of record. At that rate, the tractors are not very rapidly, as Stalin believed, "pulling up all the roots of Capitalism in the rural districts."

Great store was placed in the immense farms that were set up on former great estates, often much expanded, at the outset of the first Five Year Plan. These "grain factories" are State enterprises purely, with direct investment, hired labor, full operative

[20] *Stalin Reports*, p. 41, International Publishers Company, New York.

direction, and appropriation of crops. At the end of five years, the State grain farm sowings were to exceed those of all the sowings of Canada by 2,461,000 acres. Stalin's observations thereon at the beginning of 1934 after six years follows:

"In regard to Soviet farms, it must be said that they still fail to cope with their tasks properly. I do not in the least underestimate the great revolutionizing significance of our Soviet farms. But if we compare the enormous sums the State has invested in the Soviet farms with the actual results they have achieved up to now, we will find an enormous balance against the Soviet farms. The principal reason for this discrepancy is the fact that our Soviet grain farms are too unwieldy; the directors cannot manage such huge farms. The Soviet farms are too specialized; they have no rotation of crops and fallow land; they have no livestock element in them. Apparently, it will be necessary to split up the Soviet farms and make them less specialized. Perhaps you think that the Commissariat for Soviet Farms opportunely raised this question and found a solution for it. But it is not so. The question was raised and solved on the initiative of people who had no connection with the Commissariat for Soviet Farms."

MAKING BOLSHEVIKS

In turning to education, one reaches the field in which the second largest measure of success has been attained in the Soviet Union. Making Bolsheviks has progressed further and more securely than growing wheat, spinning cotton, generating electric power or smelting ores. A standard of universal education up to seven grades has been erected. On the way to that goal were 26,419,000 children in 1933. The figure compares with 7,478,000 at the end of the Romanoff régime. Equipment and teacher training failed markedly to keep up with the expansion of schools and enrolment. The simplest materials are widely lacking. One text to four children is the average. In remoter places, one book per school per subject is the supply.

The majority do not yet get beyond the fourth grade, but 21.5% actually reach middle school. Nearly 2% enter the higher educational institutions. The number in them is impressive—491,000 in 1933, an increase of 284,000 from 1929. The ninety-one higher educational units in 1914 have been multiplied six and one-half fold. A parallel expansion of research has taken place with 840 scientific institutes for the purpose now set up. In them much notable work goes on.

Attack on the heavy cloud of illiteracy that overhung the Russian "dark people," as the peasants called themselves, has been praiseworthy for its intelligence and vigor. The 1918 percentages for illiteracy among men and women were 20.9 and 55.9, respectively. By 1931, the rate dropped to 3 and 7.2. If these very low figures can stand, it will be with the reservation that for very many of those classed as literate the state is a most elementary one. This limitation will be not unusual among the several millions of adults reached by the admirable campaigners for the "liquidation of illiteracy."

Other steps taken for educational penetration into the less advantaged sections of the population include provision of reading rooms, cinemas, radio, and club centers for the villages and industrial centers. Outside the larger cities, the facilities offered leave much to be desired, but they represent real purpose and progress. And although these facilities have not become general, they are being progressively extended. All of them bear propaganda as well as culture, in proportions not unfavorable to the former.

Foreign educators, John Dewey among them, find marked improvement in the science of Soviet teaching compared with that of the old régime. And the system, as a whole, they rate superior in some respects to that of other countries. Professor George S. Counts of Teachers College, Columbia University, is persuaded that Soviet education leads in the way of preparing the young realistically for the life around them in which they will take their part. On this ground, he justifies the indoctrination and emotional conditioning that results, and likes the Soviet system for its frankness and efficiency in this course of action.

Soviet education went over completely at first to the pragmatic method with practically full freedom of action given to the children. Study by "brigades" in the middle schools, from which one member could not advance until all were ready, was advanced as a means of inducing the collective spirit and habit. The school schedules overdid extra-classroom work. Frequent changes in curricula drove teachers to despair. There have been recessions to correct the excess of innovation. The widely used project method, found too slow for the ground that seemed essential to be covered in a short time, yielded much in 1932 to the method of instruction from text.

As the higher schools began stiffening the courses and tests for entrance, entrance candidates from the seven-year courses were too often found unprepared.

Thereafter, more discipline and attention to the "Three R's." Certain shortened courses are being built back to higher standards. The medical colleges again require five years instead of the war-time three and one-half. A recent announcement indicates that the lower courses are more hospitable to the geography and history of other countries; and, higher up, to the Russian classics. This may or may not signify somewhat of a stepping down from his throne by King "Political Grammar." It is certain the new learning will be thoroughly Communized "before taking."

The Press as an educational medium, with large propaganda content, has attained distinction. Newspaper circulation rose to 36,500,000 in 1933, nearly trebling the 1929 issues. Its spread is complete. Foremost are the organs in the great cities for Party, Government, Labor, Peasants, Army, Industry, Transportation, Youth, Childhood. Some of them have a circulation of a million or more copies daily. The new *Pravda* plant, now building, will cover the space of two New York City blocks. The completed pressroom turns out the editions of 1,700,000 copies in two hours.

The minority languages are well represented. Every sizable town with a regional outreach has its paper—too often a weak echo of the central organs. The big factories and other groups publish house organs. The club paper of the Workers in the Food Industry in Kharkov prints 90,000 copies. "Wall newspapers" posted in the lesser mills and on collective farms afford additional media of the news and propaganda of the day or week. A parallel outpouring of books, pamphlets, and magazines takes place.

The number of copies published rose from 2,100,000,-
000 in 1928 to 3,500,000,000 in 1932.

The power of such publicity is irresistible when
so centrally directed. Stalin has called the Press "the
sharpest and strongest weapon" of the Party. A
Party man occupies each editorial chair. Over him
rules a Party censorship. Any idea, measure, or development can be cried up or down. Any person or
group that falls out of favor will be blasted into ruin
and oblivion. A shining victim of the barrage was
the once popular and mighty Trotzky. No single
page of printing exists to neutralize this force. Not
a slug of type in the Soviet land is free from Party
control.

The truth is, learning and thinking are under a
dictatorship no less relentless than that applied to
government and industry. The educational task
embraces the total mentality of the nation, whose
mind is to be emptied ultimately of every idea opposed to Communism and filled with those consistent
with Communist doctrine, formula, and program.
To this end, command of all avenues to every brain
is captured.

The Press has been cited. Add the schools from
low to highest, the movies, the radio, the stage. Most
books have Communist authors. The base for general knowledge is being laid in a new Marxist-Lenin
encyclopedia. Research may not run counter to the
Party line. A Communist checks the scholar precisely as one stood guard over every old general in
the first Red Army to keep him "loyal." Great experts are in exile for bringing forth in all good faith
findings that were used by Party minorities to support their position against the Dictator. Others are
there because outside their science they have views,

influence, and a life that ideologically is "counter-revolutionary." Only by the spoken word in discreet ears do uncommunized ideas have circulation among those 168,000,000 people. With such embargo laid from infancy to the grave on every opposing or neutralizing idea, Bolshevization of the young mind commands the field.

What might be mistaken for exceptions to the rule of denying freedom is the self-criticism for failure of performance in the execution of plans. This is widely indulged, if it stops short of challenging a doctrine or opposing a plan of the Party. The most vocal of the critics at large are the swarms of "worker and peasant correspondents" of the newspapers. Their communications are in the nature of "letters to the editor" familiar to readers of American newspapers. They are an accessory to Soviet journalism unique in the newspaper world. The Moscow organ for railroad workers in a given year has had as many as 60,000 correspondents. The *Peasant Gazette* once reported 1,000,000 letters from this source in a year. The number of these correspondents reported to the XVII Party Congress was 3,000,000. They will fiercely attack people and conditions that are blocking progress along any line of Party policy laid down. Officials and Party workers do not escape. Frequently, the editor appends to such an exposé a notice that the paper will expect a reply from those responsible in the case stating just what is being done about it.

THE COMMUNIST FAMILY

The family is another institution of society in which the Communists in Soviet Russia have made departures at about right angles to the course that has been pursued in Western Christian society. The "bourgeois" family presents to them two basic dangers. It is the citadel of private property, which they are out to abolish in effect. Also, its loyalties passively, and more or less actively, offer resistance to the domination of the State in education. Communists state a truth in saying that a complete break between the old social order and their new one is impossible if parents be allowed to pass their ideas, convictions, purposes, and habits on to the children.

The extreme Communist would meet the issue by the physical separation of children from the home at three years of age. An early edition of *The ABC of Communism* taught this procedure. Later printings omitted it. In any case, economic obstacles in the way of housing the young flocks would have blocked it. There must have been a powerful deterrent, too, in the warning experiences met with in the orphanages, swamped by the World War, the Revolution and the famine. The excess of stranded boys and girls and the dearth of resources produced the "homeless wild children" that for years lived in vagrancy.

Some of the new housing construction points the way and the distance it is proposed actually to travel in reorganization of the family. Large units for one hundred or more families provide a minimum of private living quarters for a household—somewhat more than dormitory space. The members eat, however, in a common dining room served by a single kitchen. A communal laundry does the washings. A communal nursery, kindergarten, and playground remove babies and small children largely from maternal care and their earliest guidance. The school system then picks them up for the standard courses of instruction. The system of the State thus steps in between parents and the old function of rearing children. This will be accomplished, however, without physical separation.

There are convictions behind this policy. A writer in *Izvestia* [21] insists "society can give its children much more than the best of mothers in every separate case" if responsibility be taken "from the cradle to the grave." The Communist Youth daily paper [22] appraises this as the process for "uprooting the last remnants of Capitalism" and for destroying "the strongholds of the old individualistic order of things." The goals set for the farm collectives forecast similar communal housing and living to that begun in the industrial centers. Peasant neglect tends to leave the village houses unrepaired. The Communists say "let them fall down. We will then build after the communal pattern."

At eight years of age, boys and girls, if they are to "belong" to the fellowship of Soviet childhood and are to have anything approaching a good time, enter the Pioneer section of the Party training system. Non-membership places a child under certain school handicaps as well. Pioneer status holds through the sixteenth year. It absorbs most of the leisure time of its members. Leadership is provided by the Comsomol, the youth society to which the Pioneers succeed. An official publication, *The Party, the Comso-*

[21] June 21, 1930.
[22] *Comsomolskaya Pravda*, March 16, 1930.

mol, and the Red Pioneers, reads: "The Pioneer movement is not an institution for children, but a children's fighting organization under the direction of the Party and the Comsomol." They take the pledge: "I, Young Pioneer, swear before my comrades that I will constantly uphold the cause of the workers and I associate myself with the struggle of the workers and peasants of the whole world. I will obey the orders of Lenin and fulfil the duties and obligations imposed upon me by the law of the Red Pioneers."

Between three and four millions are in Pioneer groups. On the whole, they serve useful purposes in relation to the children's pleasure, health, and supplementary education. Good psychology and planning genius are shown in enlisting these children in useful undertakings that generate enthusiasm and sense of responsibility, even of proprietorship. As a wedge driven into family loyalties the plan has probably measured up to expectations. The least enviable of the activities, encouraged by praise, is not infrequent espionage of children on their parents.

Goikberg, a high Soviet legal light, in *The Right of Marriage,* maintains that the Communist Party must extinguish that close parent-child relationship in the family which breeds egotists. The heroine of *Cement,* by Gladkov, to serve the cause better, placed her one child in an institution for children, where she saw her slowly fade out from ill care, though, be it said to the credit of motherhood, not without grief.

Lenin's blueprint called for this liberation of women from the drudgery of housework by the pooling of domestic labors. The feeding of 43% of the industrial workers in public dining-rooms and the trend in communal housing indicate a program well

on foot.   The release is not unto idleness nor gay-
ety, but for work at the machines and other economic tasks.   During the first Five Year Plan, the
number of women in the city proletariat increased
more than 250% to reach the figure of 6,263,000.
They now constitute one-third of the workers.[23]

Unquestionably, much of the urge comes from the
need to swell the family income, which in rubles increased 73% between 1929 and 1932.   Another purpose is "to draw them into socialist construction" and
win them to it as a system.   They meet no wage discrimination and may not work at night.   Nurseries
are provided in factories for mothers with babies,
and time off is given to nurse them.   More than half
of the women workers are in the "heavy" industries.
Their percentage of the total number of such workers is arresting—in coal 17.6, iron mining 21.5, metallurgy 20.4, machine building 22.9, electro-technical
33.   These women win advancement.   Their proportion among engineering and technical personnel has
reached 9%.   Their posts include heads of divisions
and of shops, specialists, higher engineers, scientific
and laboratory workers, bosses, and brigade leaders.
At the end of 1933, three hundred and five were
plant managers.   Women make up one-fifth of the
students in the industrial technical schools.

If this swing from the home as such be real progress, the status of woman has been greatly raised.
Communist pæans are sung about it as a fact.   Here
is one from the magazine *Smena* (The New Generation):

". . . If you raise your head you can see three
women at the highest span.   They are crawling along
the steel girders, high above the ground.   Sometimes

[23] *For Industrialization*, March 8, 1934.

they pull drawings out of their pockets and consult them to see if everything is in order, or if the structure will have to be strengthened. All of them are ex-housemaids. Moscow lost its housemaids in 1930, and many brooms, stoves and kitchens remained uncared for. . . . The housewives followed in the footsteps of the housemaids. The labor exchange, still unable to satisfy the demands of industry, beckoned them to its doors, which only yesterday were closed to them. . . . Some of them who were trying to brush up their long-forgotten trades, which had remained in disuse during the years of their married life, were immediately engaged by the enterprises. The others were enlisted in the section of unskilled labor. All of them were swept away along various different channels, either for training, re-training, or so-called common labor. Gone are the housewives."

Stalin found satisfaction in reporting to the XVII Party Congress that 6,000 women were chairmen of collective farms, and more than 60,000 were members of farm managing boards. Women dairy-farm managers numbered 9,000. Another 7,000 drove tractors and 28,000 were farm forewomen. In the whole range of social welfare organization and service, women are conspicuous.

Women make up about one-fourth of the Party membership. They are encouraged to activity in affairs of government. From two-thirds to three-fourths of them exercise their voting right. Hundreds of thousands serve as elected members of local and higher Soviets and as officials in executive posts. They are well represented in the All-Union Central Executive Committee of the Government, or Congress. One reached the height of Minister to a foreign power. None, however, has made the grade up to a National Cabinet post. Lenin's widow and one other woman sit on the Central Committee of the Party.

The institution of marriage has been greatly unstabilized. The bold Communist position about it is that what man and woman live together is purely the concern of themselves—not of Society, State, Church, or the neighbors. This does not admit promiscuity. Monogamy is upheld but it can be practiced seriatim, after the manner of the marrying set of Hollywood. Registration of marriage is encouraged, not to effect legality. It simply establishes the fact of marriage. There is an attending responsibility toward children proceeding from a union, whether registered or not. The "illegitimacy" of no child receives recognition; but, in the absence of marriage registration, it becomes necessary for a mother deserted by the father of her child to prove cohabitation in order to have enforced on the man the required economic provision for the child's support.

A visit to a Domestic Relations Bureau is uniformly included in the official routing of tourists. An informal atmosphere pervades the room. In a typical instance, the young woman clerk received the couple at a plain table. Each filled out a questionnaire, not differing much from one required when applying for a passport. After answering the necessary questions, bride and groom signed. The clerk countersigned. The groom paid a two-ruble fee to complete the ceremony.

Divorce proceedings are no more complicated. Either party may apply, state the case and, with rare exceptions, get released. The rights of children will receive protection. A father can be assessed up to one-third of his wages on one child's account—a

maximum of one-half if there be more than one.
The one divorce witnessed took four minutes by
the watch. Questions by the spectators were invited
by the clerk. To an inquiry about the ratio of di-
vorces to marriages, she gave the reply of one to two
in that Bureau and the same for Moscow as a whole.
In the smaller cities and rural places, which include
the great majority of the Russian population, the rate
would be very much lower. The rate for the U.S.S.R.
as a whole is not much above that for the United
States.

The pressure for large families that exists in Italy
and Germany is absent here. Contraceptive information is given freely at medical, maternity, and nursery centers. Legal, professional provision is made
for abortions in the earlier stages. A commission
hears the grounds for desiring the operation—economic or otherwise. A woman doctor in the maternity section of a large factory hospital reported
the proportion of operations to pregnancies to be
about one to three in the city and industrial centers.
The consequences to the health of women has served
latterly to check the rate.

The tenure and the measure of power for the
Communist régime will be conditioned by the youth
it produces. On the whole, the leaders may take
courage over the prospect. In almost any plant,
office force, or club are found clean-cut, healthy,
alert young men and women committed body and
mind to the ongoing movement about them without
shrinking from the admitted sacrifices. In these,
they rather glory for the time. They can be disil-
lusioned, if the fulfilment of vision tarries too long.
This is not to overlook another section of the youth
who go along in practical affairs, yet withhold ad-

herence to the political system. The elements of a great strategy for capturing a young generation are present. They have not been mismanaged.

Youth kindles in the presence of daring and resolution. When confusion and strain were at the peak in the new industries, the faint hearts were challenging the production plan as unreal and impossible to execute. Defending it at a conference of the leaders, Stalin stood his ground in the language of a conqueror:

"The reality of our program is in living human beings—ourselves, our will to labor, our willingness to work in a new way, and our determination to carry out the plan. Are we possessed of it, of that will? Yes, we are. And consequently, our production program can be, and must be, fulfilled."

And the young generation are not left to be thrilled simply and to cheer. Real tasks are put upon their shoulders. Throwing tens of thousands of youngsters into a wobbly situation in this coal field or that wheat harvest, forest project, or subway excavation reflects something other than a well-ordered, going industrial system, yet it has won real victories. And more important, the trust implied and the taste of achievement enlists hundreds of thousands willingly to the whole courageous scheme of action.

Nor is the summons all to sacrifice. An entire new line of leadership has to be reared and installed. From 1914, Russian events have taken heavy toll of the best men and women—in commerce, engineering, medicine, journalism, education, scientific research. The World War, the reprisals of the Revolution, and the waves of epidemics decreased the

doctors one-third by 1921.   Hunger, cold, abuse, and
exile left few of the intellectuals with physical reserves for further service.   The Communist leaders
are dying young from their sufferings under the old
régime and the burdens laid on themselves by the
new.   The gulf of conviction between many "former
people," as they are pathetically called, and the new
rulers makes impracticable the use of much surviv-
ing talent and experience.   The youth, therefore,
have opened wide to them a range of opportunity
without limits save those of their own capacity and
obedient willingness to be spent.   They do not have
to be of the Party, if otherwise they prove their un-
questionable loyalty and ability—the places of political power excepted.   These are reserved to Communists alone.

What has been said goes for leadership.   Enough
of it is in the making apparently to give the régime
a lease of power long enough to test out thoroughly
the economic and social theory and practice.   The
old Communists are not without doubts about "the
safety of the ark" in the younger hands to which
time will for a certainty commit it.   Can the young
hate the old order with bitterness—its political systems, its institutions, its ideas—the whole accursed
order they never saw, under which they never suffered?   Will they weaken at the points of basic
principle, discipline, and fighting quality?

Maurice Hindus [24] thus sketches the new type at
its best—"a new human being with a new form of
behavior," "a highly regimented individual," having
"a body of prejudices and dogmas all his own," "a
robust personage, with an aim and mission and a

[24] *The Great Offensive*, Smith and Haas, New York.

mentality all his own, a product of a new idea and a symbol of a new society."

About the common run of youth the leaders need not be anxious. They accept the round of life, hard as it is, just as they find it. It is there and theirs, like the rivers, sky, sun, and snow. For the many, the propagandist education will do the rest. The type has been called "a sort of gramophone record which plays without a hitch the records that are placed on it." [25] Stanley High found the only original ideas in the mind of typical Communist Youth to be "about a more complete and effective conformity." The outcome for the system appears to depend upon how much permanently creative life will flow from a society in which a minority of "robust personalities" manipulates the mass of "human phonograph discs."

A FOREMOST SOVIET ACHIEVEMENT

The provisions made toward removing from life the removable risks and anxieties that have afflicted the masses afford indubitable proof of Communist good-will and purpose for them. The administration of these provisions has been committed to the trade union organization, which embraces, along with industrial workers, the whole range of employed persons. It will be noted that the social-welfare budget for 1934, as given by *Izvestia*,[26] has a wide spread. No cost is borne by the beneficiaries consciously. This generosity is conditioned some-

[25] W. H. Chamberlin in "Making the Collective Man," *Foreign Affairs*, January, 1932.
[26] April 11, 1934.

what by the knowledge that individual incomes have such limitations as to make the population entirely dependent on the State for the services here scheduled:

		Rubles
I.	Allotments and pensions	1,514,200,000
II.	Medical aid to insured persons.	1,040,000,000
III.	Care of children of insured persons	327,000,000
IV.	Houses of rest, sanatoriums, spas	215,300,000
V.	Special invalid feeding	57,500,000
VI.	Education	750,000,000
VII.	Capital investment	884,900,000
VIII.	Inspection of labor	41,000,000
IX.	Administrative and organization expenses	50,000,000
		4,879,900,000

A distinctive departure on a large scale has taken place in a unitary medical service well established in principle and advancing. *Red Medicine*,[27] published in 1933, presents at length the findings of a survey made on the field of this Soviet socialized program. The chief surveyors were two eminent medical experts—one British and one American. By way of a summary, they say in part:

"The U.S.S.R. . . . removed the doctor almost entirely from the field of monetary competition, and has thus abolished a chief source of inadequate medical service. It has made a gratuitous (that is, State paid) medical service of an astonishingly complete character promptly available for the vast majority of urban populations, which is being rapidly extended to rural Russia: and it has given the whole

[27] Doubleday, Doran and Company, New York.

of this service an admirable turn in the direction of social as well as medical preventative measures."

The report recognizes performance to be far from perfect, as would be expected after only twelve years of operating experience. The great defects are those in meagerness of service outside the more accessible cities. What the traveler sees in the Leningrad and Moscow hospitals is not yet reproduced across the land. The farther from the centers, the more deficient are equipment, linen, medicines, and doctors. The efficiency has been high enough, nevertheless, to bring down the mortality rate 35% from the high levels of old Russia and the early post-Revolutionary period.

The free service goes beyond medical care and supplies so far as they are available. The standard set up includes also hospitalization, and treatment at watering resorts and sanatoriums. The wages of the sick, if employed at the time, continue to be paid. On the other hand, the *déclassé* population, still not small, are left outside all such provisions. Nothing could so contribute to their health and general welfare as abstention on the part of the Government from the persecutions (now without sense or justification) which act to keep them in a state between harassment and terror.

For the others in the urban centers, excellent facilities are being multiplied for the pleasant, healthful use of leisure time. These take the form of "people's houses," "parks of culture and rest," bathing facilities, playgrounds, stadiums, cinemas, theaters, and quarters for clubs. The layouts for the brand-new industrial towns rising around the mines and mills of the Five Year Plans uniformly contain these features. Their construction tends to

lag behind the schedule, but they are on paper in
good faith and time sees them increasingly realized.
The existence of plans so widely publicized creates
pressure on the officials to realize them. And enough
such facilities are in use to stimulate demand for
more. In the highest places, there is the recognition of a demand for higher standards of all-around
living that will not always be denied.

The entire water-front of Crimea is under further development as a national rest and health resort. Physical-culture circles by tens of thousands
serve healthfully their several million members—
half of them factory workers of special merit. At
the beginning of 1933, twenty-two physical-culture
technicians were training 5,000 in that field.
Within the Union, serving the same interest, were
2,000 gymnasiums and twice that number of athletic fields and stadiums. Helpful physical culture
is obligatory throughout the school system, with
some military motivation.

Central water-supply, formerly limited to the provincial capitals, now reaches 532 towns and cities.
Where before 18% of the towns had electric light,
it has been installed in 91% of them.

Another record for achievement is being made in
care for mothers and children. Hundreds of millions of rubles go in yearly to nurseries, play-spaces,
kindergartens, milk stations, and child sanatoriums.

MILITANT ATHEISM

"Religion and Communism are incompatible both
theoretically and practically" as the issue is seen by
the authors of an early text book by two Party

authoritarians.[28] Nevertheless it is not true that all churches, synagogues, and mosques have been closed by edict. They decrease rather by attrition. What then is the program of opposition? In a sentence, to let the believers indulge themselves in worship and the observances of religion; to prevent the religious instruction of the young; and, through the educational processes earlier set forth, thoroughly to indoctrinate all children against religion in every form.

Clarification is needed on the point whether the antagonism applies to all religions. A notion has currency that the Russian Orthodox Church is the sole cause and victim. An interview given to Sherwood Eddy's party in 1932 by Yaroslavsky, executive chief of the Society of Militant Godless, should correct that misapprehension once for all. The report of it appeared in full in *Bezbozhnik*,[29] Yaroslavsky's own official organ of the Society. The translated text makes nearly seven typewritten pages. Dr. Eddy had laid down what he considered to be a possible basis of understanding between the believers present and the Communists. Yaroslavsky began by saying there was no common foundation with believers. Then followed successive statements of position of which these are representative:

"We were always the foes of religion. We were atheists, revolutionary followers of Marx and Lenin. Our militant atheism is absolutely related to our revolutionary world-view. It is not a sort of appendage, which has developed only under conditions of the Soviet Union. This atheism is a basic constituent of our revolutionary world-view."

[28] *The ABC of Communism*, p. 256.
[29] Nos. 17-18, September, 1932.

"Lenin proved—and we all were of his opinion—
that religion and Communism had nothing in common. . . . Therefore we struggled energetically
against all religion and in this case made no difference between a 'good' religion and a 'bad' one.
On the contrary, we declared that the finer types of
religion demanded an even more acute struggle, and
Lenin declared that the difference between a 'good'
religion and a 'bad' one was the same as between
a blue and a violet devil."

In 1926, the Russian Church bishops in exile on
the Arctic island of Solovki petitioned the Soviet
Government to stand aloof from the religious question. After recognizing the Government's full authority in the political and economic sphere, they
asked that the Church be given freedom to have it
out on even terms with Communists and their
teachings in respect to religion. The following passages in their argument reveal an awareness of irreconcilability no less final than that of Yaroslavsky:

"The Church recognizes the existence of the spiritual principle; Communism denies it. The Church
believes in the living God, Creator of the world,
Guider of its life and fate; Communism does not
admit His existence; believes that the world was
self-organized and that no reasonable principles or
purposes govern its history. The Church believes
in the steadfast principles of morality, justice, and
law. Communism looks upon them as the conditional results of class struggle, and values moral
questions only from the standpoint of their usefulness. The Church instills the feeling of that hu-
mility which elevates man's soul; Communism abases
man through his pride. . . .

"For the Church, religion is not only the living

force enabling man to attain his heavenly destiny, but also the source of all that is greatest in human relations—the foundation of earthly welfare, happiness, and the health of nations. For Communism religion is the opium that drugs the nations, that weakens their energy, that is the source of their poverty and misfortunes. The Church wants religion to flourish. Communism wants it to perish. With such deep difference in fundamental principles separating the Church and the State, it becomes impossible that an inner nearness or reconciliation could exist between them. There can be no reconciliation between assertion and negation, between yes and no. For the very soul of the Church, the circumstances of its existence, and the reason for its being are just that which is categorically denied by Communism."

Being realistic rather than sportsmanlike, the Party, instead of welcoming a fair fight, has seen to it that the State put the Church—all religious bodies—in a strait-jacket. Nationalization swept in all church property—houses of worship, lands, hostelries at the shrines, candle-factories, presses. With the last four categories went the large revenues. Disestablishment cut away all State support. On given terms of maintenance and administration, congregations can make use of the places of worship.

Progressively, there have been shorn away the activities permissible to religious groups until they are narrowed down to conduct of the Divine Service. An early law penalizes by imprisonment the teaching of religion to children before their nineteenth year in any school. Court rulings place the Sunday school under that ban. Good people go to exile today for teaching a group in a home. A sweeping piece of legislation forbade religious Youth Societies, Women's Guilds, Bible circles, libraries, socials, concerts, and aid to the ailing, orphaned, or widowed. These later restrictions aimed directly at the Protestant sectarians, who were growing in numbers. A pastor or evangelist of theirs may serve only in a single fixed parish. Their school for training preachers was closed, and their paper suppressed.

No single institution for the preparation of priests, pastors, or rabbis has existed since. On one charge or another, the ablest of the clergy and laymen of all the Communions meet imprisonment or exile. The time must come when Orthodox, Protestant, and Roman Catholic flocks numbering millions will be without pastors. The clergy are outside the classifications entitled to recognition in the processes by which life is maintained. For shelter and food they shift for themselves or subsist on the meager fees and charity of the hard-pressed parishes. The passport system applied in 1932 entirely removed them from residence in the principal cities. For service, they must come in long distances from the places where they are permitted to live. Official resort is had to the imposition of taxes and fines to crush the spirit of any bishop or priest strong enough to bear the other economic hardships. Withal, the negligible number who have lowered the colors constitutes one of the inspiring witnesses in contemporary Christendom of enduring faith under persecution.

The State monopoly of education enables the full implementing and force of the State to be directed at raising up a godless generation. All schools work on the undertaking, down to the detail of removing the words for Deity from the text books. The

Pioneers sing as they march, "Away, away with the priests, we will mount to the heavens and throw out all gods." An elaborate press and literature for children and youth are vehicles of this atheism. Literally tens of millions of pages under anti-religious titles issue from the State publishing houses. The "Anti-religious Literary and Artistic Library for Children" takes up nine volumes. In contrast, the religious forces are denied most essential materials. Bibles and Service books wear out with no means for replacement.

The preparation of an army of experts to lead and direct the attack on religion has reached formidable proportions. The Central Bureau of the Militant Godless in June, 1933, made this summary of the year's results in organizing their program of education:

"According to the latest data furnished by the majority of the provincial, county, and republican soviets of the Central Soviet of the Militant Godless Union of the U.S.S.R., 5,020 local anti-religious groups exist (125 workers' groups, 2,671 groups of collective farmers, 1,178 school groups, and 146 Red Army and other groups). In them, 144,161 persons received instruction. In the courses and seminars of the intermediate section, 4,135 people received instruction; besides this there were twenty-six workers' anti-religious universities and one for Red Army soldiers. In the superior section we had six anti-religious higher educational institutions. The Anti-religious Correspondence Institute had six departments and gave instruction to 3,799 persons." [30]

Tirelessly, the attack by "the godless" moves along other lines of the varied tactical repertoire:

[30] *Antireligioznik*, No. 4, 1933.

"Red Corners" in buildings frequented by any considerable number of people; countless talks in the network of clubs that exist to further indoctrination; "godless cells" in factories, offices, collective farms, and machine tractor stations; museums set up to expose the weaknesses and sins of the religions at their worst, with nothing to suggest the slightest wholesome ministry.

At the times of the great religious festivals, elaborate counter-attractions are staged to divert the masses from the observances. Work in the factories and in the fields on those days is made to appear the test of loyalty to the "socialistic upbuilding." A steady attrition of the houses of worship takes place. Yaroslavsky estimated in 1932 that 20% were closed. His figure is probably low. Poverty in many parishes renders the required upkeep impossible. In 1930, the Jews reported the loss of over one-third of the synagogues in the Ukraine.[31]

The outcome can be variously speculated upon. What is real in religion has never been destroyed by oppression; and, putting aside all the pageantry, formalism, reaction, and superstition which critics of the Russian Orthodox Church dwell upon, the fact remains that the graces which Jesus exalted so reside in multitudes of Russian Christians as to make most Christians of the West seem poor in comparison. Utterances from the Militant Godless G.H.Q. alternate between shouts of victory and accounts of the strength and influence of the religious forces. The Society's membership increases. The figure given in 1933 is 5,000,000. On the other hand its organ, *Antireligioznik,* has lost circulation—from 20,750 in 1932 to an issue of 3,500 in 1933. Its

[31] *Jewish Daily Bulletin,* April 17, 1930.

estimate of active churches and sectarian prayer houses was put at 46,000 in 1932.

At best, heavy inroads upon the faith of the young are inevitable. *Pravda* reported a questionnaire test made among 12,000 workers in the large Moscow factories four years ago. Although replies were anonymous, only 3,000 came in, which leaves dark too large an area to make the result wholly conclusive. It is highly indicative, though. The index of believers fell with the age of the respondents, thus: 50 years and over, 35.1%; from 40 to 49, 22.4%; from 30 to 39, 10.0%; from 22 to 29, 4.6%; up to 22, 2.7%. As to peasants, the Leningrad Soviet, investigating 919 households in thirty collective farms, found 77% of the families with icons, 23% considering religion useful, 30% thinking it does no harm, and 18% believing it harmful.

To discover and chart the moral currents is at best a hazardous attempt. The virtues upheld are those that will undergird collectivity more than individualism. Punishments reveal this. A murderer gets a maximum sentence of twelve years: the thief of State property is shot. In Moscow, an election would not be necessary to get rid of Tammany grafters, thanks to the firing squad. The extreme license in sex life that ensued when the Communists came to power has been checked, not in deference to "bourgeois" or "priestly" morality, but in the name of "socialistic upbuilding." It was seen that the Party ends could not be served by unbridled sexual lust, passion, and irresponsibility. A rather vigorous educational campaign is put on by the Government against alcoholism, financed with proceeds from the State monopoly of vodka. Consumption is, however, heavy. The Party's theoretical influence is for temperance, but neutralized by the vodka flow directed to the villages to induce the exchange of peasant produce.

There remains enough dishonesty to require diligence for its detection and punishment. Press dispatches carry successive accounts of executions for guilty actions—now in the Kiev food supplies, then on the Moscow-Kazan railway, and again in the Moscow subway. Another headline runs "Short-changing in Soviet Stores." A scandal rose to heaven in the Gorkii industrial district over the falsifying of employment rolls in factories in order to get corresponding increases in food allotments. *Comsomolskaya Pravda* [32] listed thirty-one enterprises that had faked supplies for 61,000 non-existing workmen. Grain stealing near Smolensk brought down "the supreme penalty" on eight guilty ones during October, 1934.

The Communist discussion of these cases never gets over into the region of immorality and sin as such. Much is said about "class enemies," treason against the Socialistic State, and the hang-over of bourgeois greed. The last-named is to be cured "by educating out of the human consciousness the idea of 'my own.'" It might be added that improvement in the living conditions would serve to remove some of the temptations to "treason," for many petty offenders reason that they are only taking what is their own.

[32] November 20, 1932.

"THE WORKERS' FATHERLAND"

Doctrinally, Communism stands at the pole opposite to Nationalism. It proclaims the Soviet Union
the Fatherland of the international proletariat.
This has been a central tenet of the Party. One of
its practical applications has been extensive traffic
in world revolutionary schemes from the Soviet
base, which in past years have kept governments of
other States nervous and angry. These schemes will
be discussed under Soviet Foreign Policies.

Internally, dealings with the minorities serve best
to illustrate the different approach made from that
of the chauvinistic nationalism of the old régime.
From Imperial Russia, the Soviet Government fell
heir to a large assortment of national and racial
groups, somewhat over two hundred of them. To
the formerly dominant Great Russians and the familiar Ukrainians, White Russians, Jews, Tatars,
Armenians, and Georgians, are to be added the more
strange Karels, Mordva, Bashkiri, Kazaks, Kalmuks,
Buriats, and others by the score.

Lenin's political sagacity never displayed itself
more brilliantly than in making one of the initial
acts on taking power a "Declaration of the Rights
of the Peoples of Russia." It was couched in terms
of according all peoples equal and sovereign rights;
of the right of self-determination to the point of
separation and independence; of free development;
and of the abolition of all national privileges. After
the hard Russifying policies of the last two reigning
Romanoffs, the conciliatory effect on these populations was incalculable. It reduced materially the

insurrectionary coups with which the new régime had to reckon.

The phrases about sovereignty and independence proved most illusory. The joker lies in this Party principle read into the Act but not explicit there: "The Communist Party recognizes that the nations have the right to self-determination even up to the point of secession; but it considers that the working majority of the nation and not the bourgeoisie (class) embodies the will of the nation. . . ." [33] This automatically kept the political and all other instruments of power in the hands of Party members of the respective minorities. These in turn were directed centrally by the Political Bureau in Moscow. And when trusted servants were not forthcoming from a minority section of the Party, they could always be furnished by headquarters, and were so supplied. The Georgians provided the case of a minority seeking independence. A movement to that end, that would have succeeded if left to itself, was ruthlessly crushed with military forces sent in by the central Soviet power.

This reminder is not in disparagement of real values accruing to the minority peoples—in cultural directions first of all. Each has been given the free use of its language. This contrasts with the old autocratic prohibition of books and newspapers in the tongue of an 80% Ukrainian population. The former policy of admitting no "national" schools likewise was revised. It is notable how much revolutionary ferment is avoided by liberal language and educational privileges granted to nationals under jurisdictions not their own. Oppressive rulers would save themselves much trouble by more enlightened

[33] *The ABC of Communism*, p. 206.

action in this direction. Soviet policy goes beyond permitting the national languages to be used freely in the schools, press, theaters, and literature. The central publishing houses themselves print copiously newspapers, magazines and books in a babel of languages—some fifty-eight of them.

Apart from cultural liberality, the "self-determination" of the "Rights of the Russian People's Act" had little real meaning. The central organs of the Soviet Union of the Party in Moscow exercise Union-wide power over industry, trade, finance, transport, agriculture, labor, post and telegraphs, foreign policy, war, and the secret police. Such discretion as remains concerns local affairs.

With respect to the "national development" promised, there was reality. Parallel with the centralized overlordship, and because of it, great industries have been planted in the minority territories that the native peoples by themselves had neither the vision, resources, nor techniques to attempt. The first Five Year Plan set out to increase the capital funds of the entire Soviet Union 289%. But it scheduled the Ukraine for a rise of 308%, the Central Asian Republics for 444%, Kazakistan for 549%, and Buriat Mongolia for 966%.

This preferential treatment sprang from economic, political, and military considerations combined. The results are no less beneficial to those populations because of these mixed motives. In other directions as well, the Government of the Union has recognized the backwardness and therefore greater need in certain of the members of the Union, and has acted with intelligence. Compared with 13.5% for social and cultural purposes in the budget of the big Russian Socialist Federated Soviet

Republic, the same section of the budget for Turkmenistan amounts to 36%, and for Uzbekistan to 48%.

There are interesting ingredients in Soviet life and policies, bearing strong resemblance to nationalistic pride, and even to imperialism. A sense of genuine pride over the cumulative achievements is mounting. This is fed by the adulations of the press and the orators over this event and that. Any slight to prestige is hotly resented, such as omission of the Soviet Government from the Four Power Pact negotiations. The youth in particular inflame more as patriots than as proletarians when a clash comes with Britain over the Metropolitan-Vickers case, or with Japan in the Far East.

To its credit, this species of imperialism can be cleared of the charge of exploitation. But without the Government's exercise of something like territorial and trade ambitions, Georgia, Armenia, and Outer Mongolia would not be appendages of the Soviet Union. Nor would several statelets have been set up next to populations of the same racial stock under other national jurisdictions, such as Karelia and Tadjikistan. They came into existence to lure their brothers over the frontier. Also, there is a door ajar in the Soviet Constitution for the reception of new duly Sovietized States.

Finally, there is benevolent reasoning in *The ABC of Communism* on the subject of backward peoples that can have more than one interpretation by a cynic. This strikes out into territory where there are no proletariat to be fathered:

". . . What is to happen to nations which not only have no proletariat, but have not even a bourgeoisie, or if they have it, have it only in an immature form? Consider, for example, the Tunguses, the Kalmucks, or the Buriats, who inhabit Russian territory. What is to be done if these nations demand complete separation from the great civilized nations? Still more, what is to be done if they wish to secede from nations which have realized Socialism? Surely to permit such secessions would be to strengthen barbarism at the expense of civilization."

Again, the Soviet Union possesses the largest army in Europe. The strength sought is one to equal that of any two of its adjoining European neighbors. The standing army strength numbers over 600,000, with 450,000 additional in regular militia classes who come up for five months of training during two years, with trained reserves fit for combat service to bring the total available for mobilization up to several millions. It is believed to be a loyal army, weighted on the side of workers rather than of peasants. Those of other than worker and peasant social origin are not trained in the bearing of arms. The officers are in large part members of the Communist Party. Few are carry-overs from the old army. No equal number of the civil population are so well clothed and fed. The discipline is efficient, but far removed from the lot of the common soldier in the army of the Czar. No class difference exists between officers and privates. Off duty, the latter are released from salute. During the two years of training, there is given a liberal education in Communist principles and in lines of service beyond the military. This looks forward to their usefulness in the Socialistic upbuilding on returning to civilian life.

The equipment of the Red Army increasingly impresses observers, civil and military alike. The newly installed correspondent of the *New York*

Times wrote of many thrills over what he called Soviet Russia's show of military preparedness to the world on the first of May, 1934. The infantry and their equipment "were as well groomed as any bourgeois army." Smart cavalry, horse-drawn machine guns and mortars followed faultlessly. Tanks ranging from Whippets "to huge fast land cruisers carrying field pieces fore and after" moved past the reviewing stand in the Red Square for an hour—about 500 of them. Impressive ranks of motorized antiaircraft guns and giant searchlights and listeners for locating enemies in the air preceded a great display of air power. It was the climax. One hundred and sixty-five six-motored bombing long-range planes flew low over the Kremlin towers, followed by attack planes in squadrons that brought the total of flying fighters up to 533.

The display, to this reporter, was in demonstration of the Soviet War Commissar's recent statement that the Red Army is the most highly mechanized in the world. With this armament chiefly of domestic production, a lately returned French observer may be accurate in saying Soviet Russia in the air has twice the potential strength of France. Does this Soviet preparedness signify dangerous militarism? Not necessarily, by itself, in the present European picture. What cannot be dismissed without more reservation is the militarizing of the mind of the entire population—albeit done in that hard-worked name of "defence."

Beginning with physical and other training in the grade schools that is avowedly pointed toward the army, the system takes on more and more military color until in the higher educational institutions the standard is set for turning out personnel that can

readily be polished off into officers. *Smena* [34] called
for the quality of "staunch generals" to come out of
the colleges. It demanded 100% attendance of the
students on all the military courses instead of the
90 to 97% then attained. Each student, in addition
to his general training, must prepare in some spe-
cialty of military value. A like obligation is laid
upon the several million members of the League of
Communist Youth for qualification in general military tactics plus specialization in aviation, chemical warfare, engineering, or first aid (for girls).

Young women go in for the sterner stuff as well.
Tobenkin, Russian-born author and correspondent,
in his *Stalin's Ladder* [35] gives this account:

"Figures for the number of women in the Soviet
Union who are training for regular army service are
unavailable for the past two years. But in the year
1930, nearly a quarter-million women were under-
going such training in military schools. Fifty-five
thousand of them qualified as rifle experts and machine gunners. Something over 10,000 specialized in
war chemistry; others took up artillery and aviation.
Leningrad has a famous company of woman snipers;
Moscow has recently graduated a corps of militarized
women telegraph and telephone operators. Tomsk
and Krasnoyarsk have women's sniping companies
that are among the best-trained in the Union. In
Omsk a woman's college trains shooting instructors,
most of the graduates of this institution being used
to organize women of Siberia and Mongolia. Camps
for summer training and fall maneuvers for this
woman's volunteer army of 250,000 are maintained

[34] April 1, 1932.
[35] Courtesy of Minton, Balch and Co., Publishers, New York
(1933).

jointly with the camps for men. After the women have attained proficiency, they are organized into mixed divisions, the proportion being about 30% women to 70% men."

To enlist and wield the adult civil population, military "cells" or circles dot the map—60,000 of them is the estimate. Every mine, mill, State farm, and large commercial or office center possesses one. There is a small armory, or "corner," to correspond in each place. The members march and drill with army rifles. Shooting ranges provide them facilities for target practice. The villages have their "defense houses." Great sections of the population go through gas-mask drilling. At the "Park of Culture and Rest" along the Moscow River can be seen boys of ten to twelve years drilling with gas masks and rifles with bayonets. The time when, at twenty-one, conscription day comes is idealized to the young. Their studies, exercise, and skills of every sort they are to regard as steps on the way to that point of dedication.

Concurrently with all of this militarization, Soviet spokesmen at the Disarmament Conference offer to the nations total disarmament in common on land and sea and in the air. The relation this gesture bears to the ongoing militarization of the whole Soviet citizenship will be canvassed under the next title.

SOVIET FOREIGN POLICIES

The facts bearing on relations between Soviet Russia and the rest of the world are most difficult to reconcile. Contradictions arise out of the dual policy set up for the Communist Party by Lenin.

The Party has two arms. Both are its creatures and equally responsive to its will. One is the Union of Soviet Socialist Republics (U.S.S.R.). It is the Party's State apparatus over the peoples of the Union. The other, the Communist (or Third) International, often designated Comintern, is its instrument of world revolution. All three have the same men as directing minds—Party, Soviet Union, and Comintern.

In the earlier years of Soviet rule, the agencies of the Government abroad were used in furtherance of revolution where they served. In 1917, the Council of Commissars appropriated two million rubles "for the needs of the revolutionary internationalist movement, at the disposition of the foreign representatives of the Commissariat for Foreign Affairs."

At this period, Lenin and the Party believed most of the States of post-war Europe were about to topple into the grip of world revolution. The program for their overthrow and that of all other "unproletarian" governments was unconcealed. The other States countered with a general economic blockade. Some participated in actual armed intervention. A virtual state of war prevailed between the Soviets and the other nations.

As their dream of immediate revolution over Europe faded and normal diplomatic intercourse with "the stabilized capitalist States" became desirable, the Party leaders found it necessary to move in the direction of taking the Government as such out of the world revolutionary game. It was difficult to do and harder still to make the other governments believe it had been done, with all good Communists being the missionaries they are. The big chiefs were wont to speak after the manner of Zinoviev. This presi-

dent of the Comintern in 1922 reported officially:
"From our Communistic standpoint it is clear that
the Communist International is very important for
Soviet Russia and *vice versa*. It would be laughable
to question . . . who is subject and who is object.
It is the foundation and roof of one building. One
belongs to the other." The foreign governments,
holding in check the Russian-inspired revolutionary
agitation within their borders, insisted that the separation of Comintern and Government at Moscow
headquarters was only façade. Evidence abounded
that the charge was true.[36]

Dating from the conception of the first Five Year
Plan, the Russian Party leadership has been letting
world revolution take the back of the stage. They
recognize that their post-war pattern of a speedy general revolution is a washout. Stalin and Trotzky
split on this issue. The former had his way in the
Party, which now majors on making good at home
and thus furnishing the masses abroad the object
lesson of the superior way of Communism and the
Soviets. World revolution has not been abandoned,
but for the time, so far as the Government is concerned, is making something of a detour.

This history has left hang-overs that operate against
relations of full confidence on either side. The
Soviet leaders do not forget the foreign armed in-
terventions. Deep-seated conviction keeps them
aware of an economic irreconcilability between
Communism and Capitalism. As Communists, they
believe the issue will be settled finally by force
sometime and somewhere. They have the belief,
not without warrant, that there are economic and

[36] *The XYZ of Communism*, Chapter X, The Macmillan Company, New York.

political interests which would destroy the rising
Soviet power and what it represents, if the way
could be found to do it. Hence the professed ob-
session about imminent danger of attack and the
preaching of it to the people.

There follows logically the speeding up of armament; a strong military motivation in the Five Year
Plans; the new heavy industrial units established
behind the Urals well beyond the reach of invaders
from either West or East; the Non-aggression Pacts
entered into on Soviet initiative with every border-
ing nation except Japan and reaching over to
France; and the proposal of an Eastern Locarno, or
guarantee of frontiers.

Fear of aggression in the Far East is undeniably
real. What one reporter calls an inundation of
Soviet troops, many kilometers deep, follows the
Manchurian frontier on into the adjacent maritime
territory. They are well equipped for land or aerial
warfare. A considerable transfer of population back
from the border insures along the possible "front"
the presence of loyal peasants and trusted workers
in factories and mines. The factories in the area
are militarized. Soviet Russia will not attack there,
but will defend Siberia with a better fighting force
than the Japanese defeated in the war with Czarist
Russia. The sworn resolve is "to covet no other
nation's territory and to yield no single inch of our
own."

Then why not perfect good-will all over the place?
There remain other facts to be reckoned with and
forgotten or explained. More than fifty Communist
parties exist in as many countries—all pawns in the
Russian Party's game. The Executive Committee of
the Comintern sits in Moscow directing operations

in its fifty-odd dependencies. They proclaim and
work fanatically for the working-class revolution in
every land; for the arousing, organizing, and arming
of the workers for readiness to revolt; to worsen conditions by inciting industrial strife; to plant and
foster sedition in the armed forces of the nations.

Now, apropos of the total disarmament offer, it
may be asked what could better further these revolutionary plans than to have the protective military
forces of the "enemy" States dissolved? It would
clear the way for the scheduled revolutionary uprisings of the working class.

No Russian Party or Soviet leader by a single word
has ever renounced revolution throughout the world,
and by the class war method. This accounts for
their loathing of pacifism and all its works. Buk-
harin denounced it to the Comintern Congress of
1928 as "thoroughly rotten, bigoted, hypocritical,
lying, and false." Later than that, the great *Peasant
Gazette* referred to the League of Nations as "the
international brothel of the imperialists." The Far
Eastern and German events caused Moscow to think
again (and France also). Whereupon, the way was
smoothed for Soviet Russia's entrance into that
world body, which Stalin in 1927 thought "not an
instrument of disarmament, but of armament co-
operating with the bribed bourgeois press" making
"war therefore inevitable."

No wholesale disarmament will take place. Soviet
Russia and the other States will be armed alike. Presumably the Government there will continue the
Stalin policy of winning success on the economic
front as the major pursuit, with world revolution
left to await "the further deterioration of Capitalism

and the complete demonstration of the Communist
system in the service of the toiling masses." In such
a situation, the workers, nation by nation, would
settle scores with their respective governments.

What then, if anything, presently stands in the
way of mutual understanding and resulting good
relations between the Soviet Union and the States
outside? Probably nothing insuperable except in
respect to some specific issue that may arise between
the U.S.S.R. and a given State, or if mankind again
resorts to the madness of a general war.

In the latter event, Soviet Russia becomes one of
the factors of the first importance. The best bet
Soviet Russians make on new mass revolutions, they
lay on the inevitability of future imperialistic wars.
They will try not to be drawn in and will let the
struggles of the warring countries leave their peoples exhausted, desperate, and rebellious—and their
governments weak. The indigenous Communist
parties will then be expected to lead the workers on
to the seizure of power and the setting up of new
Soviet States. In other words, they fear war for
themselves but hope and expect others will engage
in it.

According to authoritative teachings and current
utterances by leaders, Soviet Russia will have then
a clear rôle to play. There will be the duty to support any such new Communist State with military
and other resources. The doctrine for such a situation was expounded at length to the Third International on the tenth anniversary of the Russian Communist Revolution. Here is the draft in part: [37]

"The Soviet Union is the bulwark, the greatest

[37] *International Press Correspondence*, Vol. 81, November 21,
1928, p. 1548.

achievement of the international proletariat in its struggle against the bourgeoisie.

"The Soviet Union will support with all its forces the proletarians who attempt to seize power in their own country. The fate of every revolution is closely connected with the fate of the Soviet Union.

"The intervention of the armed forces of the Soviet Union, in case of a revolt of the workers and peasants of another country, cannot be regarded as a 'foreign' intervention, but as the active solidarity of a proletarian State in the service of the world proletariat."

In *Foreign Affairs* of October, 1933, Radek, editor of the Government organ, *Izvestia,* contributed an article on "The Bases of Soviet Foreign Policy." "The defense of peace and of the neutrality of the Soviet Union against all attempts to drag it into the whirlwind of a world war" he states to be "the central problem of Soviet foreign policy." In another passage he expresses certainty "that the masses, thrust into the turmoil of new wars, will seek a way out along the same road that was followed by the Soviet proletariat in 1917." He concludes:

"And we are convinced that, irrespective of what might be the course of the war and who might be responsible for its origins, the only victor that would emerge from it would be the Soviet Union leading the workers of the whole world; for it alone has a banner which, in case of a war, can become the banner of the masses of the entire world."

PART II

FASCIST ITALY

WHY FASCIST?

MUSSOLINI'S party, in contrast to that of Lenin, rose to power in broad daylight and public places. He challenged the political state of Italy with bitterness and boldness in open print and address. Fascism marched to power on the streets with banners.

Conditions favored change and direct action. Peace had brought disillusionment to the patriots of Italy and discredit to the old political leaders. The democratic machinery of the State had jammed. The liberal parties were stalemated. National interests appeared to be sacrificed on every hand. Public order passed out of control of the forces charged with authority as factions organized to fight out their differences and to contest for supremacy. Industrial production dwindled under a combination of strikes and lockouts. Reckless bands ranged out into rural spaces, working senseless destruction of crops and other property.

At the outbreak of the World War, Mussolini was a clamant left-wing Socialist editor in outspoken opposition to Italy entering the struggle. He moved over in a few months to such advocacy of intervention that the orthodox Party of Socialism expelled him. He took the new stand on nationalist grounds, writing in his paper: "If neutrality continues, Italy tomorrow will be a nation abject and accursed: a nation condemned without autonomy and with no future. The hand-organ man, the boarding-house keeper, and the bootblack will go on representing Italy in the world; and the world of the living will again give us a little compassion and much disdain. We shall be a country beaten without fighting for ourselves, dead before born."

Consider then the picture of Italy as this hot convert to nationalism saw it on his return from frontline triumphant service against the ancient Hapsburg power. The disarmed homecoming soldiers, leaving behind 500,000 of their dead, were being insulted and mobbed in the streets by a cross-breed of Socialists and Communists, bent on gaining their class-war ends.

The year 1919 saw violent assaults on factories and towns, with all forms of terrorism rampant far and wide. The agitators bombed railways, hotels, and theaters. The Government's prohibition of public demonstrations for Lenin met with a general strike by the Red revolutionaries. They sacked shops in the principal cities. They tore the national flag in a Milan "Red Day" celebration. The Red flag was raised over great factories held by the workers for months on end. "Workmen's Councils" after the Russian pattern called on the Socialist Party to sovietize and on the proletariat to mobilize. The Bologna Labor Chamber forbade issue of bread to all who did not belong to the revolutionary organizations. Strikes gripped over three hundred communes and strangled production. Called upon to shout "Down with Italy," loyalists were shot on the spot who answered "No, long live Italy." In reprisal, machine guns sprayed fleeing workers when the gates of a factory they had seized were retaken and thrown open.

Mussolini recruited, organized, and led his Black Shirts to meet violence with equally illegal force. The Government helplessly looked on, vacillating between blows at one or the other fighting forces and doing effectively nothing at all. A virtual Fascist army came to supersede the Government in taking over public order. With members swelled to "300,000 armed men," this Party in the famous "March on Rome" moved out to try conclusions with the existing Government of the Constitutional parties in these arresting terms:

"The Army, as the reserve and supreme protector of the nation, should not take part in the struggle. Fascism renews its loftiest admiration of the army of Vittorio Veneto. Nor does Fascism move against the forces of public order. It marches against a company of faint-hearts and ineffectives who for four long years have not known how to give a government to the nation. The producing middle classes know that Fascism desires to impose only order on the nation and to help all the forces that further its economic expansion and welfare. The workers, in field and factory and offices, have nothing to fear from Fascist power. Their just rights will be faithfully cared for. With unarmed opponents we will be generous: but with others inexorable.

"Fascism draws the sword to cut the Gordian knots that bind and paralyze Italian life. We call on God and the spirit of our five hundred thousand dead to witness that only one impulse drives us, that we possess only one will, that one passion alone inflames us—to contribute to the saving and the greatness of the Country."

The single show of resistance by the Cabinet was the declaration of "a state of siege" by the Premier. On refusal of the King to support the decree, it was withdrawn and the Cabinet resigned. A compromise offering Mussolini a Cabinet post under a new Premier, he refused, on the ground that the Fascist victory was not to be mutilated. Thereupon, the King invited him officially to form a Government. He accepted. The forty thousand black-shirted marchers as a mobilization dissolved from the scene.

ONE-MAN GOVERNMENT

The Fascist Party credits Republicans, Democrats, Liberals, and Tories with having contributed nothing to its theory or practice except lessons in what not to do. Its doctrines clash head-on with those of democracy. Moreover, its partisans glory in their position. They do not plead the necessities of a period of revolution. The doctrine, formulated for most part after the events, sweeps past a philosophy of action in a crisis to a total rejection of democracy and liberalism. Manifold charges pour out against those older political schools and all their works—parliaments, majorities, public opinion, and such. They are "outdated," "futile," "decrepit," "silly," "supine," "resorts of the weak," "tools of the designing," and therefore "dangerous."

The *Duce*, Mussolini,[1] associates democracy with "the outworn ideology of the nineteenth century, repudiated wheresoever there has been the courage to undertake great experiments of social and political

[1] *The Political and Social Doctrine of Fascism*, p. 26, Hogarth Press, London.

transformation." "Fascism," he writes,[2] "combats
the whole complex system of democratic ideology,
and repudiates it, whether in its theoretical premises or in its practical application. Fascism denies
that the majority, by the simple fact that it is a
majority, can direct human society; it denies that
numbers alone can govern by means of a periodical
consultation. . . . The democratic régime may be
defined as from time to time giving the people the
illusion of sovereignty, while the real effective sovereignty lies in the hands of other concealed and
irresponsible sources."

An Englishman's work,[3] given official blessing by
Mussolini, expounds and advocates this "authority"
principle with no less candor and realism. In the
parliamentary system, the writer sees Government "a
panderer to popularity," giving power to masses to
decide issues about which they cannot possibly have
knowledge necessary to the exercise of sound judgment. In effect, they are managed by "a limited
number of wire pullers." Power falls into the hands
of "a host of amateurs" who make "a political career
their profession." The system yields no compensation of morality "for the premium it sets on mediocre
intelligence." A business corporation so ruled would
arrive directly and shortly in receivership. For "no
Government can carry on the business of the State
properly if it has to take truck of purely captious
criticism, . . . or depends for its continuance in
power on popularity only."

Nietzsche, Barnes states, lodged with Mussolini
"the truth that the multitude must be led by the

[2] *Ibid.*, p. 14.
[3] *Universal Aspects of Fascism* by J. S. Barnes, pp. 100, 101, 106,
126, 128, 145, 150, Williams and Norgate, London.

few, and hence the necessity of an Aristocracy which represents the refinement, the exaltation, the embodiment of that kind of individualism which is worthy of encouragement, namely, the capacity of individuals to realize themselves in harmony with the good of the community to which they belong. . . ." The correct system, therefore, "should be such as to throw up in effect an Aristocracy of intelligence and morality." Within this circle will exist, to be effective, "one office of outstanding or unifying authority."

This defender of Fascism meets squarely the question, "Who is to decide the form of Government?" He answers (in his own italics): *"Whoever is, in fact, the efficient authority at any given phase of social development;* . . . the question of sovereignty is a question of power. The body wielding it is continually shifting and it is for the historian and not the jurist to designate the body that happens to be wielding the sovereign power at any particular moment." "Mussolini," he states, "considers that the best form of Government is the one which, in the given circumstances of a particular country, works best."

Under Fascism, the Party and this "indispensable Aristocracy" have become identical. Fifteen Fascists and an equal number out of four old parties made up the first Cabinet of the new régime. No Socialists were recognized. With Fascists in the House of Deputies still a minority, the first speech of the *Duce* to the body left the majority members in no doubt as to just where they stood.

"Revolution has its rights, and I am here to defend and carry forward the revolution of the Black Shirts. I refused to make an utter conquest as I could have done. I put a limit on my actions. With my 300,000 armed men, ready to dare everything and ready, almost mystically, to obey my orders, I could have punished those who have defamed and bespattered Fascism. I might have made this bleak hall into a bivouac for my platoons. I might have closed Parliament altogether and set up a Government of Fascists alone. I could have done that, but such—at least for the present—is not my wish."

This they heard with their own ears—and not long afterwards voted him "full powers"!

Similarly, he reminded the Senate: "I am not at all intoxicated with victory. I have not abused it. What was to have kept me from closing Parliament and declaring a dictatorship? Who could have resisted a party which has not only 300,000 enrolled names but 300,000 rifles? No one!" . . . "I have at once put the Fascist movement on the tracks of the Constitution. I have made a Ministry from all parties in the Chamber, . . . but I look to practical values. Political niceties do not interest me."

The years immediately following saw policies laid down that brought the non-Fascist parties and personalities into open opposition. Their progressive exit from governmental affairs resulted. The conflicts found expression in the press, on the floors of the House and the Senate, and in riots. Those who held out were met with more and severer restrictive measures, climaxed by the dissolution of the other parties and the silencing of the entire opposition press. This state continues until now.

The interim was stormy. Gun-play, assassination and reprisals, many arrests, and some executions marked the period. Repeated attempts were made against the life of Mussolini. A "Special Tribunal

for the Defence of the State," though disavowed officially as another "Cheka," [4] had all the powers needful for getting results.   One round-up of "subversive
elements" in 1923 netted over 35,000 firearms and
more than 1,100,000 rifle cartridges.   Grim work was
performed by the Party "militia," armed with pis-
tols, castor oil bottles, and clubs that one observer [5]
has described as "making Irishmen's shillelaghs look
like toothpicks."

Irreconcilable leaders of the opposition fled the
country, were outlawed, and had their property confiscated.   Abroad they spoke, wrote, and conspired
against the régime at home.   The violent among
them for long carried on murderous attacks against
Fascist foreign officials.   One plot struck at the life
of the Italian Crown Prince when he was visiting
Brussels.   The "Tribunal for Defence" sentenced
variously over 1,000 offenders.   As revolutions go,
this one will not be reckoned reckless of human life.
The total recorded toll from the beginnings did not
much exceed 4,000, about equally divided between
the Fascists and their enemies.   Numerous Russian
revolutionary episodes cost more lives, the last one
not more remote than 1930.

With violence subsided, a gesture of forgiveness
to the "outcast and deluded" marked the tenth anniversary of the "March on Rome."   Fewer than
eleven hundred people were then reported to be imprisoned under conviction for anti-Fascist crimes.
Of these, two-fifths were released by amnesty.   Another fifth received reductions in their terms of sentence.   Out of another one thousand or more who

4 The first Soviet organization for combating counter-revolution.
5 Ian S. Munro in *Through Fascism to World Power*, p. 209,
Alexander Maclehose & Co., London.

were in, or on the way to, detention camps over one-half were given freedom.[6]

The Fascist Party itself needed parallel discipline, and got it with rigor. The first inmates of detention camps were Fascists. Adventurers, and worse, such as attach themselves to revolutionary movements, were cast out. Others, given to excesses of zeal, required taming. Not a few, by provoking violence, prolonged disorder. They found themselves jailed. Abuses of power abounded. Some strong men held out on differences in policy. For one or another offence thousands of Fascists were imprisoned. More thousands met expulsion from the Party.

Relentless imposition of the single will at the top cost the Party numerical strength. It demoted from high governing posts loyal men who had been capable in revolutionary action but who proved to be without capacity as executives. This course broke long-time friendships. One former secretary of the Party was executed. In no respect did the *Duce* show himself so unmoved by temporizing considerations as in intra-Party dealings. On the single occasion when an important decision of his was formally rejected by a not very consequential minority, he resigned until, three months later, the Party Congress called to meet the resulting crisis by acclamation pledged him implicit obedience to the end.

Changes in the Constitution marched side by side with the measures for stern public order and Party solidarity—all in the direction of Party supremacy. They centralized the State's executive power and vested it solely in the Head of the Government. The Chamber of Deputies, formerly the popular and commanding legislative body of liberal Italy,

6 *Ibid.*, p. 245.

has little left that is recognizable beyond the building in which it sits. It sits by courtesy only. It has
become the humblest of rubber stamps. No bill nor
item for debate may come before it without pre-
vious approval of the same imperious official and personage.

The *Duce* as Head of the Government is more than
a Premier among equals in a Cabinet. In no way
is he controllable by the House of Deputies. He is
called to office by the King and is responsible to the
King alone. The other Ministers are responsible
to himself. They can be removed and replaced at
his will. He can combine or abolish Cabinet portfolios, or assume them in person. He has held as
many as eight at one time. A complete ministerial
renovation can take place without "the Government
falling" or the Deputies being so much as consulted.

This Cabinet enjoys the power (limited in theory
though not in fact) to emit legislation by decree.
The decrees have full legal force at once. A later
confirming vote by the Deputies is a matter of
course. The Party Grand Council reserves to itself
large powers for the initiation of legislation and the
exercise of decision in respect to most major issues.
It prescribes such feeble functions as remain to the
Deputies.

The method by which the House is chosen is insurance against rebellion in that quarter, or even
hesitation. Preliminary to an election of members,
lists totalling one thousand names go up to the Party
Grand Council from the several occupational and
other groups having the right of proposal. The
entire number will have been nominated for their
"character, expertness in their calling, and loyalty
to the interests of the nation." The Grand Council

sifts the number down to four hundred. These
nominees then go to the electorate on a single national ballot for a "yes" or "no" answer by the individual voter. If miraculously the majority vote
should be negative, the process of selection and submission would be repeated. A campaign takes on
the character of high-powered promotion to secure
overwhelming approval of the one and the same
policy of Government, Party, and *Duce*. The
March, 1934, referendum brought out a 95 per cent
expression of registered votes. Dissenters were insignificant in number. The Church lent its influence to the desired end by the priests numerously
organizing the vote of the parishes and going to the
polls with their flocks.

The Chamber itself, so representatively meaning-
less and otherwise shorn of reality, is already on the
skids. In the ultimate Corporative State System it
will have no place. Mussolini pronounced its doom
before the 1934 election: "The Chamber of Deputies
has never been to my taste. The Chamber has become anachronistic even respecting its name. It is
an institution which we found, and it is alien to our
mentality. The Chamber stands for the world we
have demolished. It presumes a plurality of parties
and, since the day we annulled them, it has lost the
essential reason for which it was created."

The Senate, Upper House of liberal days, fares
better in the *Duce's* estimation. Beginning with
Royal Princes, it is constituted on the whole more
to his taste, chiefly from among those successful in
the varied ranges of national life—academic, literary,
scientific, legal, economic—with a few of the famed
in military, diplomatic, governing, and high tax-
paying circles. Largely outside active politics, these

more grave, elderly men conducted discussions of the successive revolutionary steps, not without criticism, but with greater urbanity. Mussolini in turn has shared with the body a more full and quiet account of his principles and policies. Like the King, the Senators had more concern for the permanent values in Italy and society, and less for the ups and downs of partisan political fortune.

On the Monarchy, Mussolini shifted gears during a period when the winning of political strength called for strategy. It is not the only major instance when he chose deliberately to limit the number and strength of his enemies. The German *Führer* might have profited by this example. The *Duce's* reasoning on the subject combined expediency and historical sense. To effect the coup within the Monarchy would raise no question of recognition by foreign States. In September, 1922, he said: "I think it practicable to renew the régime in a profound way without disturbing the Monarchy. . . . We will therefore leave it out of the game, which has other more obvious and more important goals. We will also leave it apart because a great section of Italy would look with suspicion on a change of the régime that would go to such a point. We might have regional separatism. I do not think the Monarchy at heart has any interest to put obstacles in the way of what now must be called the Fascist Revolution. It is not in its interest; for, if it did, it would then become a target, and, once a target, it certainly could not be spared by us, since we should be facing life and death ourselves. . . . The Monarchy should stand for the historic continuity of the nation. . . . We must avoid having the Fascist Revolution place everything at hazard. We must not give the impression to the people that everything must fall and everything be rebuilt."

Neither was a break with the army risked, although in the early stages of Fascist activity, the Government used troops feebly a few times against the movement, and took some Fascist lives. There is a presumption even that Government, King, and army looked indulgently, if not gleefully, on the Black Shirts' progress in beating into submission the violent elements in the serious post-war agitations. With the new Party acclaiming the virtues of the army's war services and silencing its attackers, a breach between them would have been unnatural. It is highly probable that discreet collusion existed in certain army quarters. The manifesto of the "March on Rome" asked and received a hands-off attitude on the army's part. The first Mussolini Cabinet brought into the Ministry of War the victorious General Diaz, and into the navy portfolio the admiral who had won distinction against the Austrian fleet. Consistently, the Party's armed forces that fought the Fascist battles have not supplanted the army in any sense. The army is integrated with Fascist power, body and soul, and rates ace high with the *Duce*.

The executive power extends by direct line from the Head of the State to the respective units of population. No elective governing bodies or persons exist at any point on the way down. Each province receives a Prefect by appointment of the Crown. His duties include those of magistrate, the maintenance of public order, and the coördinating of administration throughout his jurisdiction. He presides over the all-important Provincial Economic Council. A *Podesta* appointed from above directs the affairs of each lesser town. He is responsible to his Provincial Prefect, whose approval is necessary for validating all local regulations. In the larger towns this official is given assistants. Advisory committees, partly representative in character, and a communal secretary are attached to the office. The *Podesta* serves practically without salary.

The chief cities receive a ruling official of greater dignity with larger powers. An inspection system, reporting to the Ministry of Interior, continuously informs the Center of conditions and keeps in perfect alignment the one-piece, iron-riveted administration of the entire nation.

If anything of control or direction by the State be lacking, the authority of the one and only legal Party will supply it. The interlocking relations with the State have become such as to make Party superior to State. A pruned membership of somewhat more than 1,000,000 in the local *fasci* form the base of the Party. By categories, the picked Party body reaches out to nearly 2,500,000 men, women, and youth in an affiliated capacity. Through them the Party leads, influences, and controls universities, the civil service, railways, post offices, militia, sports, and leisure time. Party members on admission take the oath: "I swear to follow without discussion the orders of *Il Duce,* and to serve the cause of the Fascist Revolution with all my strength and, if need be, with my blood." Instructions to the members descend to them from federal, provincial, and area Party secretaries. The provincial secretaries constitute a National Council. Above them, a Directory functions as the executive organ of the supreme Party body, the Grand Council, the *Duce* always in command. His immediate executive aid is the ranking Party Secretary—a figure second in power to the *Duce*. This Secretary sits in the Cabinet of the Government.

The Grand Council tops the hierarchy of power. Beyond being the high controlling organ of the Party machine, it is the mentor of the State. In deliberations that are secret, without legislating directly, it prescribes legislation for the House of Deputies and the Cabinet decrees, and actually drafts them. In respect to Foreign Affairs, Church Relations, Labor, Industry, and Succession to the Throne, the Grand Council acts directly and decisively. It will present to the King the nominees from among whom he will choose a future Party *Duce* and his own Prime Minister—the two offices now constitutionally prescribed to be administered by the same person.

As a further organ of Party solidarity, the Disciplinary Court for Fascist members is not to be overlooked, nor the Black Shirt Militia, 300,000 strong. They are a legalized subsidiary armed force functioning as State police. Intelligent speculation on the likelihood of Fascist power being able to survive Mussolini's lease on life must take into account this formidable structure of discipline and control. And there remains to be fitted into the apparatus of power the all-embracing, intricate, economic framework that reaches every vocation, and thereby into every household. The description of it follows.

A REVOLUTIONARY ECONOMIC
STRUCTURE

This new form has been conceived and set up to secure a planned national economy on Fascist lines. Since the lesser parts of the system have functioned longer and with enough success to have the new superstructure erected upon them as foundation, an account of the whole will best begin with them.

"Occupational Associations of the First Grade" are formed within the area of one commune or of many. It is basic that employes and employers be organized in separate Associations. A unit Association, then, will consist of workers in a given category—let it be a textile product in a prescribed territory. It becomes recognizable by the State if 10 per cent or more in that textile category in the territory are embraced. The body then becomes official. It can make labor contracts with employers and otherwise act for and toward all their fellow workers in the area, including the collection of dues from all. The yearly amount collected legally may not exceed one day's wage. Joining is not compulsory for the workers, but all are bound by the contracts entered into by the Association in the given area, whether they are members or not. Beyond its economic office, the Association has political, educational, and other welfare functions for which it is held responsible by the State. Non-members may not share in the election of Association officers, nor in the social activities and benefits accorded to members. The State limits recognition to a single employe Association in a given category and territory.

The employers in that category set up a parallel

Association. The territorial size may be the same, but not necessarily so. To secure State recognition and legality, the members must be employers of as many as 10 per cent of workers in that textile category. The Association then becomes official. It acts for all fellow operators in the prescribed area. It makes labor contracts, levies the Association assessments, and performs other functions.

The law specifies the qualifications for officers in both employe and employer Associations. It demands character, ability, experience, patriotism, and loyalty to Fascist principles. The State reserves the right to pass on the fitness of the officers chosen. It may give or withhold recognition to an Association. The State justifies its intervention at these vital points on the ground of the responsibilities committed to the bodies. They become in effect State organs.

For practical operating purposes an occupational Association, whether of employes or employers, has an Assembly of all the members. It meets at least annually. A Directorate, meeting several times a year, acts as an executive committee of the Assembly. A secretary is the ranking officer and chief of staff. The business is manifold. It covers wages, hours, and labor standards for all within the jurisdiction. The Associations enter into varied working agreements with those of other categories. The contracts have the validity of law and involve enforcement on members and non-members alike. Educational and welfare activities are conducted, funds collected and disbursed, headquarters maintained, and staff employed and directed.

An Association of the First Grade, whether of employes or employers, may have three "vertical" orien-

tations.   Our textile employe unit will unite in a
Provincial Union with the employe units of the
other categories.   The Provincial Union is styled an
"Association of the Second Grade."   It too secures
State recognition on the Government's terms.   That
status carries recognition of all lower Associations
grouped in it.   The latter must contribute of their
funds to the Union.   The Association of the Second
Grade has power to impose collective labor contracts
on the inferior Associations in case they have been
handed down from its own superior body (the Confederation to be described).   Otherwise, its powers are
concerned with overseeing and directing its member Associations when they conclude labor contracts;
and with service as conciliators in matters affecting
their dependents.   The Provincial Union deals with
its several categories through corresponding sections
(textile, etc.).

The Association of the First Grade may also join
itself to another higher body (of the Second Grade
also) known as its National Federation.   In the case
of textiles, it will be a body concerned with the
larger interests of that category directly, and with
its relations to the Federations of other categories.

The two Associations of the Second Grade—Provincial Unions and National Federations—then rise
into their appropriate "Associations of the Third
Grade," called Confederations.   Of these, under the
1934 laws, there are nine—one each for employes and
employers in Industry, Commerce, Credit, and Agriculture; and a single one for the Professions and Fine
Arts.   This completes the vertical organization.   The
newer regulations aim at simplification to give the
utmost practicable freedom of activity and development to the category Associations.   In principle, As-

sociations of the Second and Third Grades are calculated to provide the framework in the higher ranges of policy through agreements and rules within which those of the First Grade will operate. They are without any operating authority over the businesses and individuals that make up the units of the First Grade.

Besides having their place in the vertical economic edifice, the occupational Associations have their corporate or horizontal orientation. This differs from the other alignment in two essentials: first, both employe and employer bodies now come into combination; secondly, the State has representative members at every stage to assert the interest of the nation, and to subordinate both of the other interests thereto. The organs of this horizontal structure are Provincial Corporations, National Corporations, the National Council of Corporations, and the State Ministry of Corporations.

The paragraphs below, sketching the form and functions of the Corporative System, are drawn from a translation and abridgment of *Elementi di Ordinamento Corporativo,* published by the British Empire Fascist Party as *The Structure of the Corporative State.*

A Provincial Corporation, presided over by the Prefect, groups the Associational representatives of all categories (employe and employer) existing within the radius of each Province.

The several National Corporations unite the employe and employer representatives of all categories engaged in their respective lines of production. They are constituted by decree of the Ministry of Corporations, which determines their composition, attributes, powers, and administrative organi-

zation. Their entire activity is directed towards
the general interests of the nation in which are
united and absorbed the interests of the different
categories. They are, in fact, organs of the State,
and the expenses incurred in their work are borne
by the State, which allocates to them a part of
the contributions that come up from the vertical
occupational Associations.

The function of the Corporations is dual: social
and economic. They can, with the consent of the
representatives of employers and employed, establish
general rules for conditions of labor. (These rules
have the same value as those contained in a collective labor contract.) They also function as conciliators in any controversy that may arise between Associations affiliated to them. Recourse to the Labor
Courts is not permitted until such conciliation has
been attempted and has failed.

The Corporations engage themselves with the problem of unemployment. The placing of unemployed
in industries in need of labor is effected through special Labor Exchanges, established by law and directed by an administrative commission composed of
an equal number of representatives of Associations
of employers and of employes. The exchanges are
controlled by the Provincial Corporations. The Corporations exercise control over the training of the
workers, the conditions under which industries can
employ apprentices, and the professional education
of apprentices. They have the task of seeing that
employes and employers observe the laws regarding
hygiene and prevention of accidents.

The objective of the economic activity of the Corporations is defined by law as the "coördination and
improvement of the organization of production."

They cannot become producers nor take over the management of a business, nor intervene on their own account in national production. Their action turns toward dynamic activity in coördinating and improving the organization of private production. This rejects the Socialist ideology of State ownership and management, limiting it to exceptional cases where private initiative is insufficient or lacking, or exercising it in the political interests of the State.

The Corporations act directly on the different forms and factors of production, stimulating, encouraging, and coördinating business, eliminating dangerous competition, bringing backward industries in line with the more advanced, spreading the knowledge of modern systems of organization, connecting similar industries in different regions, and interesting the worker in the progress of the business in which he works. They coördinate, in fact, all production, beginning with individual business, followed by the different industries in a given district, then the different commercial interests in each branch of production, and finally the different branches of national production.

The National Council of Corporations is composed of an equal number of representatives of employers and employes in the occupational organizations, according to the importance of the branch of production. It unites the representatives of all the great categories of interests that comprise the nation. It can function in general assembly, in assemblies of sections, in assemblies of categories, and in conjunction with the representatives of employers and employes. It can give judgment on a wide range of subjects dealing with economic life, and formulate rules and laws for the regulation of discipline in labor and production. It coördinates the different collective contracts; also all forms of activity in the field of social assistance. It regulates collective economic relations between different recognized occupational Associations, between employer and employed; between producer and trader; between producer, trader, and consumers; between the different categories (such as industry and agriculture); and between industry and banking.

The National Council, therefore, is the organ through which the State can exercise its rights in full and perform its duties in superintending the economic life of the nation, which is the rôle given to it by the Fascist doctrine. The Central Committee of the National Council coördinates the activities of the Council and can, in urgent cases, act without calling a general assembly. The Central Committee is composed of selected members of the National Council, the President being the Prime Minister.

The National Council of Corporations itself, beyond being supreme in the widest ranges of economic policy, is on the way to superseding the vestigial House of Deputies. W. R. Duell, *Chicago News'* correspondent, sees the Council as "the lobbies made into one house of parliament." According to Mussolini, there has not been haste about substituting it for the House of Deputies. In the Senate, he raised the point, then commented: "We do not in any way hasten events because we feel sure of ourselves, and because, in so far as the Fascist Revolution is concerned, we have the entire century before us."

The functions of the Ministry of Corporations are to superintend and direct the consultative activities of the Corporations; to intervene in attempts at conciliation in disputes which have been referred to the Corporations; publish and ratify the deliberations of the Corporations and supervise their execution; control the services instituted by the Corporations; coördinate the actions of the Corporations between themselves and with regard to the National Council; coördinate the data of production to form a criterion in order to proportion the general interests of categories and classes with each other and with the superior interests of national production. The Ministry becomes the supreme disciplinary organ of labor and production, in that it completes and performs the two forms of State intervention in the social and economic life of the country—social intervention and economic intervention—which constitute the two fundamental principles of the Corporative doctrine.

The principle used in fixing the scope of a Corporation is that of the productive cycle. To illustrate, there is one for each of the chief products of the land covering growth, processing, and distribution: thus, Cereals; Vineyards and Wine; Wool; Beets and Sugar. To complete the list, are named Horticulture, Flowers and Fruit; Oils; Zoötechnics and Fisheries; Textile Products; Metallurgy and Engineering; Chemicals; Clothing; Paper and Printing; Building and Public Works; Water, Gas and Electricity; Glass and Ceramics; Mining Industries; Sea and Air; Internal Communications with Sections for Transportation and Internal Navigation, Auto-Transport, Auxiliary Traffic, Radio, and Telegraph; Insurance and Credits with Banks, Savings Banks and Insurance Sections; Professions and Arts, with Legal, Medical, Technical and Arts Sections; Tourist Industry; Theater.

How the many strands of interest in "a productive cycle" lead into a Corporation, there to be interwoven, may be illustrated in our standard textile category. The body of constituent members is apportioned thus: to the Fascist Party, 3; Cotton (employers and employes), 3 each; Sheep Growers, 1 each; Wool Industry, 1 each; Silk Worm Egg Producers, 1 each; Silk Producers, 1 each; Silk Weavers, 1 each; Rayon Spinners, 1 each; Rayon Weavers, 1 each; Linen and Hemp Producers, 2 each; Jute Industry, 1 each; Textile Dyeing and Printing, 2 each; Carpet and Related Industries, 1 each; Textiles Trade (retail), 3 each; Farm Experts, 1; Artists, 1; Coöperative Dyeing Plants, 1.

The Buildings Corporation affords a sample type in heavy industry. It is representative of the Party and of the employers and employes in Building Construction and Public Works, Building Materials, Cement Manufacture, Lime and Plaster Industry, Refractory Materials, Trade in Building Materials, Building Property, Professional Engineers, Architects, Surveyors, Building Experts, Crafts, and Building Coöperatives.

The powers of the Corporations within their "cycles" extend to setting limits to the annual output of an industry or the kind and quantity of a crop. By decree of the *Duce* as Government Head, these can be amplified to deal with the wage system, use of machinery, taxation, international competition, and customs duties.

It is scarcely a matter of surprise that the *London Times* correspondent, commenting on the reception of the new economic measure, reported "among the industrialists and capitalists certain misgivings" and an element favorable "among the Socialists of yesterday." He remarked too "a sense of greater and growing trust" noticeable in the masses, and "a general tendency among Italians to consider the liberal economic system as finished," because it was argued that "it has not been able to rescue the world from the chaos into which it has fallen."

The claims advanced in support of these and other revolutionary steps begin with the contention that the older established political and economic order is no longer competent to meet successfully the present-day problems. The old economy is termed "anarchistic." The new is calculated to forestall the production of anything for purely private interest. Also, production must rise above class interest whether of Capital or Labor, which "may not struggle at the public's expense." To the end of securing these objectives, the State must enter in with a final authority up to the point where the principles, framework, and regulations of the general economic order are determined. Beyond that stage, operation is held to be "free."

The Trade Unionists, Laborites, Socialists, and Liberals flatly charge this Fascist economic structure as a whole with being a studied scheme of things to perpetuate the Capitalistic system and to save private property from the rising organized power of the working classes. John Strachey,[7] lately a convert to Communism, has this to say about it: "We must define Fascism as the movement for the preservation by violence, and at all costs, of the private ownership of the means of production. This and nothing else is the real purpose of Fascism. . . . Fascism is merely the militant arm of the largest property owners, who are of course already in power."

[7] *Menace of Fascism*, pp. 124-25, Covici, Friede, New York.

An official pronouncement, issued in England by the National Joint Council representing the Trade Union Congress, the Labor Party and the Parliamentary Labor Party, gives this warning: "Here in Britain, a Working class, united in its fundamental faith, can stem and reverse the streams of Reaction in our midst. It has already successfully resisted attempts at disruption both from the Right and from the Left—from 'National Labor' on the one hand and from 'Independent Labor' on the other. If the British Working class, however, hesitate now between majority and minority rule and toy with the idea of Dictatorship, Fascist or Communist, they will go down to servitude such as they have never suffered."

Carmen Haider [8] writes of "The Meaning and Significance of Fascism": "Mussolini rose to power in Italy when the industrialists and landlords found themselves incapable of subduing the agitation of the masses. . . . Fearing the spread of Communist sentiments, the Capitalists and middle classes united for the preservation of the present order of society, which to the one group assured their rights as property owners, and which apparently appealed to the other group because it protected them from the dangers of the unknown."

The motives of others are easily invented and ascribed. Here the issue seems to turn on method and result more than on motive and principle. The responsible man in the case states the governing principle to be that the economic interests of the nation as a whole have a claim superior to those of any class; and that he has set out to protect them by the way of national collaboration. Whether, as between Capital and Labor, the balance weighs down

[8] *Political Science Quarterly*, Vol. XLVIII, pp. 558-59.

on one side or the other, there is yet no way to determine except by declamation.

As for private property and enterprise, they are retained and defended with conviction. But, if for them life has been saved, it has been by losing it. They survive only as "useful to the nation." The State holds them responsible for this result. Private property, Mussolini believes, rounds out the human personality; but it must be considered in the light of a social function. If unused or abused, it is subject to confiscation. Increased production and lowered costs are enjoined. Economic inefficiency invites State intervention in varying forms up to State management. The political interests of the State justify intervention at any time or place. Capital must share equally the misfortunes of financial crises. It bears proportionately the costs of social protection of the worker.

The lockout is illegal. Suspension of work, when employed as pressure on employes, is punishable by heavy fine; and by imprisonment if used to constrain a decision of a State body or organ. An enterprise does not operate or close wholly on its own volition. A department store, purposing to liquidate, found that 6,000,000 lire would be the sum necessary to pay off its employes under the collective labor contract. It continued in business. The State can enforce either the extension or liquidation of trusts. It tells a firm whether to build or not to build. For a given period, the Finance Minister reported 152 building applications. Eighty-eight were approved, 41 refused, and 23 sent back for more data. No new producers can enter a field without Government sanction. In all relations with Labor, the employer is yoked with his workmen on even terms up the lad-

der of the Corporative State, with the State standing master of the situation on every rung. All of
this spells old King Profit confined to a country far
from the land of *laissez faire*.

Italy under Fascism has undertaken no industrial
expansion comparable to that afoot in the Soviet Republic. There was no incentive so to do in the more
advanced state of Italian production. Progress there
has been, markedly in respect to discipline and efficiency in all industrial, commercial, and agricultural
operations. Service on the railroads and highways
compares favorably with the best in Europe. A fleet
of superb new ships has been launched. The consumption of electric power rose from the pre-war
figure of 1,785,000,000 kilowatt hours to 5,105,900,-
000 in 1933. Italy has become self-sufficient in the
output of iron and steel, although from imported raw
materials. Development of hydro-electric power will
soon bring independence from foreign coal. The
volume of oil refined increased tenfold between 1927
and 1933. Sugar production now meets the domestic
demand. Export in cheese, vegetables, and fruits has
reached large proportions. The 1933 foreign trade
balance for foodstuffs was favorable to the extent of
832,500,000 lire. (The lira is worth between eight
and nine cents at the current exchange rate.) In 1928,
before the checks on international trade choked down
the exchange of goods, the balance for finished goods
was 2,345,800,000 lire in Italy's favor in contrast to
the deficit of 192,400,000 in 1913.

The depression has taken its heavy tolls here as
elsewhere, subjecting the national income, the State
budget, and the people's scale of living to the pressures familiar across the world. Old and new semi-
public credit agencies have been called upon to give

saving aid to large and small industries, to agriculture, to provinces and communes, and to public works. Although industrial production in 1934 was running 5 per cent over 1933, unemployment rose from 866,570 in August to 887,345 during September. The widespread drought over Central and Eastern Europe in 1934 brought the wheat harvest considerably below the normal requirement for consumption.

The national budget for the fiscal year ending June 30, 1934, closed 3,766,000,000 lire in arrears on the regular account, plus 3,000,000,000 more for extra expenditures such as public works. The shortage was covered in part by a 4,000,000,000 lire bond issue. The 1934-35 budget ran a deficit of 565,000,000 lire in the first quarter—still large but nearly 600,000,000 less than for the corresponding period of 1933, thanks to drastic cuts down to a total budget of 20,636,000,-000. The public debt amounted to 103,251,000,000 lire on September 30. A 1933 refunding operation on a large scale has resulted in a substantially lessened interest charge through a lowering of the rate to 3½%.

From March to November, 1934, the gold losses of the Bank of Italy amounted to 1,034,400,000 lire. This brought the "firm cover" for the currency down to within less than three points of the legal minimum of 40%. In the first nine months of the year, the adverse foreign trade balance was 1,830,820,000 lire—an increased deficit of 764,000,000 over 1933. Disquiet over the security of the lira in December led to the call upon all Italian holders of foreign securities to place them at the State's disposal for conversion into lire at the market price, if and as needed to protect the currency. Mussolini pledged himself in 1926 to defend it "to the last breath, to the last drop of blood." Under these compounded adversities, the common life is difficult, though far from catastrophic. The Fascists stoutly maintain that their régime and system have averted a débâcle.

NO STRIKES OR LOCKOUTS

Labor is not more free. Strikes are tabooed along with lockouts, with penalties up to prison terms for violation of the laws against them. The Labor Charter presumes to provide the workers with all of the benefits for which strikes have been instituted—at least all that can be granted if the public welfare is to receive recognition. Collective bargaining with the Associations of employes is enforced upon employers. Wages and conditions of work are fixed under State supervision on the principle of the highest level justified by the condition of the enterprise, and not below the living wage minimum. Workers receive night and overtime pay on a higher scale, a weekly rest day and annual vacation on pay. Data for determination of the wage level are supplied from official and scientific sources. Nationally invoked and supervised societies for insurance against involuntary unemployment, accident, and industrial diseases have the support of compulsory legislation looking toward the general provision of such benefits.

Official labor employment bureaus have power to shift labor personnel geographically. Government recognition of an employe Association depends upon official approval of its membership list, aims, working relations with other bodies, location of offices, and use of funds. The Government may enforce the admittance or expulsion of members, the removal of

officers, or the dissolution of the entire Association.
Often the secretary will be appointed from above,
and sometimes not a worker; whereas employers
choose their own executives. Dues are deducted from
wages, of which 10 per cent are set aside to guarantee
labor contracts.

Labor Courts of equal standing with any in the
legal system have compulsory jurisdiction if a deadlock with employers has been reached. Their decisions are final. The judge has the advisory assistance of two experts—one each from the category of
employers and of workers. Conciliation is often effected, the more easily, Pitigliani [9] says, "Inasmuch
as the parties are convinced that the State, as impartial arbitrator, will always endeavor to effect the settlement of the dispute by making an equitable ap-
portionment to the parties."

From 1927 to 1933, the Ministry of Corporations
received for conciliation 497 collective labor disputes. Of these, 339 were settled by written agreement. In 62 cases, no agreement was reached, and 96
were postponed for more evidence. The distribution
of the cases follows: from Industry, 346; Agriculture,
74; Commerce, 25; Communications, 21; Banks, 18;
Sea and Air Transport, 13. In a corresponding
period of seven and a half years, only 36 collective
labor disputes reached the courts. Alfred Rocco,[10]
high legal authority, considers the entrance of the
State into disputes of this character progress in the
same direction as when it intervened to check violent self-defence on the part of individuals.

The Corporative scheme, as one piece, bears no re-

[9] From Fausto Pitigliani in *The Italian Corporative State*, p. 83.
By permission of The Macmillan Company, Publishers, New York.
[10] *The Transformation of the State*, p. 336.

semblance either to industrial democracy, to an "all-power-to-the-workers" system, or to "capitalistic exploitation." It does evidence a purpose to arrive at social justice handed down from above. Fascism claims to have sorted out and appropriated substantially the values for welfare and protection of Socialism while rejecting its principles of class war and suppressing its political party strategy.

In contrast to the general public sitting at the ring-side while Capital and Labor fight; or in tighter situations finding themselves at the receiving end of bricks, bullets and tear bombs (and always paying the bill), Fascism presents the picture of all the social-economic groups coming to terms in the constraining presence of the big State referee and policeman.

Even the lowly and original "forgotten" white-collar folks are caught up and integrated in the system with a seat and voice at least. Intellectual workers have their legally recognized Associations. These form part of the territorial unions of pooled interests, and rise into the National Confederation of Professional Men and Artists. They penetrate, too, into the National Corporations. Thus, they sit in as representatives at every point where the give and take of separate interests goes on. The twenty-one sections of their Confederation embrace Accountants, Farm Overseers, Appraisers (industrial and commercial), Architects, Artists, Chemists, Druggists, Economic and Commercial Experts, Engineers, Journalists, Lawyers, Legal Assistants, Midwives, Musicians, Notaries, Physicians, Private Teachers, Surveyors, Veterinarians, and Writers. These classifications embrace 159,442 persons in the population of Italy. Of this number, 105,484 in 1933 were inscribed Confederation members.

Membership in any occupational Association, it will be recalled, is voluntary, while all pay dues, and are bound by the agreements and contracts of the category. The extent of member participation varies in the different pursuits. Among industrial workers 1,813,463 out of 2,994,961 belong to their occupational Associations. This membership figure compares with a 1914 total of 534,229 industrial workers in the several pre-war labor organizations. Then 460,208 represented Socialist trade union strength. Nearly 58 per cent of the industrial firms, engaging somewhat more than three-fifths of the workers, have joined their legal bodies. In Commerce, the proportion of employing members of the Confederation is 4½ per cent lower—385,483 from a total of 722,969. The employe membership in that category runs still higher—368,175 out of 565,502. The highest employe ratio in any large category is found in Communications, where it is over 68 per cent.[11]

MAKING UP AGRICULTURAL DEFICITS

Farm owners and farm laborers had a class-war history before Fascism. Socialism took early root among the relatively large numbers of rural workers. Their organization leaned violently radical along with the Italian Socialist Party. Finally, the stage of violence was reached. Their "land to the workers" slogan, as they returned from the war, echoed events in Soviet Russia. The many small farmers, rather than the large owners, bore the brunt of the onset. The latter, mostly resident in the cities, remote from the actual happenings, kept aloof. For a period, the

[11] *Fascist Era Year XII* (December, 1933, figures).

small farm owners entrusted their interests to a loose
organization with uncertain policies that made no
headway against the increasing destructiveness of the
laborers' movement. Whereupon, they began joining the "Fascisti of Combat," and to meet force with
force.

Happily, rural peace came early. The two National Federations of farm owners and of workers
came into being. Proceeding on the basis of full
equality of rights, enforced by the State, they formed
the first of the Corporations with owners, laborers,
and experts in collaboration. Credit must be entered for such an achievement, following so soon
after crop burnings, killings, and reprisals between
the contending forces. The new system lent itself
to majoring on the practical aspects of agriculture
and on gains for the owners, the laborers, and the
nation at large. Owner members in the Confederation of Farmers number 662,692 from among 2,742,-
764. In the farm laborers' body, 1,926,931 belong
out of 2,815,788.

Pitigliani [12] states the Fascist case as opposed to the
Socialist Party position—that "small landed property
is a form of agricultural exploitation" out of date
and "incompatible with the interests of agriculture
and the general progress of humanity." He says on
behalf of Fascism:

"This orientation . . . is not intended chiefly to
unite the rural laborers for the purpose of raising
their money wages as far as possible, such having been
the constant tendency of red syndicalism, but rather
to represent this great labor category as regards all
problems in the national economic life in which it is

---

[12] *The Italian Corporative State,* pp. 167-68. By permission of
The Macmillan Company, Publishers, New York.

an interested party. Accordingly, it becomes part of
the business of the syndical (Association) organizations to deal with questions relating to self-sufficiency
in the supply of cereals (the Wheat Campaign, *bat-
taglia del grano*), the reclamation of marsh lands,
their cultivation and resettlement for agricultural
purposes (*bonifica integrale*, or comprehensive land
improvement), the regulation of internal migration
from one district to another according to the requirements of the various crops, the use of improved
methods of cultivation, the adoption on the part of
occupying owners and tenant farmers of a certain
quota of labor, etc."

He asks that the farm wage questions be understood in terms of the principles of the Corporative
theory. The purpose here, he says, "is to secure for
agricultural laborers, and particularly for those categories among them which are economically less favorably situated, wages commensurate with the new requirements of the times. Such wages must take into
account length of service and be so paid as to give
the agricultural laborer a certain joint interest, the
ultimate goal in applying corporative legislation in
the rural classes being to foster in them a stable at-
tachment to the land on which they work."

Mussolini has these appreciations and purposes for
his rural Italy: "To increase the fruitfulness of Italian soil as much as possible, to elevate the condition
of the millions and millions of countryfolk who work
with such sacred tenacity—there you have one of the
fundamental aims of the Fascist régime." "The real
fount, the real origin, of all human activity is the
earth." "Industrial concentration in cities leads to
the sterility of the population. Monstrous cities
with their geometrical development end up by mak-

ing a desert all around them; and in the desert life dies. This old land of Italy can give bread to her sons today and tomorrow, when once man knows how to harmonize these elements,—the sun, water, work, and science. The hydraulic, agrarian, and sanitary transformation of a region is a long job which demands the most generous force and labor of the Government."

Action follows on after this man's dreams. The disparity between agricultural and other prices (which in America and other countries brought rural catastrophe) Italy went far to avert—an easier feat to be sure than where the problem is one of surplus production. Drainage, irrigation, and clearance to bring new land into production proceeds over several million acres, while the United States, according to the Secretary of Agriculture, contends with croppage of 40,000,000 acres too much. A conspicuous project is on foot to drain the Pontine Marshes near Rome to provide homes and means of livelihood for tens of thousands of inhabitants. Sixty thousand are already there.

The notable "Battle of the Grain" was won on practically the same acreage as had been bearing the inadequate yield. It changed the 1925 import figure for wheat from 65,500,000 quintals [13] to one of self-sufficiency. Fertilizers, better seed, and cultivation did it—induced by price stimuli. Not only was a heavy duty laid on the foreign product; the milling charge allowed was very small. To keep up the price under the present self-sufficiency, the Government provides for holding back the crop by furnishing storage and advancing to the farmer a large part of the sale value. He sells when called on for delivery.

[13] A quintal equals 3⅔ bushels.

He is relieved of interest on the advance for six months. The effect is to remove the grain from speculation. Rice growers receive similar favoring facilities.

The State has taken other highly enlightened measures in the agricultural interest. The "Fowler Steam Plow" service works a revolution in the uses of great stretches of the land. Engines at each end of a field pull a plow back and forth, turning a furrow with a depth of two or more feet. The cost of 1,000 lire per hectare is advanced by the State or by consortiums of the farmers who repay over a term of years. This process redeems from low-profit sheep-grazing land that formerly could not be cropped because of underlying soils impervious to growing grains. On one given tract of land that had maintained eight families, the deep-plowing system has enabled sixty families to live. This plowing is enforced upon big landowners and companies. They have the alternative of selling to the Government for a nominal appraised value.

New waters are being channeled down to land that irrigation will make productive. Elsewhere, erosions are being checked. The present reclamation projects will provide additions of arable land equal to 14 per cent of that now under cultivation.

Corresponding to the "county agents" of the United States, "moving chairs of agriculture" go among the farmers in cars. They give practical counsel and assistance in varied ways. They offer premiums for exceptional crops. They further connections with the State agencies that aid financially in the erection of silos and community plants for storage, fruit sorting, and packing, cheese aging, and cocoon drying.

Electric lines conveying light and power begin to reach and serve the farms. Supervision and pressures secure a better adaptation of crops to climate, soil, and the national needs. The small model farms in the newly developed areas of cultivation with accessible school, church, playground, and baths look like kin to the New Deal's subsistence homesteads. The State finances the undertakings by borrowing from the Insurance Reserves. Its protection lies in the better yields of produce. Increases of ten- to twenty-fold occur. In one region, the products rose from a value of 130,000,000 lire to over 1,000,000,000, and the tax collections from 400,000 lire to 600,000.

EDUCATION BY AND FOR THE STATE

Four features stand out in education as Fascist departures from the system of liberal Italy. Fascism has introduced or greatly heightened emphases to secure creativity of spirit, physical vitality (with a military touch), a passionate nationalism, and faith unto death in one man and his leadership.

Substantial gains in the usual facilities for instruction of the young have been registered, it is true. They are simply not distinctive in the new order. Expenditures on formal education increased from 922,400,000 lire in the fiscal year 1922-23 to an estimated 1,757,000,000 in the 1934-35 budget. Attendance at elementary schools rose from 3,350,774 in 1921-22 to 4,544,368 ten years later. In the same first decade of Fascist rule, 11,000 school houses were built in 2,764 communes to serve 620,000 children. The compulsory school age has been raised to fourteen years. About 10 per cent of the young go on into courses of the American high school level or that of the German *Gymnasium*.

The ideals and principles of this formal education are more significant. Giovanni Gentile, the first Minister of Education under Mussolini, swept the whole school system with renovating breezes. His aim was that teaching should "cease to be a mere transmission of knowledge and to become . . . a live spiritual force acting on the mind and stimulating creative activity." He changed the standard of success for school, teacher, and pupil from volume of information to maturity of mind and character in the product. What a pupil was capable of doing became more important than what he had done. The courses took practical turns away from multiplying white-collared, black-coated bureaucrats, with which Italy was already choked. Most of the youth leave school prepared for the common tasks of shop, farm, and household, and nurtured in the discipline and dignity of work rather than looking for an easy life. They go out commissioned to carry on the Fascist Revolution by fashioning its spirit into objective reality throughout Italian life and beyond.

A second pronounced accent is placed on training for health and physical stamina, with military fitness and proficiency an unconcealed consummation. The pointing of mind and habit in this direction begins as early as the child's sixth year. Supplementing the formal school in this field and, indeed, taking chief initiative and control are the four youth organizations: for boys the *Balilla* and *Avanguardisti;* the *Piccole* and *Giovanni Italiane* (Little and Young Italian Girls) for their sisters. All of them are integrally under the Ministry of National Education. Membership is voluntary and with consent of parents.

At the close of 1933, it totaled for both sexes 3,454,069.

The *Opera Nazionale Balilla* in itself is a major institution in the Fascist system. It is an incorporated body that receives a brooding attention from the *Duce*. He proposes the Central Council of twenty-six members to the King, who names them by Royal Decree. The direct administration from top to bottom has more than Party complexion. It resides in the black-shirted, armed Fascist Militia—beginning with the President, who is one and the same with the Commander General of the Militia. It is nation-wide. The Central Council has its provincial counterparts—each commune its president with councillors.

The Royal Decrees of 1928 directed dissolution of all unaffiliated juvenile organizations and clubs. A building program supplies each chief city with a *Balilla* house center, with the goal to equip every town similarly. The "houses" with playgrounds and "gyms" are headquarters for activities. These include entertainment, recreation, educational development, and moral guidance. The financial support comes from Government grants through the Ministries of Education, the Interior, and Corporations, contributing members, bequests and gifts.

The grouping for program follows the ancient Roman army formation: eleven boys to the *squadra* (band); three bands to the *manipolo* (platoon); three platoons to the *centuria* (company); three companies to the *coörte* (battalion); three battalions to the *legione* (legion). Leaders by the ten thousands are required. To get the right combination for instruction and drill, these are recruited chiefly from among teachers who are in the Fascist Militia. Volunteer doctors and chaplains contribute their services. The program majors on physical training and Fascist-national indoctrination and action.

For health and physical culture, the highly favoring climate and terrain of the country are capitalized to the full. Sports, drills, induction into special avocations, and camping claim chief attention. Athletic competitions, with awards for excellence, bring forward the strongest and most competent. At an annual national meet, the *Duce* in person distributes the prizes. Each large Italian city has two camps bearing its name: one in the mountains, one by the sea. Three-fourths of the children of Italy's working class go each summer to one of these camps for three weeks.

Children to the number of 100,000, selected by doctors as in need of special treatment, are given the required facilities and attention for physical upbuilding or cure. All boys inscribed as members are automatically insured against accidents up to 30,000 lire for total disability. Sections for developing interest and skill in aviation, navigation, motors, cycling, and skiing are regarded of strategic importance and advanced accordingly.

The *Avanguardisti* are a military auxiliary, pure and simple. The leaders will have reached officer status in the Militia. The camps can be distinguished in no way from an army set-up and discipline save by the youth of the members. The armed controls, equipment, salutes, drills with arms, and rifle ranges are all preparatory for soldiering. The boy who entered *Balilla* at eight years, on coming into *Avanguardisti* ranks at fourteen is received with solemn ceremony. At the completion of his eighteenth year, he, with 100,000 of his comrades, graduates into the

Young Fighting Fascists and receives his rifle. Two years later, if he has shown promise, he enters the full fellowship and responsibilities of the Militiamen, whose prayer voices the Fascist spirit at the height of its exaltation:

"O God, who lightest all flames and strengthenest all hearts, renew each day my passion for Italy. Make me always more worthy of our Dead, in order that they themselves more strong may answer 'Present' to the living. Nourish my book [thought] with Thy wisdom and my rifle [action] with Thy will. Make my vision more sharp and my feet more steadfast on the sacred passes of my country: on its highways, by its coasts, in its forests, and on its fourth shore [North Africa] which once was Rome's. Make me worthy when the future soldier marches beside me in the ranks, so that I hear his faithful heart-beats. Make me worthy when the insignia and flags are carried so that every one may recognize in them the Fatherland: the Fatherland which we will make more great by each faithfully adding his little to the work. O Lord! Make the cross the ensign which precedes the banner of my legion. And save Italy in the DUCE, always and in the hour of dying in harness. Amen."

Such a petition, in so far as it has reality, is not the product of chance, but of tutelage from infancy. This, Fascism purposes to give to the childhood and youth of Italy. The intellectual, cultural, and emotional food supplied all are meant to induce the passion of the Fascist. The very name of the Cabinet Portfolio to which the task is committed bespeaks its purpose: Ministry of *National* Education. The control is from the center and political. No places remain for teachers not Fascist. The teacher's oath subscribes to fulfilling the duties "with the idea of forming industrious citizens, upright and devoted to the Fatherland and to the Fascist régime." The school-room decorations invariably include the *fasces* emblem, the Cross, and pictures of the King and *Duce*. The school text books and manuals for youth and youth workers bear always the motto, "Mussolini is always right."

The study of Latin now has place in all secondary schools. The "destiny of Italy" receives emphasis on every occasion. The histories and museum guides have been rewritten to relate the glories of Roman culture and power to this generation. Occasions to glorify Italy are regularly contrived. Anniversaries of events from the founding of the city by Romulus to the 1918 victory at Vittoro Veneto and the "March on Rome" feature the national calendar. In the language of the present Minister of Education, all is conducted to "contribute validly to the formation of the political conscience of the rising generation," and "to popularize Fascism among the masses." The goal has been set by the *Duce:* "All within the State, nothing outside the State, nothing against the State."

MORE ITALIANS

The weight of Fascist speech and print on the subject of family, beginning with the Party's founder, might well lead the facetious to say the chief objective is more and better children. Mussolini experienced disquiet over the continuously falling birth rate from 1921. In that year 568,000 Italian families had seven or more children. The maximum fertility was recorded in 1876, with 39.3 births per thousand. In 1929, the rate was 9.1.

Nothing daunted, the *Duce* has set the mark for an increase of 10,000,000 to the present population of about 40,000,000. He lays down the policy in terms of broad national interest. Such accession of consumers he expects will make profitable all kinds of industrial production in Italy; render the nation independent of staple food imports; provide permanently for agrarian employment for the overcrowded and workless in the cities; take up present unemployment by the public works involved; and yield rapid transport between agriculture and industry for the exchange of goods.

He further observes that added millions will serve to make "the weight of their mass and their force felt in the history of the world." These prospects explain the large outlays of funds and labor on arterial roads, model villages, flood control, irrigation projects, and the actual land reclamation measures which are bringing into cultivation areas comparable to the tract developing under the Tennessee Valley Authority.

Taking for granted that sustenance will be found for all the present and future Italian millions, the Government proceeds to have the 10,000,000 produced. The *Duce*, father of six, sets a superior example to Hitler, who also advocates a larger population but remains single. Bachelors have had the punitive tax on them doubled to yield 50,000,000 lire. Families with seven children, if in State service, have their income tax reduced to a nominal sum. (If not in State employ, a family needs ten children to win like exemption.) Up in the super-brackets of fecundity, families secure substantial bonuses, unless they are in favorable circumstances financially. Unmarried men and women meet discrimination in the employment market. Together with small families, they are also handicapped in respect to housing.

What the laws of other lands have not done to restrict Italian immigration, the new laws of Italy do to prevent emigration. In the flood tide of seeking other lands, roughly 500,000 Italians left their country annually. Now few are released, and they to adjacent Mediterranean lands. To give Italian citizenship to their babies, the Government aids expectant mothers to come to their native land for confinement. And 20,000 young Italians domiciled abroad are brought annually to the *Balilla* and other camps for vacations for the preservation of their national loyalties. An organization of Fascist origin national in scope concerns itself solely with the welfare of mothers and infants. It will be referred to again under the next title.

More is to be said for these policies, of course, than that they aim at a growing population. The family as such is central in Mussolini's ideal for society. In *My Autobiography* he pays tribute to his home as a source of spiritual refreshment. He associates private property and the family as twin pillars of civilization. To this view the Church gives solid support. It would be difficult to ascribe intelligence to a revolutionary who would undertake to found on the ruins of the family a constructive system and régime among a people of Roman Catholic nurture.

The youth product of Fascism has attractive qualities. Improved health and vigor are to be seen on all sides. The author of *Universal Aspects of Fascism* [14] writes of them thus glowingly: ". . . If we move

[14] Pp. 166, 167, 169, 170.

about today among Italy's young men and women, especially of the upper-middle classes, the nobility outside the international cliques, the sons and daughters of the professional classes, and of the peasants, the signs are extraordinarily encouraging. These young modern Italians seem to be set on combining the sporting, fair-play, chivalrous qualities of the public-school class in England, with greater intelligence, greater alertness, far greater consciousness of responsibility, a more genuine sense of Religion and artistic sensibility. The children of the new generation, the born-after-the-war, are a veritable joy to behold. They are already immeasurably superior to the children I remember in the days before the war —and this of all classes. They are healthier in their bodies, better fed, healthier in their minds, better educated. They have learned to make thought and action one, to do what they say, to say what they do, to stand up for their opinions, to be courageously sincere and sincerely courageous."

The hammering of the leaders on the rank and file who will not or cannot live the Fascist ideal, this admirer finds getting results in "a new generation growing up who promise to make a governing class really worthy of the ideal. . . ."

"The *Weltanschauung* of Fascism, in putting a premium on creative and recreative activities," he testifies, "has gained for Italy a notable victory of the cause of chastity and sobriety." "The knight chivalrous that Fascism exalts" presents "the very antithesis of the gay Don Juan," "the type that Fascism will not tolerate in any disguise or at any price."

There will be need for a great deal of this excellence to maintain dynamic where dead weight effects also must flow from a social order of one-man power (howsoever superb), a minority monopoly of initiative, Party standardization and a servile press. Senator Corbino spoke of this with rare tact and grace on January 13, 1934. The eminent scientist and former Fascist Minister said to his colleagues and the nation:

"The Italians, persuaded more and more every day of the exceptional qualities of their chief, inclined as they are to that tendency to avoid fatigue which is partly the fruit of our splendid sky, begin to grow every day more and more accustomed to throwing off the duty of overcoming by themselves the difficulties which they meet in their economic life, finding it more simple and convenient to turn to Signor Mussolini so that he may solve them. When one wants to get over a difficulty, one must first of all think of a way of doing so, then persuade those who have the same interest that the way is good, and lastly overcome the obstacles put forward by opponents. Now, all the doubts of friends and the obstacles of opponents are immediately eliminated if one is able to say that he is following the path traced by the *Duce*. Let me deplore the spread of such a habit, which might even give rise to a generation of individuals averse, either by laziness or fear, from assuming the necessary responsibility. The fact that the Chief becomes every day bigger should not authorize the Italians to make themselves every day smaller."

BETTER ITALIANS

Fascism recognizes and upholds the obligation of society to afford its members protection against life's hazards, and a level of living consistent with human

decency and dignity. It legislates to enforce these
services throughout the social and economic order.
It creates agencies whereby the authority and facilities of the State are brought to bear to guarantee national scope, coördination, and efficiency to the entire welfare system.

The policy contrasts with Socialist and Communist theory and practice in that the State does not
assume the responsibility either for administering the
services or paying for them. The principle pressed
as far as possible is that social protection and welfare
benefits shall accrue from financial participation of
the persons concerned and not from State gratuity.
Likewise the continuing private charities are con-
strained so to administer that the educational effect
will lead away from a perpetually dependent body
of the population.

The régime found Italy retarded in providing protection against sickness, accident, and old age. The
economic groups that enjoyed such protection to a
fair degree of adequacy were exceptional. A National Social Insurance Fund had been instituted in
1919. This has been continued and extended in
scope. It grew out of a voluntary Workmen's Fund
of twenty years' standing. Insurance is now compulsory against vocational diseases and tuberculosis. Affiliated with it are certain autonomous provident
schemes covering unemployment, maternity, and sea-
man's disability. Its resources reach up to several
billions of lire, invested in large part in the Government's public works, housing, and reclamation
projects.

The National Accident Insurance Fund exists to
give compulsory protection in its field. That also
dates from a pre-Fascist period when participation

was voluntary. The occupational Associations, both employer and employe, are obligated to provide their members protection in both these directions, to be financed from the funds in their treasuries. Under this policy, the number of risks covered has multiplied together with the assets and the benefits paid. It enjoys the confidence of both employers and workers. The staff includes six hundred medical men. There are carried on parallel with the service important studies in the problems of labor and its social betterment.

The social insurance costs on a purely contributary basis much exceed 1,000,000,000 lire, or about 5% of the total taxation load. Employers provide 66.6%, employes 33.2%, the State 0.2% (for seamen and a special mothers' project). Tangible results have followed these more liberal and vigorous provisions and expenditures. The death rate from tuberculosis, for example, during the first ten years fell 36%.

Immediately on coming to power, Mussolini led Italy in ratifying the Washington Convention of 1923, laying down the eight-hour-day standard. Italy has not lagged subsequently in going along generally with the agreements proposed through the International Labor Office in Geneva. Few of them remain unratified. The many accepted concern working hours, unemployment, night work for women and children, age limit for industrial and agricultural workers and firemen, weekly industrial rest, method for determining the minimum wage, the use of health-destroying substances in manufacture, compulsory insurance against occupational diseases, and numerous provisions for the protection of sailors.

Italian influences around the I.L.O. steadily exert pressure in two directions: one away from action

determined by the class-war principle and toward the
inclusion of the professional trades and farm interests; the other, for a comprehensive international
Labor Charter instead of a fragmentary approach.
Both proposals will be recognized as Fascist in principle.

Conspicuous among social welfare institutions is
the *Opera Nazionale Dopolavoro* (National Leisure-
time Institute)—in name shortened by common usage
to *Dopolavoro* (After Work). The Charter makes its
task to promote "the coördination and encouragement of institutions for the physical, educational,
and moral betterment of the intellectual and manual
workers during their 'after-work' hours." In 1932,
as many as 89.7% of the 7,249 communes in the country had their branches, with 17,809 institutions affiliated. In 1933, over 2,000,000 members were enrolled from the categories of Industry, Transport,
Commerce and Banking, Agriculture, and Public
Service. Obligatory appropriations from the funds
of the occupational Associations provide most of the
financial support. These are available, one reporter [15] observes, in the absence of need for a chest
to finance strikes and other forms of Labor-Capital
warfare.

Control issues directly from the Party. Copious
national (Fascist) instruction is supplied all down the
line along with recreation, vocational guidance, and
other educational features. In addition to contributions made to the general funds from the treasuries of
the employer and employe Associations, many of the
larger firms have branch institutes under their own
auspices. (They had been established as welfare
projects before the advent of the Fascist system.)

15 *Universal Aspects of Fascism*, p. 193.

Certain State enterprises also make separate provision for their personnel.

The *Dopolavoro* has been described as a Young Men's Christian Association, Playground Movement, Carnegie Trust, People's Institute, and the like, rolled into one. Its activities are truly multifarious— sports, camping and tours the length and breadth of Italy; radio, moving picture, theatrical and musical performances (to the extent of travelling opera companies of quality reaching rural and village audiences of many thousands); technical, cultural, and folk-lore classes; home-making, furnishing, and economy; practical hygiene, medicine, and nursing; handicraft and needlework. In these early years, a major handicap in execution of the program is the dearth of trained leadership. The surpassing achievement has been in the advance of sport and athletics. Credited largely to *Dopolavoro* is the winning by Italy of second place in the World Olympic Games in Los Angeles. The other European teams were simply outclassed.

Another conspicuous work in welfare goes on under the plans and driving force of the National Maternity and Child Welfare Institution. The enactment creating it provides for ninety-two provincial branches and for committees in every commune or village. Their service covers protection and aid to mothers before and after childbirth; the care of nursing mothers and of babies; the physical and moral protection of children under and of school age; and the protection and care of abnormal, neglected, and delinquent children. The central institution and branches are charged with coördinating the related activities of other institutions, public and private; inspecting and controlling them; attending to the enforcement of laws and regulations applying to maternity and child welfare; and carrying on educational processes favorable to the causes in hand.

Since 1925, the death rate of babies has been lowered over 24%; in the ages up to four years, 19%. Seven per cent fewer mothers die in childbirth. The care of unmarried mothers and their babies has been raised to a level where no discrimination against them remains in respect to care. Among the less favored southern and island populations 1,500 dispensaries are established to advise and assist pregnant mothers and nursing or weaned infants. Foods and medicines are provided as necessary. Traveling chairs of obstetrical aid and child culture traverse wide areas. Several hundred thousand mothers and young children now benefit each year from these ministries.

This *Opera Nazionale Maternità ed Infanzia* undertakes aid to depraved children or those in danger because of evil influences. The Children's Courts; the homes that look after children taken in charge by the police; the refuges for the care of minors awaiting trial in the special Courts; the maternity homes established in women's prisons; the study of legislative provisions to diminish delinquency among children; special dispensaries for morally tainted children (who are such a formidable factor in the degeneration of a people)—all are facets of the program for the moral regeneration of the young.

At this stage of observation and reflection, the question presses on the student—What is the driving urge at the heart of this Fascist system? In the presence of such policies and measures and others, only to be named (more constructive action toward juvenile crime, intemperance, white slavery, and prostitution), one answer in all fairness has to be flatly rejected.

It has not been conceived and set up to perpetuate the exploitation of the common man by privilege; nor has it been suffered to become the tool of oppressive wealth. Though widely propagated, such accounts sound more like the angry accusations of other schools of revolution which Fascism has balked by its strategy and program. It is not Capitalism but Nationalism that has marked this child as unmistakably its own.

PLACE OF THE CHURCH

Settlement of the Roman Question, "the torment of two generations," will be one major accomplishment under the Fascist rule certain to go down in history. After sixty years of deadlock between the Kingdom of Italy and the Vatican over the removal of Rome from the temporal Papal power, events had moved to bring both State and Church into conciliatory moods. The motives naturally varied. On the part of the Church, with the Austrian power broken by the war, need existed for the support of a strong, truly Catholic state. Although the Fascist Party had destroyed the Popular (Catholic) Party in Italian political life, it held the gate against the rising Socialist and Communist forces that had so menaced religion and the Church. Mussolini and his régime by conviction stood with the Church on such fundamentals as the Christian family, religious education, and morality.

Influencing the *Duce* and Head of State were his own Catholic moral and spiritual principles. He was not without need of political support. The democratic-liberal forces were making their united stand against him to a finish. The Church's backing might be decisive. The war, by the brutal weight of its materialism oppressing the soul, had recalled the Italian people, 99 per cent Catholic, as a whole, to a higher appreciation of true religion. Millions, more deeply than ever, were distressed by the division of their loyalty. They yearned for reconciliation. Time had removed on both sides the original clashing personalities, and replaced them with new and unembittered leadership. It was time for rapprochement, and the two able Italian men, each with unlimited power in his sphere, seized it—Benito Mussolini and Pope Benedict XV.

The terms of this 1929 settlement (known as the Lateran Agreements) created an entirely free State, City of the Vatican, in the very center of Italy—Rome. The Italian Government gave the Church the sum of 1,750,000,000 lire in cash and securities as compensation for the usurpation of the past times. It recognized the Catholic Church as the sole Church of the State and accorded special favors to all ranks of priests and religious orders. Teaching of the Catholic religion in the elementary as well as the secondary schools was pledged. Marriage by the Church was made obligatory for Catholics. Mutual recognition was given to the full sovereignty of the two States. The question of tolerance to other religions was omitted from mention. In practice, freedom has been accorded them. The Italian State, not the Church, is their supervisor.

A sharp conflict in interpretation arose over education of the youth. Fascism claimed supremacy in the field and independence of any other influence. Fascist education of youth, aiming to create a dominating nationalistic mentality, lacks accord with the

spirit of the Catholic Church in this and other respects. The fight was acute between two opposite
and absolutist finalities. A Papal encyclical letter
claimed the real education of youth for the Church,
preëminently, as a supernatural motherhood; and,
secondly, for the family as a right, precedent to that
of the State, but under the tutelage of the Church.
Publication of this document (which had great effect
on public opinion) was followed by a practical agreement between the Fascist Party and the Vatican. All
religious education in the Fascist organizations—
Balilla, Avanguardisti, and the rest—was placed in
the hands of special chaplains. The hours of instruction were fixed not to conflict with those of Mass.

To teach the special courses on religion in the
schools, many hundreds of priests entered the schools
as teachers of Catholic doctrine. (This teaching is
not compulsory for non-Catholic people.) They were
not accepted without opposition by the lay teachers,
especially by the professors of philosophy, who as-
serted the rights of philosophy against the rights of a
definite dogma. But the priests remained.

Another bitter conflict arose over the Catholic lay
organizations. The Church reiterated its appeal and
right to increase their efficacy—especially in the social
domain. This assertion met in Fascism the most
open opposition. Some meetings of the Catholic
university youth were forbidden. In an official
speech, the Secretary of the Party declared certain
aspects of the Catholic Action Society must be considered as "perhaps useless and perhaps dangerous."
The Pope answered personally in reaffirming the
right and duty of the Church and the Hierarchy to
form and to direct the Catholic Action and so "to

exercise its influence in the social and industrial domain."

By June, 1931, the situation had become acutely aggravated. Some Italian newspapers began a wide campaign to show that under the Catholic Action banner a vast anti-Fascist organization was concealing itself. It provoked on the part of the Fascist youth a reaction, often violent, against the Catholic youth. The police authorities closed all Catholic youth circles of both sexes. Many Catholic circles were invaded and sacked and their members insulted and caned. The institution of the Church itself, the priesthood, and even the person of the Pope were disparaged. Newspapers and periodicals vied with one another in every sort of accusation. The most vulgar anti-clerical literature emerged.

After long and laborious parleys carried on in secret, an agreement was signed in which the Italian Catholic Action passed officially under the supervision of the Bishops, adopted the national flag as its own, and limited itself to spiritual and religious aims, renouncing every other activity. The youth sections of Catholic Action received recognition with the same limitations—enjoined thus from any activity in athletics and sports. They confine themselves entirely to activities of recreative and educational nature having religious ends. Disagreement ceased, leaving the impression of a clear victory for the Government. It took from the Catholic circles every possibility of entering the field of politics and of sport, and retained for the State alone the right and the care of the total secular education, formation, and preparation of Italian youth.

Polemics ceased. Subsequently, the Pope conferred the Order of Christ upon the King and the

Crown Prince, and the Order of the Golden Spur upon Mussolini. The total impression left is that the accord is more political than spiritual. Along with moral principles and social ideals they hold in common, there remain some fixed gulfs between Fascist and Catholic ideology and objectives. Convincing evidence of this is the recent placing of the writings of Professor Gentile on the Index of books forbidden to Catholics. He is the preëminent philosopher of Fascism and its outstanding educator. (He will be recalled as the Minister of Education who renovated the entire State system of instruction.)

No prominent Fascist leader can be pointed out who has concern for the interests of the Church in the ecclesiastical sense. It is most doubtful if the Fascist contribution to the uprearing of youth has a churchly content apart from that which the Church itself provides through its access at organizational points. All of this must be patent to the all-seeing mind of the Church. Yet, at that, the Church fares better than under the liberal régime which the Fascists displaced. The position of the Protestants also has been clarified and made legally secure.

"LONG LIVE ITALY"

In Nationalism, Fascist ideas find unification. An assertion so sweeping calls for evidence. Mussolini broke with the Socialist Party and his Socialist comrades on the issue of Italy's intervention in the World War. He took the stand for the nation's interests and honor. Nothing connected with the step indicates any conscious or implied disloyalty to the cause of the working class, nothing to suggest the man had forgotten, who as a youth under twenty knew the aching muscles of brutal work, hunger, and the night shelter of a barge, a bridge, or a lavatory. He took on the cause of the "Italian land and people unredeemed" from Austrian rule.

This opposed the internationalism of the Socialists, which he abandoned because he saw it crumbling. "The unit of loyalty was too large." [16]   To love of nation the road brought him after travel with Russian Nihilists, Anarchists, Radical and Moderate Socialists, Syndicalists, and Republicans. The tomes of Marx, Hegel and Sorel, which he ransacked and discarded, are now presented in the Fascist Revolutionary Exposition in Rome as burdens on the workman's back, bowing him to earth. Somehow during the sacrifices of the Carso trenches in his Bersaglieri regiment, a sense of the worth and needs of Italians moved in and took complete possession. He came under ministries of inspiration from Dante, Mazzini, and Garibaldi.

Peace came without the full compensation which he thought Italy merited. The Government at Rome was giving away the birthrights. Over the evacuation of Albania, he wept. "As if by a revelation," he says in *My Autobiography,* "I came to realize that Italy would be saved by one Historic agency—in an imperfect world, sometimes inevitable still-righteous force." "Save Italy"—let it be noted. The blunt instrument of this salvation, the "Fascisti of Combat," he "consecrated to the solution of the fundamental problems of our nation," amid which twenty-seven different Italian political parties were floundering.

The Socialists alone seemed to know where they were going. They announced officially in the spring

[16] *My Autobiography,* Benito Mussolini, p. 36, Charles Scribner's Sons, New York.

of 1919 the policy of a revolution to establish proletarian power. The current defamation of the returned army and the proposed despoiling of its
costly victory roused him to fury, and to this language: "Stand back, you Socialist jackals! It is forbidden to divide the dead. They are not of Party
but of Country and of Countries." "Do not fear,
O Glorious Spirits, we will defend you even at the
cost of digging trenches in the plazas and streets of
our cities."

The triumph of Fascism set up the power of no
class. The former "great ones" are little in evidence
in the high places, less than in any democratic State
that can be named. The Fascists have been called
"a minority, possessed of a creed and the zeal of
missionaries, who seized power in the first instance
by violence, albeit with the passive consent of the
vast majority of Italian citizens, sick to death of the
old order." [17]

Foreigners and Italians alike testify to the existence of a new Italy. A change in spirit has taken
place widely enough to be identified. The quality
is above that of devotion to country "right or wrong."
It partakes more of the sense of honest pride, of aspiration for a yet greater Italy in all that is worth
while. Recognition that among the prices to be paid
are unity, work, responsibility, governs millions now
who before thought much of rights and little of
duties. Changing the celebration of corner-stone
laying to that of placing the capstone on a piece of
construction is a characteristic bit of stimulus to
achievement applied by the *Duce,* with a touch of
grim humor. One Scotchman [18] thinks he has

[17] *Universal Aspects of Fascism,* p. 15.
[18] Munro, *Through Fascism to World Power,* p. 406.

changed the spirit of a race, individually and collectively.

There is an almost religious content to zeal for
one's country like this: [19] "The only things at which
I aim are those which identify themselves with the
greatest objects of life and civilization, with the highest interests, and the real and deep aspirations of my
country." He has been credited with this prayer—
"O my God, let me perish if only Italy may be made
great in the eyes of the world and in Thy eyes."

Here is the driving passion behind measures of
force, hardship, and sacrifice that will have to go
down as acts of cruelty or vengeance if they are to be
otherwise explained. It is a passion unspent on domestic affairs. There are international policies that
have their source in these high altitudes of his purposes for Italy. The Associated Press relayed from
Rome on the eleventh anniversary of the Fascist
régime the wish of Mussolini "to give the Italian nation a hard but magnificent task, that of obtaining
primacy on earth and in the skies"—primacy "both in
material things and in the spirit."

THE BIDS FOR POWER

A voice like that ringing out across the world arrests attention. It invites examination into the specifics of a national aspiration so expansive. Does it
foreshadow selfish imperialism, or a certain sublima-
tion of national ambition that bodes only good for
mankind? Data are plentiful. The *Duce* has spoken
his mind freely, even volubly, on the entire range of
external affairs.

[19] *My Autobiography*, p. 205.

There are rather profound stirrings in the Fascist heart for reviving and diffusing "the spirit of ancient Rome." There exists a "Committee of Action for the Universality of Rome," under Government patronage, with purposes expressed in terms wholly benevolent. It works under the conviction reflected by Alfredo Rocco, Minister of Justice. In writing on "What is Fascism and Why?" he calls on the Fascist State to "fulfil in the world the civilizing mission entrusted to peoples of great culture and great traditions . . . beyond its own borders."

This language means more than merely employing on a universal scale the methods by which classical culture over the world appropriates from the enormous values in ancient Roman law, history, and art. It envisions world-wide reëmbodiment of the old worths and glories after the pattern of Fascism, but by peaceful means. This outreach marks a long distance traveled from an early dictum of Mussolini that Fascism was not exportable. Witness this confidence expressed by him in October, 1932: "Today, with full tranquillity of conscience, I say unto you that the Twentieth Century will be the Century during which Italy will return for the third time to be the director of human civilization, because outside of our principles there is no salvation for individuals and far less for nations."

In the years before he spoke in what might be called the mood for peaceful penetration of the world, the spectacular Italian revolutionary leader gave it a shuddering case of nerves with sword-rattling exhibitions. The fires raged in his soul over what had taken place at Versailles against Italy. The combination of forces against Italy's claims had overpowered the representatives of the weak Govern-

ment, which he held in contempt for its pacific helplessness. As the Treaty neared completion, he had
publicly denounced French ingratitude, Wilson's
broken faith, and Anglo-Saxon imperialism. He
came out for banishing foreigners from the Mediterranean "beginning with the English." He had proposed aiding the Egyptian revolutionaries in "that
ancient Roman Colony, the national granary of
Italy." As for France, she must lose her Mediterranean Empire, "beginning with Tunis." . . . "The
decisions of the four old idiots in Paris (Clemenceau, Lloyd George, Orlando, and Wilson) should
have no sanction by the Italian people." And now
this bristling Italian was in the Quirinal!

His later responsibilities as Premier softened somewhat the Fascist Chief. He toned down his former
fearsome revolutionary language; but it still lacked
greatly in the quality that the jumpy diplomacy of
the period preferred to hear. His first speech to the
Italian Senate was punctuated by declarations like
these: "Our policies will not be that of imperialists
who seek impracticable aims, but equally it will not
be a policy of submitting to everything sooner than
to use force." "I think I have made the Allies, and
perhaps the other European nations, understand the
change that has come over Italy; . . . an Italy which
. . . proposes with its own strength, its own labors,
its own passion, to create its own future."

The abrupt dealing with Greece over the killing of
some Italian surveyors in Albania temporarily made
the worst fears appear to be coming true. A one-day
ultimatum to Greece read no less peremptorily than
that of Austria to the Serbs in July, 1914. Anything
might have followed. The Greeks bethought themselves of the new League of Nations. That body,

which held the world's hope for peace, Mussolini proceeded to flout. At the zero hour, the Italian fleet
bombarded Corfu. He did accept mediation by the
Council of Ambassadors still engaged in remedial
political surgery over Europe. (It was the Council's
surveying party that had been shot up.) Greece
bowed to a settlement that met the severe terms first
laid down. These included payment of an indemnity
of 50,000,000 lire, which Mussolini turned over to be
used for the relief of refugees in Asia Minor.

The short-changing of Italy by the Allies in paying
what the Treaty of London promised gave the new
Head of Government the motive and grounds for
his early and continuing foreign politics. The chief
defaults in payment were along the eastern Adriatic
coast, in Asia Minor, and in Africa. At London, the
Italians were assured of positions in Dalmatia and
Albania to give complete command of the Adriatic.
Versailles required these to be divided with the new
French ally—the Kingdom of the Serbs, Croats, and
Slovenes (Jugoslavia). Between the belligerency of
Kemal and the acquiescence of Britain and France,
the coveted province of Adalia was saved to the
Turks. The Italian share in the African colonies of
which Germany was dispossessed, the two big Allies
kept finally for themselves.

Although important new factors had come into the
total situation after the London agreement (such as
the entrance of the United States into the war and
the collapse of Russia), Italy's grievances were real.
Nearly 6,000,000 soldiers had been mobilized. Well
over one-third of them went into front lines of combat. They suffered nearly 1,750,000 casualties.
These included more than a half-million dead.
Towering debts had been incurred to press upon a

relatively poor population as daily reminders of the sacrifices and the bad faith. Hence the steadfast lining up of Fascist Italy on the side of the countries demanding Treaty revision.

France has been envisaged as the *bête noire*. The clashing interests of the two powers make an impressively provocative, not to say ominous, list. Italy covets Tunis for colonial expansion. France got there first and feels none too comfortable over the 130,000 Italians resident in the land. Measures for de-Italianizing them have consumed the time of much Franco-Italian diplomacy. Orlando, at Versailles, sought better frontiers around the Libyan colony of Italy in North Africa. Clemenceau tendered a rebel-infested desert parcel, conditioned on Italy protecting the abutting frontier of the French possession. The offer was declined, along with that of the Georgian Caucasus proffered Italy as consolation for being denied Turkish Adalia. Tagging Italy with Georgia would have served two purposes. It would have forestalled Soviet rule there, and kept Italy preoccupied with defending it from the Bolsheviks.

France financed and armed Jugoslavia in her encirclement of the defeated Central Powers. According to repeated public statements of Mussolini, the measures aim directly against Italy. The baking at the London Naval Conference came out with no more than half a loaf because France refused to concede Italy naval equality in the Mediterranean. The basic conflict of interests concerns the command of these waters. France, therefore, bars the way to Italy becoming a first-rate Power. Mussolini proposes to liberate the "prisoner of the Mediterranean" from the menace of a superior and not over-friendly neighbor able to intercept coming and going through Gibraltar, Suez, and the Bosporus.

To aggravate the troubled situation are other grudges, old and new. In the period of Italian unification, Savoy and Nice fell to France through a half-kept, half-broken promise of Napoleon III. The same French Emperor's troops kept the new Italian State out of Rome until he withdrew them for the 1871-1872 war with Prussia.

Following the Mussolini-Fascist coup, France, famed as refuge for the politically persecuted, has been headquarters for the *Fuorusciti* ("gone-out") émigrés from Fascist rule. From this base, their organization has taken heavy toll of Italian State officials and property across the world. The leniency which the French Government has shown known offenders appeared to the Fascists something near to collusion. At one stage the *Duce* protested: "The culpable and unheard-of tolerance given beyond our frontiers must cease if the friendship of the Italian people is desired—friendship which might be fatally compromised by episodes of this kind." This experience affords the background of Italy's refusal to surrender certain alien refugees charged with helping to assassinate King Alexander of Jugoslavia in October, 1934—a plot which also cost the life of the French Foreign Minister.

The total effect has been to align Italy and France on opposing sides of most of the post-war issues. In the Franco-German grand drama or tragedy occupying the European stage, Mussolini until 1934 was prominent in the pro-German cast in every act except when the curtain rose on the German-Austrian *Anschluss*. Often he had the stellar rôle. He began calling early for an end to the odious distinction be-

tween the victorious and the defeated nations. The
French occupation of the Ruhr displeased him,
though he took the precaution of being there in the
person of technical representatives to protect Italy's
share in reparations. He came soon to favoring can-
cellation of all the war indemnities and debts. Certain of the new frontiers were to him "immoral and
barriers both to economic recovery and to peace."

His influence throughout the Disarmament Conference was consistently exerted toward reduction of
the swollen armaments set up and maintained to
keep the territorial *status quo* of Europe. Failing in
that, he stood for the permissive rearming of Germany. This concern for the defeated extends to
Austria, Hungary, and Bulgaria. It reflects the east-
ward thrust of his ambitions for Italy—partly commercial and peaceful toward the Danubian and Bal-
kan areas—but not less to check French hegemony
now exercised in these parts through the Czechs,
Roumanians, and Jugoslavs.

With alliances and understandings brewing outside
the League of Nations, the progress of disarmament
has bogged down in the welter of conflicting national aspirations. Dissatisfied Central Europe still
confronts the sated Western and Eastern parts. The
Nazi threats to the independence of Austria first seriously weakened the Italian-German working relations. The summer events of 1934 quite halted the
former team-work.

They did not change the basic community of interests of the two nations unless France, at a handsome
price, induces Italy to join in the permanent encirclement of Hitler's Germany. Two items on the
Italian bill will be Mediterranean naval equality,
and the breaking of the French-Jugoslavian alliance.

The late King Alexander was en route to Paris to
block such a bargain, when the French Foreign Minister and he were shot down in Marseilles. If Mussolini gets his price, the Little Entente (Czechoslovakia, Roumania, and Jugoslavia), blessed by France
to keep Hungary and Bulgaria shackled, will be
broken. Small wonder all Europe is under tension.

Whether Fascist power over Italy spells war or
peace remains for time to reveal. Mussolini speaks
much of the Italian people's right and will to live.
He deplores the scant resources of the peninsula
and islands, for the support of forty-odd millions of
them. They increase at a rate approaching half a
million annually. The surplus formerly emigrated.
By reason of less hospitality overseas and domestic
restrictions, these now accumulate at home to be fed
and clothed. He seeks to stimulate a birth rate that
will make 50,000,000 to employ and support, and
then 60,000,000. Lately he acted as host in Rome
to mothers who had brought forth 1,000 *bambinos*
on a scale averaging fourteen per mother. With
intelligence he labors to create more fruitful fields
and profitable factories. By more than a score of
trade treaties, he has had Italy reach out to foreign
sources of the needed raw materials, and to markets
that will be an outlet for Italian industrial and agricultural surpluses.

He makes few surveys of Italian foreign policy
without bringing territorial need to the fore. There
are five possible courses (or combinations of them)
for such a statesman and people to pursue. He can
intensify production to meet all requirements (which
seems impossible for Italy). He can encourage a
lower birth rate. (This Mussolini says he will not do.)
He can let the standard of living decline. (The

Duce has often implied he will fight before it comes to that pass.) He can try to induce the gift of lands by other nations. Finally, if they will not give, he can try to take more territory by force.

Le Temps of Paris, in the temper of international realism, believes:

"None of the peoples which found their unity in the framework of frontiers fixed by treaties will ever voluntarily consent to the abandonment of any single part of their territory. . . . If war is to be avoided, the idea of treaty revision must be set aside." This squares with Continental Europe's history.

The French *Figaro* warns: "There can be no improvement in Franco-Italian relations unless our friends and Allies are not asked to make sacrifices incompatible with their vital interests and their dignity as sovereign states." The logic of it all is war, however peaceful the declarations. Whether or not Mussolini is leading his people toward or away from the ways of peace, his foreign policies have brought Italy into a place of prominence and influence incomparably higher than when he initiated them. In this fact the *Duce* delights and exults as partial fulfilment of the dream of national grandeur and an earnest of the future. If war ensues on the modern scale, he stands more than an equal chance of proving the ruin of his people rather than their savior.

PART III

NAZI GERMANY

"HOMESICK FOR DESPOTISM"

FROM the beginning of the World War, life for the German people has been a cumulative breeder of revolt. To the strain of the exhausting struggle was added the surprise, shock, and bitterness of defeat. Peace brought no respite. The charge of sole war-guilt, admitted now by most historians to be false, rankled increasingly with the years in every German. The pyramiding of penalties in the Versailles Treaty, as if the indictment were true, was so oppressive that the single item of reparations had to be reëxamined three times. The best economists of all the powers found the terms impossible of fulfilment, and progressively reduced them. Meanwhile, the recuperative power of the people was being extinguished under the load. The prophecies of Keynes and Hoover that the Treaty would wreck the economy of Europe came to pass. It helped prostrate the financial order of the world.

The attending evil of inflation wiped out the Government internal war debt, but ruined the entire middle class. Far from experiencing the beginning of recovery, this bulwark of German stability was pressed ever harder to maintain existence until it became the soil in which the Nazi ideas sprouted, took root, and spread. With general buying power restricted sharply, agriculture soon fell under eco-

nomic blight. The farms yielded insufficient return
to meet the multiplying taxes, the accumulating
farm debts, and wages of the extensive rural proletarian labor. Economic extremity, the forerunner
of revolution, then had the two most sober sections of
the population in its grip. Under such conditions,
rising murmurs against the Government and its supporting parties had resonant national sounding-
boards.

The air was full of questions and charges. What
about the whole republican system? How can it
cure our ills? Did it not create them? Its sponsors
signed for the war-guilt shame and for reparations
to break the backs of three German generations.
Its ministers have been subservient to our vindictive
and merciless neighbors. They sit with them in conferences without end, but we remain as we were.
The historical lie is unrecalled. Helpless before the
heavily armed nations that encircle us, we are made
to pay unjust and impossible tribute out of our economic misery. After $9,538,000,000 (gold before de-
valuation) [1] in reparations have been bled from our
economic arteries, yet more is demanded. Taxation
and assessments for social protection consume more
than one-third of our lessening incomes. We are
being led away from life and hope.

National elections, following one on the other,
grew in bitterness. They resulted in ever-tightening
party deadlocks in the Reichstag. Near the crisis,
two of the major blocs fought out their hatreds on
the floor in physical combat. Their followers emu-

[1] This is the figure of the Brookings Institute of Economics. The
amount named by Germans is nearly twice as large; by the French
about half as much. The true net is smaller than the Institute
figure by as much as $3,000,000,000 of German foreign borrowings
during the period.

lated them in the streets with firearms. The aged President, unable to find a Chancellor who could command a parliamentary majority, had recourse to the constitutional provision for ministerial rule by decree. He gave three successive Chancellors virtually dictatorial powers. Even before Hitler, the Republic was dead.

It is reasonably certain that the Republic never enjoyed the favor of a German majority, even at its inception. President Wilson had led the Allies in making a German Republic an advance condition of peace. But for the German people life during the whole fifteen years the Republic endured brought almost nothing but misery. That most of the unhappiness would have ensued, in all probability, under any régime, is here beside the point. The man on the street only knew that these were bad years, and he hated the Republic accordingly.

For whatever of distress the Republic was blamed, the Social Democrats were certain to be charged. They had brought in the new order and had had most to do in determining its forms. They constituted the major bloc in the coalitions that governed through most of the republican period. To be sure, they have to their credit achievements that will be enduring; when passions have cooled, these services will be recognized and honored by Germans without regard to party. Conspicuously, the Social Democrats averted an immediate post-war demoralization of German public order. Their improvement of housing for workmen in the cities advanced it beyond that of any State in Europe, if not in the world.

Parallel with good works they made fatal mistakes. They had unprepared leaders. Not all of them were honest. Weaknesses sapped away the

Party strength until its exit from power took on the character of abdication rather than of well-resisted defeat. They were not realistic revolutionaries. They did not crush their enemies. They placed blind trust in democracy. They met the fate of the Russian Mensheviks and Socialist Revolutionaries, though less summarily.

Changing the flag of the nation was a costly blunder in judgment. For the body of German people, the old tricolor had sacred attachments. On the "Day of Potsdam," when Hitler's inaugural was celebrated, the exaltation of the Nazi revolution reached its height. The old standard, its legality restored, leaped to flagstaffs throughout the land that had flown no insignia of the State until again the one could be raised under which brave men had gone out to die from homes that loved them.

In 1918, the Socialists and other republican parties took over rule from an administration that had been strict, honorable, efficient, and respected. The new one developed enough corruption to shock the German sense of civic honor. What several flagrant scandals in high places and much petty grafting did not do to shake confidence in the new system, was done by propaganda in skilful and unscrupulous hands.

The Social Democrats proved sufficiently incapable in the administration of the social institutions of the State to alienate widely their natural constituency. Here they revealed their most vulnerable side. German protection against sickness embraces millions of the working and middle classes. Extravagant buildings, swarms of job-holders, fat salaries, red tape, and other sins of bureaucracy came to enrage the whole citizenry. On this ground, more

than any other, the Brown Shirts penetrated deeply
into working-class ranks.

An eminent, close friend of Social Democrats,
warmly sympathetic with their cause, when asked to
account for their sorry show of strength in the revolutionary crisis, replied: "Social Democracy is eighty
years old with the weaknesses of age. Its leaders had
become tired, bureaucratic, and comfortable. They
no longer had a Movement." In 1920, they stopped
the Kapp reactionary *putsch* in its tracks by calling
a general strike of the Trade Unions. Little more
than a military gesture then had to be made. Twelve
years later that might was reduced to a shadow.

German life also experienced the sagging of
morals common in the post-war period throughout
the world. The administration of the Republic,
especially in Prussia, lent itself to the loosening of
social sanctions. Literature, art, the press and stage
had full license. Sexuality expressed itself un-
checked. The busiest Berlin streets became crowded
with undisguised prostitutes day and night. Well-
known houses for the patronage of homosexuals,
both male and female, were unmolested. The no-
torious El Dorado, a few doors from the American
Church, off Nollendorf Platz, until closed by the
new Nazi rule, harbored scores of men dressed and
adorned as women. All facilities for assignation
were provided—café, dancing, and private rooms.
Upholders of religion and morality of all Confessions
saw the national character sinking in quagmires of
unbelief, immorality, and pessimism. For this condition, they blamed the ruling order.

It is nothing remarkable, that after fifteen years
of grinding economic pressures, flagging morale,
moral decadence, and collapsing public order, the

Germans, as Edgar Mowrer puts it, "got homesick for despotism." And if out of the compounded adversities, griefs, resentments, and fears, no leader had emerged with a sense of mission for deliverance, history would have furnished a striking case of failure to repeat itself. In Adolf Hitler, one presented himself, who after thirteen years of revolutionary campaigning was called by Hindenburg to the Chancellorship with a Reichstag majority behind him.

The objectives of the revolutionary movement are set forth in the Program of the National Socialist German Workers' Party. This Party (usually abbreviated to Nazi) has been the vehicle and instrument of power created by Hitler and his first colleagues. A mass meeting of the Party, held in Munich in February, 1920, announced "to the world" the Twenty-five Points summarized below:

1. Union of all Germans to form a Great Germany on the basis of the right of the self-determination enjoyed by nations.

2. Equality of rights for the German people in its dealings with other nations, and abolition of the Peace Treaties of Versailles and St. Germain.

3. Land and territory (colonies) for the nourishment of the people and for settling surplus population.

4. None but those of German blood, whatever their creed, to be members of the nation, and therefore citizens.

5. Any one not a citizen of the State to live in Germany only as a guest subject to foreign laws.

6. All official appointments, of whatever kind, whether in the Reich, in the country, or in the smaller localities, to be granted to citizens of the State alone.

7. The State to make it its first duty to promote the industry and livelihood of citizens of the State, to the exclusion if necessary of foreign nationals.

8. Non-German immigration to be prevented, those having entered Germany subsequent to August 2, 1914, to be required forthwith to leave the Reich.

9. All citizens to be equal as regards rights and duties.

10. The first duty of each citizen to be to work with his mind or body, and within the framework of the community and for the general good.

11. Abolition of incomes unearned by work.

12. Ruthless confiscation of all war gains.

13. Nationalization of all businesses which up to the present have been formed into Trusts.

14. The profits from wholesale trade to be shared.

15. Extensive development of provision for old age.

16. Creation and maintenance of a healthy middle class; immediate communalization of wholesale business premises, and their lease at a cheap rate to small traders.

17. Land reform suitable to the national requirements, with provision for confiscation without compensation of land for communal purposes; abolition of interest on land loans, and prevention of all speculation in land.

18. Ruthless prosecution of those whose activities are injurious to the common interest, with death penalty for sordid criminals against the nation, usurers, profiteers, etc., whatever their creed or race.

19. The Roman Law, which serves the materialistic world order, to be replaced by a legal system for all Germany.

20. With the aim of opening to every capable and industrious German the possibility of higher education and of thus obtaining advancement, a thorough reconstruction of the national system of education, the curriculum of all educational establishments to be brought into line with the requirements of social life and with the State idea, beginning with the first dawn of intelligence in the pupil.

21. To raise the standard of health in the nation by protecting mothers and infants, prohibiting child labor, and increasing bodily efficiency by obligatory gymnastics and sports laid down by law.

22. Abolition of a paid army and the formation of a national army.

23. In order to facilitate creation of a German national Press, all editors of newspapers and their assistants employing the German language to be members of the nation; special permission from the State to be necessary before non-German newspapers may appear; non-Germans to be prohibited from participation financially in or influencing German newspapers; prohibition of papers not conducive to the national welfare; legal prosecution of all tendencies in art and literature of a kind likely to disintegrate the life of the nation; the suppression of institutions which militate against the requirements mentioned above.

24. Liberty for all religious denominations in the State, so far as they are not a danger to it and do not militate against the moral feelings of the German race.

25. Creation of a strong central power of the State, unquestioned authority of the politically centralized Parliament over the entire Reich and its

organization; and formation of Chambers for classes
and occupations for the purpose of carrying out the
general laws promulgated by the Reich in the various
States of the confederation.

ONE-PARTY GOVERNMENT

The war closed with Hitler in a hospital recovering from temporary blindness caused by British mus-
tard gas at the front. On his discharge, he returned
to Munich, his adopted city. Already having committed himself to politics, he soon fell in with a few
kindred spirits, whose nationalism made them feel
the terms of Versailles intolerable. The republican
Government which had accepted these terms they
anathematized. Moreover, they did not stop with
talk; they organized to overthrow the Government
and to cast off the Treaty. They campaigned
against policies hated by the people: the one-sided
disarmament of Germany; the payment of reparations; the French occupation of the Ruhr; the Dawes
and Young Plans; the hypothecation of the German
railway properties; and also the social measures and
trends generally that they saw "destroying German
culture and life." They launched a *Putsch* for
power in Munich in 1923, dubbed by reporters "the
beer-hall revolution." It got nowhere and was
laughed at. The leaders were imprisoned. Leader-
less, and with its property and funds confiscated, the
young Party went into decline.

Released after a few months in jail, Hitler resumed
the rostrum and the Party leadership, now with supreme power. The platform of sole authority for the
Führer (leader) was no detail or accident but basic

in his philosophy and strategy. In *My Battle*,[2] he
states the position without qualification:

"The young movement is in its essence and organization anti-parliamentarian; i.e., it rejects, in principle and in its composition, any theory of the majority vote implying that the leader is degraded to
being merely there to carry out the orders and opinions of others. In small things and great, the movement stands for the principle of unquestioned authority of the leader, combined with fullest responsibility. . . . For the task of organization is to communicate a definite idea—which always originates in
the brain of one single man—to the general public,
and also to see to its conversion from theory into
reality."

Audiences of thousands came to listen. The Party
grew slowly at first, then by the hundred thousands.
The Program of the Party of Hitler places the membership figure in 1925 at 27,000; in 1926, at 49,000;
in 1927, at 72,000; in 1928, at 108,000; in 1929, at
178,000; in 1930, at 389,000; in 1931, at 806,000;
and early in 1932, at "something like 1,000,000."
The methods of campaigning, thrilling to friends,
were highly provocative to foes. Bitter denuncia-
tion and threats invited attacks in kind, sometimes
with acts of violence.

Large political armies had previously come into
existence in the distraught land. Uninformed or
purposely misleading accounts of these had represented them as a device to circumvent the disarmament terms of the Versailles Treaty. They really
meant that the leaders of all the parties foresaw Ger-

---

[2] Pp. 139-40. The quotations from *My Battle*, by Adolph Hitler,
are used by permission of and by arrangement with Houghton
Mifflin Company.

many heading into revolution, in which the weight
of organized man-power would have much to do
with the outcome. The Communists led off with
their "Red Fighting Front," its size estimated in six
figures at the peak. Made illegal under the Republic, it carried on underground with force enough
to throw large bands into action at almost any time,
anywhere in city, town, or country. The Social
Democrats had their *Reichsbanner* forces of some
hundreds of thousands. The German Nationals
(Conservative and Monarchistic) controlled the
equally large *Stahlhelm* formation of war veterans.
The *Centrum* Party (Catholic) also had formidable
marching forces.

The Nazis were bound to build up a counterpos-
ing force. They did it quickly, stimulated by Communist and Social Democratic interference with
their meetings, often in no pacific fashion. Mutually
provoked acts of violence multiplied on all sides.
The brown-shirted Nazi Storm Troopers soon
reached sufficient strength to take initiative. They
assumed the function of "clearing the streets." By
the summer of 1923, they proceeded systematically
"to break down the Red Terror" in Bavaria, spe-
cializing on key centers like Ratisbon, Hof, Beyreuth,
Nuremberg, and Würzburg. Often this brought on
bloodshed. If the local Storm Troopers were not
equal to the occasion, reënforcement came from
Munich. For the job in Coburg, Hitler personally
led a unit of 800 men.

The rank and file did not carry arms uniformly
unless on special assignment. A dagger became part
of the standard equipment for merit. As violence
increased, the *Schutzstaffel* emerged, set apart for
protection of the leaders. Black in the uniform dis-

tinguishes the "S.S." men from the "S.A's." (*Sturm Abteilung*). Since the establishment of Nazi power in the Reich, the "S.S." units command a full complement of small arms and are trained in the use of them. The "S.A's." enrolled 2,500,000 at their maximum; the "S.S's.," about one-fifth as many. Together they were a determining force in the march to power. They "cleared the streets." Much of the ugly treatment of Jews, Socialists, Communists, and others took place in their local headquarters. The campaigning casualties of the Nazis and their enemies totalled several thousands, the deaths some hundreds, about equally divided between the contending forces.

For many Germans, the "S.A's." by 1934 were becoming superfluous and, in no small measure, an irritation. The actions taken before, on, and after June 30, 1934, followed recognition high up in Party and Government that the formation presented some grave problems. The leaders charged with dangerous conspiracies were ruthlessly blotted out under the *Führer's* personal direction. The rank and file were submitted to severe discipline and subordination of function. The "S.S." contingent promises, after the Fascist "black shirt" precedent, to become a national militia having auxiliary police duties in peace time and a military reserve status. Its forces executed the *Führer's* grim orders of June 30 against the "S.A." leaders.

Hindenburg must be credited with having played fair with the Republic. He kept to the end his oath taken under the Weimar Constitution. Under that Statute, in the absence of a majority party of coalition in the Reichstag, it had been possible and necessary for the Brüning, Von Papen, and Von Sleicher Cabinets to legislate and govern by decree.

Dictatorship was only a step away. The President still refused to make Hitler Chancellor, on Hitler's terms. The election at the turn of the years 1932-33 gave the Reichstag a working majority of Nazis and German Nationals, who had pooled their strength. With no better alternative in the situation, the German National Party heads, actively aided by Von Papen, successfully used their good offices with Hindenburg on behalf of Hitler becoming Chancellor.

Those "in the know" of high politics believe that the two expected to capture the leadership from the *Führer*. They did succeed in attaching to him a Cabinet with a Nazi minority. The *Führer's* ideas were consistently different. When previously invited into Cabinet membership, without a free hand, he had as often declined. He held tenaciously to the theory and practice of power which he had evolved in prison after the 1923 *Putsch* and had elaborated in *My Battle*—that mixture of discernment and fanaticism. His German National patrons would have been better advised had they taken seriously such clear passages as this, written by Hitler under the caption, "The Strong Man Strongest Alone":

"It ought never to be forgotten that no really great achievement has ever been effected in this world by coalitions; but it has always been due to the triumph of one individual man. Successes achieved by coalitions, owing to the nature of their source, contain the seeds of future disintegration from their very start, to the extent, indeed, of forfeiting what has already been attained. . . . The National State, therefore, will never be created by the unstable volition of a nationalist union of organizations, but only by the adamantine will-power of a single movement,

after that movement has won through, having defeated all others." [3]

Hitler had made it a condition of accepting office
that his government be given full authority and responsibility for four years. This required changes
in the Reich Constitution by a two-thirds vote of the
Reichstag. The Communist Party had already been
made illegal and its dissolution ordered. This served
to cancel the franchise of the several scores of Communist seats in the Reichstag. To reach the two-
thirds vote it was still necessary to have the support
of the *Centrum* Party's members. With Von Papen's
influence, this was secured in direct negotiations by
the Chancellor. It left the Social Democrats with
their votes offering the only considerable opposition
to the measure on its passage.

The Act is known as the "Legislative Project for
Saving the Nation and the Reich from Distress."
The text states that by the Resolution having passed
the Reichstag and having received the consent of the
Reichsrat (Reich Council, or Senate), "the requirements of the legislation changing the Constitution
have been complied with." It supplements the
process of legislation prescribed in the Weimar Constitution by adding that "laws of the Reich can be
emitted by the Reich Government also"—in short,
by edict. The same power extends to making the
budget for expenditures and the raising of income.
The Act has validity until April 1, 1937.

The edict laws become effective the day after
proclamation. Reservations specified that the original process of legislation remains legal, that the Institutions of the Reichstag, the Reichsrat, and the
Reich President may not be altered under its pro-

[3] *My Battle*, p. 219.

visions. Under the Act, the President yielded the
former right of approval or veto but retained the
power of removal and appointment of the Cabinet,
including the Chancellor. Also, the President could
invoke a plebiscite. With the death of Hindenburg,
and the concurrent merging of the powers and functions of the Presidency and Chancellorship, the reservations relating to the former presidential office
became ineffective.

Another stride toward unchallenged power was
taken by the measure completely divesting the several States of the Reich of the administrative
powers held by them under the Republic. Then
States like Prussia, Bavaria, Saxony, and Thuringia
chose legislative bodies. Out of them rose executive
organs and personnel responsible to the electorate.
Now the ranking official of each State is appointed
by the Chancellor and is responsible to him. Every
State legislative body has been dissolved. The only
substitute is an Advisory Council. The Prussian
Governor has the rank of Minister President. In
the person of Hermann Göring, he is an important
member of the Reich Cabinet. These major posts
all go to Party men in the confidence of the *Führer*.
Germans generally look upon this centralization of
power either with satisfaction or equanimity. Many
regard it a step for German unity long overdue.
There was much in the old political structure that
was loose-jointed, overlapping, and expensive.

More revolutionary, if not more significant for the
gathering in of power, is the suppression or dissolution of all other political parties throughout the
Reich, leaving the open field solely to the Nazis. Demolition began on the Communist organization,
which had fought it out with the Nazis on the street.

In Nazi speech and press this Party had been one of the salients of persistently bitter attack. The Communists had become formidable. They had polled up to 6,000,000 votes in an election. They consistently held the third-largest number of Reichstag seats. Their vote in Berlin led all the others. The Nazis convinced most Germans that they had to choose between the Nazis and the Communists. The memory of 1918-19 was still fresh. Several thousands of Germans had perished during that thrust the Communists made for power. Almost the initial act of the Nazis was to outlaw them politically, seize their headquarters and network of lesser centers, silence their presses, and subject the leaders and many followers to arrest, prison, and the concentration camp. Some executions took place, and many beatings, administered by rampant Storm Troops. Not a few were shot down "while escaping arrest."

Large numbers of Communists have been taken into "S.A." ranks. Some went to bore within, others because the more radical economic features of the Nazi program attracted them. More came in for safety, with the Nazis willing to have them under supervision, and so knowing where they are and what they are doing. Although it is claimed that the Communist threat is finished, it is not intelligent to believe that an integrated organization of some consequence does not survive and function. In Wedding, Berlin's reddest district, one Communist in 1933 said to his American friend, "There are a million of us—enough for seed."

With scarcely less determination and fury, struggle against the Marxism of the Social Democrats was instrumented and directed by the Nazis. Less physical violence attended it, thanks only to the modera-

tion of the Socialists in the use of force. They used
it much too little for dealing successfully with revolutionaries of the Nazi type. In the Social Democrats, Hitler succeeded in incarnating all the failures,
shames, and villainies of the past two decades—loss
of the war, accepting the accursed Treaty, servilely
trying to fulfil its wicked terms to the impoverish-
ment of the German people. They were pilloried
as pacifistic, un-German, de-Germanizing, half-led by
Jews, the tools of Jews, addicted to parliamentarianism, infidels, libertarians, bureaucrats, civic corrup-
tionists, apostles of the Class War, and as such guilty
of disuniting the German people.

This Party, at first left with the shadow of legality,
was shortly suppressed. Thousands of its leaders
were put under arrest or went into hiding. Nor
were they left unsubjected to terrorism. Several of
the chiefs fled the country to set up a directing
center in Prague. The Party's great press was si-
lenced and so remains. The ease with which the
job was done would be incredible if not a fact.
Here was a party organization reduced to scrap that
had the official backing of the great trade unions,
a powerful press, and comparatively large financial
resources. Throughout the period of the Republic,
it had consistently commanded the largest voting
strength. Nothing illustrates more realistically the
state of mind for change into which the German
nation had been led.

Two other organized political bodies of importance then remained: the Catholic *Centrum* and the
Deutsch National. The latter represented interests
most hospitable to a return to the order of things
before the war. It enlisted monarchists, large landowners, old army men, big industry, and sections of

the intellectual élite and the upper middle class. Its leaders had engineered the election and the Reichstag collaboration which elevated Hitler to the Chancellorship. One chief was Minister of Economic Affairs. An ally was Vice-Chancellor. Other members were in the Cabinet, including the head of the Stahlhelm. Yet this great party voluntarily dissolved. The war veterans became subordinated to the Storm Troopers, but with resentment.

The Catholic party was the instrument first created and used by the Church to defend its interests against those policies of Bismarck which were regarded as unfriendly. It majored with the Social Democrats in supporting the Republic through coalition governments, and furnished several Chancellors. Since membership in a Marxist Socialist Party was always denied to Catholics by their spiritual Authority, the alliance was a strange one. Yet it persisted, until that Reichstag division took place which gave the Hitler Government four years of rule virtually independent of a parliament. Catholic assent to the Act, however, brought no longevity to the Party. Its dissolution was implicit in the terms of the Concordat between the Vatican and the Hitler Government. This called for complete abstention from politics on the part of the Church. The smaller Bavarian People's Party, also Catholic, went into the discard by the same route.

The wiping out of independent political action for the period has been sealed by the new system of voting for the Reichstag membership. It is almost a facsimile of the Italian Fascist pattern. It presents to the voters a single national ticket of names picked by the Party. The option left to the voter is that of registering by secret ballot a "Yes" or "No." The watchful eyes of the Party machine can make observations only on those who fail to vote. The result is a practically solid Reichstag membership of Nazis, whom a foreign press correspondent disrespectfully called "voting rabbits."

GOALS OF ECONOMIC SELF-SUFFICIENCY

A reader of the *Party Program*, without other information, will expect from Sections 11, 12, 13, 14, 16, 17, and 18 that Germany was slated for a radical economic overhauling. So thought numerous elements in the Party and among its supporters, although there did not develop any very articulate left wing. It will be noted that the economic demands range out over a wide spread of interests—those of the smaller industrial enterprises, shopkeepers, retailers, farmers, consumers, and debtors in general. The Program, as a whole, has been called "a consensus of discontent"—in no part more pronounced than in the economic field.

As soon as practical remedial measures were undertaken, however, some of the interests involved were found to be in conflict with others. These clashes within the Party have been serious enough to check the execution of the Program at several vital points. In general, the radicals have been held back, and probably have lost their opportunity for aggressive action on a large scale, unless the country goes on into much deeper economic distress. Then all forms might be broken up and anything happen from red left to reaction. Certain of the men shot in the summer of 1934 were identified conspicuously as leaders of the left.

The point of departure in the Hitler-Nazi economic policy is Section 10 of the Program. This makes it the primary duty of everybody to work with all his powers within an order set up to serve the common good. The conception is of a system to serve the community as against the grasping individualism of Capitalism and the class selfishness of Socialism and Communism. One of the Nazi boasts is that the Party grew without class stratification. A bitter and passionate campaign charge had been made against the other political parties that they stood for the economic interest of a class or group.

With the parties suppressed, there remained to be reckoned with the self-interested employer, organizations, and the class trade unions.

The word *Gleichschaltung* has come into Nazi use with a special significance. It is translatable as "adaptation" or "coördination." One figure to illustrate its meaning is that of plugging the switch of a machine into the main current of power. If well done, the process of *Gleichschaltung* amounts to Nazification or, at least, to the surrender of independence. In effect, it enforces the new Party-State ideas, plans, and power over the institutions of society. In the economic field, organized industry and Labor came in for the treatment early, the latter in drastic form.

The last Section (25) of the Party Program refers to "Chambers [or Estates—*Staende*] for classes and occupations." A sketch of the whole structure of which the Chambers would be a part is here essential. Mussolini's Corporative scheme evidently provided a part of the pattern, but it will have anciently German features as well.

It is proposed to set up certain all-embracing divisions of the national economy. In a given division, the constituent unit in a local area is to be made up of leaders selected out of all the plants engaged in the same line of production (such as mining and metals). In the unit will be represented the owners, managers, labor, clerical employes, and specialists. Out of the several locals so engaged in an industrial area, will rise a regional body of leaders, drawn out by some selective process, but again representative of all the interests concerned. At the top there will emerge from the several regional mining and metals bodies, a national body. This national unit then is expected to tie in with parallel sections built up in like manner for machinery and electrical equipment, leather and textiles, metalwares, foodstuffs, pottery and glass, chemicals, and pulp and paper. These unitedly form the Industrial Chamber. Other Chambers will consist of Handicrafts, Commerce, Transportation, Banking, and Insurance. The tie-in with the State is effected through the Ministry of Economics. Together, the Ministry and the Chambers, it is proposed, will plan and order the total national economy.

Such was the dream castle. Much about it and its ultimate operation was indefinite and remains so. Sharp differences exist about the measure of freedom which each Chamber and its parts down the line are to have for operating within the national plan. Whether the pyramid of leaders reaching up into the National Chambers will be constructed democratically from the bottom, or be handed down from the top by Party or Ministerial selection has been debatable also.

The trend of thinking, so far as it is done aloud, points unmistakably toward State control by an organization handed down from the *Führer*. If the Chamber type most nearly in prospect materializes, it will have a central governing committee of members chosen by the Government on the basis of character and place in their category. Their authority and control will lead downward to regions and communities through occupational committees limited geographically. There will be power, as in a Corporation in Italy, to make regulations within the sphere of the Chamber that will have the force of civil law, and in large part will supersede the latter.

Vital differences within the Party on economic policies, the mountainous difficulties in sight, and the tightening of the financial cordon around Germany constrain the Chancellor and Government toward conservatism and low speed. Schacht at the head of the Reichsbank and dictator in the Ministry of Economics is no revolutionary. The plan for the Chambers became the subject of inside study for six months. During this time, open discussion of it has been forbidden. Action will be taken, it is said, "in the *Führer's* own good time." The snuffing out of the Roehm-Gregory Strasser group at the end of June, 1934, served further to remove pressure for a faster tempo of change. The less patient radicals were in that camp.

Although there has been no one master operation on the entire economic corpus, industry and commerce have been on the table for considerable surgical attention. The Government actively employs its wide powers to correct abuses here, to extend aid there, and steadily to enlarge control. In no material respect have these interests that might be called capitalistic received favors at the expense of the general population. An outpouring of laws descended upon everybody. From March 23 to December 27, 1933, 147 items of economic legislation came forth. The titles of the Acts selected below read like a race with the New Deal. They are forceful reminders of the restless, uncertain seeking among the nations for ways to make the capitalistic order a better minister to the whole people:

Consolidating the sugar industry

Revision of stock exchange regulations

Regulating savings banks

Revising the regulations for coal mining

Organizing bank supervision

Regarding foreclosures

Regarding concealment of items in balance sheets

Regarding reduction of capital incomes

Protection of the small retailer

Regulating the grain monopoly

Punishing the flight of capital

Regulating minimum prices and minimum profits in retail groceries

Regulating the boards of directors of public companies

Promoting the public interest in home building

Regulating cartels

Establishing compulsory cartels

Regulating the bank for German industry obligations

Regulating department stores and branch stores

Prohibition of cigar-making machinery

Revising the commercial code

Regulating the milling of domestic wheat

Regulating the powers of the Federal Commissioner of Banking

Regulating advertising

Regulating the merger of mills

Funding of short-term debts of cities and communes

Regulating grain prices

Promoting exports

Regulating agricultural foreclosures

Regulating price discounts

Establishing the Federal Office for the Control of Foreign Exchange

Regulating the potash industry

Income tax law

Regulating the sale of oils, fats, animals, meat products, milk, eggs, honey, garden produce, fruit, cocoa, brandy, ice cream, wallpaper, linen thread, fertilizer, and seed.

Immediately on taking over the Government, the Nazis installed Party men at the head of the great national organizations of industry and commerce. Commissars with large powers were established in high places of business administration. In numerous cases, former heads of the firms were removed. Some were placed on trial for dishonesty or exploitation. Not a few received punishment by imprisonment. Conflicts of authority resulted. Business stalled sufficiently to bring about abandonment of the "Commissar Plan" within six months. The purposeful policy toward control and reform, however, did not abate.

Private ownership remains in name, though with a status resembling little of the past. The Minister of Economics is empowered to act directly in the matter of cartel agreements and to compel cartelization. This carries along price-fixing powers. Stabilization of prices had proceeded, by the end of 1933, to the extent that prices of 40 per cent of the turnover

were fixed by cartel and other agreements. There
are cases of imprisonment for unauthorized price
changes. The expansion of an old plant and the
setting-up of a new one can be forbidden; likewise
the closing of a business or the reduction of employment. New department and chain stores are prohibited. In some States, the first are heavily taxed
and have propaganda directed against them.

The licensing of retail dealers is seriously discussed. Protests from owners of empty stores secured the easement of a law forbidding the opening
of any new shop. Older ones may move or expand
10 per cent. A *numerus clausus* under debate may
fix the number who shall engage in any occupation.
Small industries and shops receive encouragement at
the expense of large ones and of consumers' coöperatives. Pressures are applied to use hand labor more
and machinery less. In the glass and cigar industries
the former has been made compulsory. The scaling
down of large salaries has gone far. Advertising can
be done only by the owning or managing individual,
or by licensed professionals.

A major emphasis in policies is on the diffusion of
industry, checking the growth of large cities, linking
industry and agriculture, and simplifying distribution by making districts more nearly self-contained.
State monopolies and price regulations operate
against wholesaling. Fifteen district organizations,
for example, collect and distribute all eggs.

As in every other land, the new measures must
receive their test in the grinding mill of the general
economic depression. Nowhere has it ground more
relentlessly than here. The more detached observers
believe the issue turns on ability to hold out for salvation by a world recovery.

The German case may not be hopeless, if desperate. Industrial production, which was down one-half from 1928 in 1932, rose 12% during 1933. Up to the end of the third quarter, the 1934 level was keeping about 20% above that of the preceding year. The gain was for the domestic market principally and in capital goods induced by Government public works. Iron and steel led, with railroad transport well up. Removal of a burdensome auto tax markedly stimulated that industry. The bonus to marrying couples helped furniture makers. Makers of brown-shirt uniforms and boots prospered. The retail turnover that went down 15% in 1931 and 20% in 1932 rose 5% in 1933 (7% in December). The 1934 scale for the first nine months has run consistently higher than during 1933.

Unemployment fell from 6,013,612 to 4,058,000 during 1933, and to below 3,000,000 during the first half of 1934. At the end of October, the figure was 2,268,000.[4] The official figures given out check with the number of employed making payments to the organizations that insure against sickness. The reduction has been brought about through various measures. Public works on roads, rail-beds, canals, harbors, land reclamation, and power plants are extensively undertaken. Subsidies to house owners and tax relief for building repairs or enlargement reëmployed many. The sharing of work absorbed others. That this was a considerable factor is shown by the total of wage income not rising with employment, while hourly rates remained the same. The use of servants increased under a regulation allowing the same income tax reduction for such an em-

4 *Weekly Report,* German Institute for Business Research, November 28, 1934.

ploye as for a child or other dependent. Displacement of women is not general unless they are married and the husbands employed. Female employment actually increased 11.2% compared with the male rate of 27.1%.

Government financing drags heavily. It constitutes an immediate major economic concern. Taxation on all sides has reached heights beyond which lies danger. The budget, weighted by the extensive public works, is being balanced by the sale of assets, borrowings from insurance funds, and fresh obligations at the Reichsbank. The foreign trade balance so long in Germany's favor and so essential to German economic strength has vanished with world trade locked in the grip of economic nationalism. Apart from tariff barriers, quotas, and boycott, the adherence to the gold value of the mark keeps German goods out of many markets. And what German Government will risk inflation? The "firm cover" of the mark has fallen at times below 2%. Almost no exchange will be released by the Reichsbank. Without it, there can be no buying of raw materials; further reduced export of manufactured goods follows—a vicious circle.

The foreign debts press heavily, with a favorable balance the sole way to pay. These debts, that stood at 23,800,000,000 marks in 1929, had become 12,800,-000,000 in 1933, the result in part of payments and the buying up of depressed German bonds by the Reichsbank, more largely by reason of the two chief creditor nations devaluating their pound and dollar. Payments have reached a practical standstill, even of the service charges—a condition from which Germany derives more ill-will than sympathy. It looks like an impasse which only a greatly revived international trade can break. For that Government and people it cannot come too soon. The one-time Nazi vision of a self-contained German economy has not been abandoned but it pinches the consumers by reduced supplies, higher prices, and adulterations. If long-enforced either by design or by an unyielding world situation, the none-too-high living standard of the population must be materially depressed.

THE "LEADER" PRINCIPLE AND LABOR

If ownership and management in German industry moved rapidly toward a change in status under Nazi rule, Labor arrived overnight. Hitler began his political career with a strong dislike of Marxist trade unions, which made up the great body of German organized Labor. (Others were Catholic in character, numerous but not controlling.) The opposition to them dated from the Vienna days, when at seventeen Hitler went there to become an artist. He found it necessary to become a common workman to live. First as a mixer of building mortar and then as draughtsman for an architect, he grew critical of the Marxist outlooks and techniques, and of the loyalties of the workers.

In *My Battle,* he has stated the grounds of his criticism. Their class-war principle "sets up the mass and dead weight of numbers which denies the value of the individual among men, combats the importance of nationality and race, thereby depriving humanity of the whole meaning of its existence and culture." In "the madness of internationalism," Marxists proceed "without regarding the common welfare and preservation of the nation's economy."

Their unions become less "an instrument for defending the social rights of the employe and for fighting for better living conditions for him" and more "a party instrument in the political class war."

Neither Hitler's words nor official acts have as yet proved anything other than genuine consideration of the workers' true interests. With Trade Unionists, Socialists, Communists, and others declaiming that Labor has been sacrificed, it remains for time to show whether the new Labor Front renders the German workers an equivalent for the really distinguished service performed by their trade unions over the long period of their strength.

The Nazi attack on the working relations between Capital and Labor is a revolutionary departure from orthodox trade unionism. It opened three months after Hitler took the Chancellorship by an order dissolving all trade union organizations. Their headquarters were seized. Their great economic and insurance institutions were taken over, with their assets, for administration. The leaders met about the same handling as that given the Social Democratic Party leaders. In many cases the identity was the same. Charges against them were made implying that something like prevailing financial corruption had existed. A few proven cases failed to substantiate the general innuendo. To justify their suppression it remains highly incumbent on the new order to serve Labor's interests with equal fidelity and success. Much grumbling is heard over the absence of financial accounting by the Labor Front officials, and its leader is an unpopular figure.

Industrial workers and employes of all categories have been joined in this German Labor Front. In each factory or other establishment, a local unit

exists.   Pressures to induce joining have given the
Front a nearly national spread. The locals are much
in evidence in popular demonstrations. The Nazi
Party nuclei, or cells, control the locals. They are
known as National Socialist *Betriebs* (Occupational)
Organizations.

The "N.S.B.O." cells functioned with vigor at the
start. Many of them undertook what grossly exceeded their powers. The heads of the shoemakers
and the hairdressers in Berlin directed offhand the
raising of the trade prices in their lines. The directors of a large concern in Hamburg were waited
on by a delegation from the N.S.B.O. to request the
election of some of their members to the Board.
This was done. The chief executive of an important Leipzig industrial plant entered his office one
morning to find a minor employe in his chair who
believed himself commissioned as director to act
with full power.

Such playing of the game out of bounds speedily
brought down from the top the blanket order to
desist from the usurping of authority and from all
unauthorized actions. The abuses were not so easily
stopped. It was not easy for those on whom demands
were made to know how much real authority resided
in a shirted visitor blazing with insignia and with a
revolver on his hip. The issuance of the prohibition order, however, gave evidence of confidence in
power at the Center sufficient to begin reining in
the impetuous forces in the ranks, whose interpretation of revolutionary slogans was much too naïve
and literal. Later orders against the excesses imposed severe penalties. By the close of 1933, these
had brought to an end the reign of irresponsibility
in that form.

The new enactments made strike and lockout alike "treasonable." In the absence of functioning trade unions, the principle and practice of collective bargaining went into discard. Pending the elaboration of the complete Labor Code, announced in January, 1934, and made operative May 1 of the same year, the *status quo* in respect to the wage rate has been generally maintained. The average of wage hours lengthened from 6.96 to 7.35 up to December, 1933 (7.31 for July, 1934). The pressures on employers very materially raised the number on payrolls. Price controls have been keeping the cost of consumers' goods nearly stable. From January, 1933, to March, 1934, the index of living cost rose 3.2 points—not enough to bring on complaints from housewives of whom inquiries were made by the writer during the summer of 1934. (By October an additional rise of 2.1 points had taken place.) [5] That the pinch was not being felt more with the index rising and when the sharing of work and therefore of income was going on, may be accounted for in part by the use of substitute and inferior materials in the processing stages of consumers' goods.

The New Labor Code represents a serious effort to organize relations between employer and employe in accord with the Nationalist Socialist philosophy and program. These demand that the common good of the nation take precedence over every other interest. They repudiate the principle of conflict between worker and employer and set up instead the ideal of mutuality of interest. They counterpose social solidarity of the forces of production and co-operation to the system of bargaining and concilia-

[5] *Weekly Report,* German Institute for Business Research, November 15, 1934.

tion, which, if it breaks down, ends in industrial warfare.

Taken apart from those premises, these opening paragraphs of the new Act do not read well for Labor:

"In each establishment, the owner of the undertaking as the leader (*Führer*) of the establishment and the salaried and wage-earning employes as his followers (*Gefolgschaft*) shall work together for the furtherance of the purposes of the establishment and for the benefit of the nation and the State in general.

"The leader of the establishment shall make decisions for his followers in all matters affecting the establishment in so far as they are governed by this Act" [including wages, hours, etc.].

"He shall promote the welfare of his followers. The latter shall be loyal to him as fellow-members of the works community." [6]

In every establishment employing twenty or more persons (including home workers), a "Confidential Council" is created by the leader from among the followers "to strengthen mutual confidence within the works community." A Council's task is "to give advice respecting all measures directed toward the increase of efficiency; the formulation and carrying out of the general conditions of employment (especially the establishment rules); the carrying out and promotion of industrial safety measures; the strengthening of the ties which bind the various members of the establishment to one another and to the establishment; and the welfare of all members of the community." Also "the Council will undertake and must settle disputes within the works community,

[6] From the *Act for the Organization of National Labor,* official translated text of the Reich Ministry of Labor.

and be heard before penalties are imposed under the establishment rules."

In March of each year the leader proposes the membership of a given Council, in agreement with the chairman of the Party cell in the establishment. The followers then vote by ballot for or against the list. If the leader fails to act or the vote be adverse, a "Labor Trustee" appoints the Council. In making up a Council, salaried employes, wage-earning employes and home workers must be taken into account. The qualifications required are: age, twenty-five or more; one year in the establishment or two years in a related industry; possession of citizenship; membership in the Labor Front; and "exemplary human qualities, guaranteed devotion at all times to the National State." On the National Day of Labor (May 1), they take a solemn oath before the followers "to perform the duties of their office exclusively for the benefit of the establishment and of the nation as a whole, setting aside all private interests, and to set an example to the members of the establishment by the life which they lead and the way in which they perform their duties."

For the purposes of the Act, thirteen Labor Trustees have been appointed over as many districts. They are Government officials under the supervision of the Minister of Labor. As such they are bound "to observe the principles and instructions laid down by the Federal Government." The duties and powers of a Trustee are to supervise the formation and operation of the Confidential Councils and to give decisions where disputes occur; to appoint confidential men for establishments and remove them from office for cause; to decide respecting appeals from Confidential Councils; to overrule the decision of the leader of an establishment and issue the necessary ruling if the case warrants; to decide respecting proposed dismissals; to supervise the observance of provisions respecting establishment rules; to cooperate in the exercise of jurisdiction by the "social honor" courts; and to keep the Federal Government supplied with information respecting social progress, in accordance with detailed instructions respecting social progress issued by the Minister of Labor and the Minister of Economic Affairs.

Trustees may associate with themselves an Advisory Council of experts from the several branches of industry in their territory for purposes of general consultation. Three-fourths of the members of such a council will be nominated by the Labor Front, the remainder by the Trustee. Leaders and members of Confidential Councils are included in equal numbers. A Trustee may also appoint a committee of experts to advise him in individual cases.

The machinery is completed by Social Honor Courts. They have final jurisdiction in appeals by leader or followers that may rise through the Confidential Councils and Trustees. A district Honor Court consists of an official of the judiciary appointed by the Minister of Justice in agreement with the Minister of Labor, who shall be chairman. One leader of an establishment and one confidential councilor are associated with him as assessors. The leader of the establishment and the councilor shall be selected by the chairman of the Honor Court from lists of candidates drawn up by the Labor Front, taken in the order in which they stand on the list. It is provided that, wherever possible, persons shall be selected who belong to the same branch of industry as the accused.

Taken altogether, it is a rather comprehensive and detailed set-up. The nature of the breaches of "social honor" are defined for both leader and followers. The corresponding penalties are prescribed, together with all procedures for determining where justice lies. There is apparent the desire and intention to secure impartiality. Some very important terms, however, are vague. The common good as laid down by the National State is kept paramount. The power of the State is there to enforce its priority. Neither employer nor employe is free, nor are the two together free. The purpose and effect with which the plan is executed must with time determine the degree of its success. Employer-worker relations have changed for the better. The improvement is attributed to a general abandonment of class war spirit and tactics.

STRENGTHENING THE FARMER CLASS

National Socialism makes basic in its policies elevation of the rural population to a higher status in the national whole. This purpose goes far beyond economics to recognition and protection of the farmer class as the essential stock of the nation because of its purity, fecundity, and fidelity to the folk-ways of the race. The initial manifesto of the new Government on February 1, 1933, announced, along with the "rescue of the farmer from the ruin of the preceding fourteen years," a "back-to-the-land" movement. In the Chancellor's inaugural address on the same day the farmer's "salvation" was made the first of two primary economic tasks to "be achieved at all costs," however "hard on the consumer." Otherwise, "collapse of the German body corporate" impended. In April following, addressing the representative of agriculture, Hitler reverted to the subject with like conviction, and more explicitly:

"When I survey all the individual economic phenomena of the time and all the political changes, the essential thing is always the question of the maintenance of our nationality as such. A favorable solution of this question can be provided only if the problem of the maintenance of the agricultural class has been solved. History has taught us that a nation can exist without cities, but history would have taught us one day, if the old system had continued, that a nation cannot exist without agriculturists. All fluctuations can be borne in the end and all blows of fate can be survived if there is a healthy agricultural class. So long as a nation can rely upon a powerful agricultural class, it will constantly derive new strength from this class. Any government that overlooks the importance of such an essential foundation can only be a government of the moment." [7]

There was need for action. The cash income of the farmers from the sale of products had fallen from 10,170,000,000 marks in 1928-29 to 6,460,000,000 in 1932-33. Their debts in 1930 totalled 11,500,000,000 marks. They carried an interest burden of about 1,000,000,000 marks, or nearly 14% of the debtors' gross farm income. The purchasing power of farm products, reckoning 1913 as 100%, in January, 1933, had declined to 80.9% (72% if relation to industrial prices be considered). Foreclosures would dispossess

[7] *The New Germany Desires Work and Peace*, pp. 27-28, Liebheit and Thiesen, Berlin.

the owners but realize only 60% of the mortgage indebtedness, besides jeopardizing production. The frozen credits were rendering unstable no small part of the national economic structure.

A vigorous Minister of Agriculture, Herr Darre, has advanced the organization of the Agricultural Chamber of the new planned economy to the point of an actively going concern, dating from its recognition by the Government, September 13, 1933. It has made long jumps in advance of industry and of commerce. By forming ahead of them, it swept in both the processing and distribution of farm products. Headquarters are set up in a medieval town in Lower Saxony. The Minister is "leader," with nearly unlimited powers, which he has used freely.

Economically, of all the German population, the peasant farmers have been placed in the most favored positions. They raise and sell their products behind an impassable tariff wall. The pre-Hitler customs duty on wheat had made the German price two to three times that on the Chicago market. This advantage for the farmers was retained at the expense, of course, of the consumers. The Government establishes a liberal fixed price at the initial market for nearly all farm products. Monopolies set up against the intervention of speculation between the grower and consumer afford further security. This protection now covers wheat, corn, rye, milk, butter, cheese, eggs, animal products from hides to lard, and vegetable canning. Flour must have a 97% domestic content at the mills. These measures have brought the agricultural wholesale index up to 90.6 compared with the 80.9 of January, 1933. It is estimated that the cash income for the 1933-34 crop increased about 12%.

Parallel favoring legislation includes pressure for downward ranges in the cost of what the farmer must buy, such as machinery and fertilizer. The nitrogen cartel yielded a 7% reduction. The sales turnover tax of 2% was halved. Farm real property taxes were lowered 100,000,000 marks. The farm hands and their employers have been relieved of payments to the Unemployed Insurance Fund.

Debt-relief measures greatly lightened that burden. More will follow. The Brüning and Von Papen Governments had lowered the interest rate 2% for a four-year period. With additional reductions, service charges have now been brought down to a net of almost 50%. A law of June 1, 1933, boldly aims to reduce the debts to correspond with the real land value and earning power. This will be accomplished by conversion or forced settlement. In this process, the Government assumes heavy obligations to the mortgage banks. The interest rate has been lowered generally to 4½%; on debts to foreign creditors, to 4%. The Government now pays the ½% difference but is not expected to continue doing so.

A recent law prohibits incumbrances on what are to be known as hereditary farm lands. At present these have 8,000,000,000 marks of debts settled upon them. It is on the schedule to convert these debts into annuity bonds, with creditors reducing their claims and the Government undertaking large ultimate responsibilities for their liquidation.

Strong controls were imposed necessarily, some irksome, if accounts of peasant unhappiness be reliable. There is the lack of balance in crop production to be corrected, if the principle of self-containment in respect to foods and other consumers' goods is to be a governing one. The stimulation through price raising brought cereal grain up to and beyond self-sufficiency, whereas the domestic share of production in the vegetable oils consumed is only 1%, in wool less than 9%, in flax 17%, and in tobacco 30%. The corrective prescribed is the regulation of croppage adapted more nearly to demand. Farmers are required to plant and till accordingly. This means fixed acreages, and more or less rebellion of spirit among the nation's hope and pride over being told what to plant.

Crop shortages by reason of the summer drought of 1934 induced further irritation. Fixed prices operated to forestall the increases. The former minimum prices were ordered to be the maximum. The high grain tariffs were suspended for one year. Grain could be sold only to the Government agencies. The farmers were required to deliver, by October 1, 30% as much rye and 25% as much wheat as during all of a normal year. The effects were to take control of animal feeding from them, and to bring home the fact of the Government grip on their affairs.

To anchor an hereditary people to the land, a law (already familiar in parts of Germany) has been extended over the Reich, whereby the homestead goes to the eldest son, whereupon he must assume a somewhat big-brother rôle to the rest of the family—dependents and indigents included. As further security of title, the mortgaging of the land is forbidden. Credits therefore are available on notes alone. This makes for reluctant lenders. Sale of crops on farms up to 125 hectares is placed under official control. The independence of the farmer thus disappears in the gigantic government system now in the making.

Along with ordinary agriculture, this Chamber is gathering in forestry, fisheries, market gardening, the agricultural coöperatives, dealing in farm products and implements, and the processing of agricultural commodities. The composite is known as the Agricultural Section of German Society. The system is being designed to secure for the farmers deliverance from the terrors of an unstable market, to assure them "fair" prices for what they buy and sell, and to protect their land holdings permanently from the menace of debt—all in the interest of the nation. It is a revolutionary subordination of the agricultural part to the German whole.

GERMAN THINKING STANDARDIZED

The marked turn the Nazis are giving education is in the direction of bending the mind of the people to the Nazi conception of reverence and service due the Nation and State. To this end, *Gleichschaltung* has been enforced on all the media of instruction. The Germany that once gloried in objectivity and a scientific spirit now matches Fascist Italy and Soviet Russia in subjection to a propaganda scheme that is German only in its thoroughness.

Fortified in the very structure of the Reich, there sits in the Cabinet a Minister for Propaganda and Enlightenment of the People. Joseph Goebbels is easily the third most influential man in the Party. At propaganda on his level, he is a genius. He has not been called upon by the *Führer* to operate on any lofty height. "All propaganda," the latter writes, "should be popular and should adapt its intellectual level to the receptive ability of the least intellectual of those whom it is desired to address. Thus it must sink its mental elevation deeper in proportion to the numbers of the mass whom it has to grip. If . . . the object is to gather a whole nation within its circle of influence, there cannot be enough attention paid to avoidance of too high a level of intellectuality." [8]

In reaching the mass mind, these men do not neglect strategy. Hitler [9] wrote thus on the theory of doing it, and later made its demonstration complete: "An immense majority of the people are so feminine in nature and point of view that their thoughts and actions are governed more by feeling and sentiment than by reasoned consideration. This sentiment is, however, not complicated, but very simple and consistent. It does not differentiate much, but it is either positive or negative, love or hate, truth or lies, never half one and half the other, and so on." "Fine oratory by a dominant apostolic character" would be more successful in the evening in persuading men. Their powers of resistance are then sensibly weakened. They are not "in full possession of their energy of mind and volition." [10]

Again, "mass assemblies are necessary because, while attending them, the individual, who feels on the point of joining a young movement and takes alarm if left by himself, receives his first impression of a larger community, and this has a strengthening and encouraging effect on most people. . . . The desires, longings, and indeed the strength of thousands is accumulated in the mind of each individual present. A man, who enters such a meeting in doubt

[8] *My Battle*, p. 76.   [10] *Ibid.*, p. 201.
[9] *Ibid.*, p. 78.

and hesitation, leaves it inwardly fortified; he has become a member of a community." [11]

The great mass audiences that Hitler and his colleagues swept along their path to power have been too often described to merit space here. The effects were incalculably great. Goebbels is now the impressario for a succession of immense, moving observances and demonstrations studiously calculated to maintain the emotions needful to sustain popular faith, courage, and contentment, while the fulfilment of many promises tarries behind the making of them. Hence the Day of Potsdam; the Day of National Mourning (over the Versailles Treaty); a Storm Troopers' mobilization in Nuremberg; the Nazi Thanksgiving Day (for peasants chiefly); the Day of National Labor, with 2,000,000 persons assembled under perfect organization on Tempelhof Field; a nation-wide election campaign, the result of which is known before the fact. All lest they forget.

This Propaganda Minister is also forehanded in getting on foot his Chamber for the organization and control of what Germans are to know and think. The body is known as "The Reich Chamber of Culture" in six Sections: Music, Creative Arts, Theater, Literature, Press, Broadcasting. For public expression in any one of these fields, membership is compulsory for a person, either directly or through an affiliated society that has already "coördinated" its roster and program with those of National Socialism. Thus what the nation shall know will first be approved as correct and safe at the Center.

Each of the six Sections has power to determine, with the force of law, the opening, closing, or operating conditions for any establishment or enterprise

[11] *My Battle,* pp. 202-203.

in its sphere. This goes for the theaters. Under the
Press Section, the newspapers had become so color-
less that even Goebbels asked for the injection of
some spirit. A Frankfurt-on-Main editor who took
the call seriously got savagely rebuked. Half a million former buyers of newspapers in Berlin alone
now get on without them. When Von Papen spoke
up for some constructive criticism, the propaganda
end of the Ministry apparently did not consider the
Vice-Chancellor's speech to be anything "enlighten-
ing" for newspaper readers. It was suppressed.
Numerous foreign papers and magazines are debarred from the Reich. On the *verboten* roll are
the *Manchester Guardian, Statesman* and *Nation,
Harper's, Time,* and numerous French and other
Continental organs. Offending issues of all foreign
papers get held up. Radio, cinema, and stage play
the Party and Government game no less faithfully.
Happily for the German intelligence, there remains
even after the expurgation more food for the mind
and soul than a censored servile press affords. But
performance for the newspaper is 100 per cent up to
the goal set by the *Führer*—"control of that instrument of popular education with absolute determination to place it at the service of the State and Nation." [12]

The changes made and proposed under the Ministry of Education have more substance to commend
them. Some of them are not new in German life.
They mark rather a return to emphasis familiar
under the Empire. One is training for love of
country. The liberal mind can go along some distance with this reasoning: "For only when a man
has learned through education and schooling to

[12] *Ibid.,* p. 109.

know the cultural, economic, and above all the political greatness of his own Fatherland can he and
will he gain that inner pride in being permitted to
be a member of such a nation. I can fight only for
what I love, love only what I respect, and respect
only what I at any rate know about." [13]

For the furtherance of these ends, the school
schedule, curriculum, and books are well furnished,
beginning in the tender years with the flag salute
and "Heil Hitler." A certain militancy seems over-
done in the songs for school and marching. Many
of them will be found to be pre-Nazi and pre-
Republic. Non-militant Nazis insist that their revival is inspired more by the purpose to lift the
nation out of its post-war mood of depression and
helplessness than to implant a martial spirit dangerous to neighbors. The great stress placed on the
schools as ministers to the health of childhood,
youth, and race invites no just quarrel with its fundamentals. Its bearings on militarism will be further commented upon later.

NAZI WOMEN AND YOUTH

On the institution of the family, the Nazis stand
four-square with the old German tradition. It is a
small minority of the people—men, women, and
youth—who do not stand with them by conviction.
The lack of defence of the family on the part of the
Social Democrats made one of the breaches in the
wall through which the National Socialists took their
city. The others had placed no obstacles in the way
of influences that were undermining the best in the

13 *My Battle*, p. 10.

German home by way of the stage, film, literature, and generally lowered moral sanctions. Looking "at the bill of fare offered by the cinemas, playhouses, and variety theaters," Hitler called the prevailing public life "a forcing bed for sexual ideas and attractions." It must be freed "from the asphyxiating perfume of our modern eroticism, as it must be from unmanly and prudish refusal to face the facts." [14]

Some vigorous lines in his book, sometimes called the "Nazi Bible," strike out for sterilization of the unfit, against birth control by the healthy, and against the economic conditions which prescribe the small family. They demand that the State use the most modern medical aids in the light of accepted facts, declare unfit to beget children any one clearly diseased or having hereditary disabilities, and back up its decision with action, while insuring that "the fruitfulness of a healthy woman is not blocked by the damnable régime of finance which makes the blessing of children into a curse for the parents." [15]

On January 1, 1934, a sterilization bill came in force. It provides for "Courts of Eugenics" composed of a magistrate, a medical health officer, and a physician whose special province is the study of hereditary hygiene. Persons suffering from "hereditary illness" are subject to the provisions of the law. These specify congenital feeble-mindedness, manic-depressive insanity, schizophrenia, congenital epilepsy, St. Vitus's dance, blindness and deafness, bodily malformation, and habitual alcoholism. Hearings by the court are secret and all parties to the case throughout are bound to silence under penalty.

14 *Ibid.*, p. 112.
15 *Ibid.*, pp. 163-4.

The exposition accompanying the bill explained that it was not designed to include such cases as minor forms of mental disturbance or the healthy bearers of inheritable disease, but only those making diseased posterity highly probable. A subject may himself propose sterilization; but it can be enforced and is in process at the present time. The further explanation characterized the operation as "a simple, harmless one, impairing neither the being nor the sexual sensitivity of man or woman." The law may be extended to cover criminals, but among law-breakers only perpetrators of rape are affected—and in their case by emasculation only for a third offence.

Although troubled over the hemmed-in German population already cramped for productive land, the National Socialists call on those of the race sound in body and mind to bring forth at least the sizable family of four children. Only so, it is pointed out, by the law of averages can there come about any material increase in numbers. In the Nazi view, the birth rate in the cities has been falling alarmingly. The 32,000,000 Poles have been yielding a larger annual baby crop than double that number of Germans. Accordingly, earlier marriages are urged and facilitated.

Since the war, large numbers of marriages have been held back because of inability on the part of many young women to provide the dower fund for house furnishings after the German custom. The State now advances 1,000 marks for the purpose to a woman who gives up a position she has held six months or more to marry. This advance is repayable without interest at the pace of 1% a month, but it can be more quickly paid off with children. Each baby reduces the debt one-fourth. A tax on unmarried men and women of given ages provides this subsidy fund. In approximately one year, 100,000,000 marks were claimed by brides on these terms. Marriages came to be celebrated by scores in a single church service. Moreover, dividends are coming in. During the first quarter of 1934, the thirty-six largest Prussian cities recorded 9,954 more births than for the same period in 1933—a gain of 23.4%. The marriage rate went up 52.5%. Emphasis placed on male employment further induces marriage on the part of single women. The fact that they are barred from office-holding also leads them homeward. Limits are placed on their higher education also. (Only 10% of future entering university classes may be women.)

All of this seems to bother the German women themselves very little. Feminism and "emancipation" had never reached a vogue among them. It is certain that far more approve the Nazi emphasis than resent it. The fact is, "Woman's place in the home" in the tradition of that people is not a belittling statement. Otto Tolischus, Berlin correspondent of the *New York Times*,[16] quotes the leader of the Nazi Federation of all women's organizations on this point: "The State of Weimar (in the German Republic) did not win the love of the German woman, despite the political rights which it conferred on her. Its center was the individual; his rights and his happiness were the only concern of the democratic State. National Socialism has arisen out of the soul of the people for their rescue. Despite the fears of many women to whom it seemed ungentle, National Socialism maintains far more intimate contact with the woman than the vanquished epoch because it seeks to return her

[16] September 10, 1933.

to her real field of work, namely, to the family as the basis of the community."

Frau Siber, in the Ministry of Interior, liaison representative of women's organizations, further exalts the home ministry of the mother: "She is the guardian of all national culture, which she transmits to the child in fairy stories, legends, play and customs, which, in turn, determine the child's attitude toward the nation and the race throughout life. National Socialism is the battle for the redemption of the German woman from the domination of her own tiny self. National Socialism does not mean the crippling of the woman, but her highest development." Tolischus, himself, adds, "If anything, the women are more ardently for this part of the Nazi program than the men."

The upbringing of the youth is by no means left wholly to the home and school. The Party takes a strong hand in their education and training, beginning at the early ages on to the eighteenth year. Its direct instrument is the *Hitler Jugend* (Youth), composed of boys and girls. This body, beyond recruiting its own mass following, has forced into its ranks the membership of other youth movements, either by dissolving them or by a "coördination" (*Gleichschaltung*) that means the surrender of independence. The objectives are National Socialist indoctrination and training for physical and moral stamina. These may come to be bent more or less toward militarism, but that is not now the emphasis.

Hikes and week-end camping under leaders constitute the most conspicuous activities—often over-strenuous in the zeal of a new enthusiasm turned into rearing a generation with courage, decision, and endurance. The aims exalt discipline and sacrifice.

Many families find relief in having the boys taken from the streets during leisure time. On the other hand, family protests brought about an adjustment of the excessive claims on children's time. A six-day school regimen with Hitler youth, taking the after-hours twice a week and long week-ends, came near to removing the children from home life. In June, 1934, the Ministry of Education reduced the school claim to five days a week, and apportioned to the Youth organization Friday night and Saturday, leaving Sunday to the family.

The Youth movement suffers from lack of enough capable, trained leaders. Poor ones bring boredom to the children; good ones inspire loyalty and zeal. The girls' program is distinct from that of the boys, modified to suit their status, yet with much stress placed on health. This assumption of leisure-time training by the Party is not new in German life. From the end of the World War, the Communists and Socialists gathered their young in organizations with activities that practically set them apart from the rest of the community and nation. Protestants and Catholics paralleled those largely anti-religious bodies with others having Christian aims. It was in the stars that a Party obsessed with the claims of nationality should act to create and control a single all-German youth order.

In the period of its rise, National Socialism caught the imagination of the university students and won almost mad allegiance. The aroused and flaming patriotism quenched the spirit that after 1918 had placarded the universities with "No More War" slogans. The student bodies in 1933 were aggressive in helping oust from their chairs conspicuous liberal, internationalist, and pacifist professors. They led the rank and file in proscribing "un-German" books. Some slackening of zeal can now be noted. The Party claims on student time have had to be reduced. The attempt to enforce the Aryan clause on the university Corporations, or fraternities, met refusals here and there and, in some instances, physical resistance. In Heidelberg, serious rioting took place between Nazi loyalists and the resisting men of the Corporations. The former believe that the Corporations are institutions that, at best, have outlived usefulness in the new day.

Student restiveness increases over the Nazified history, social science, and economics ladled out to them to the exclusion of other interpretations and points of view. In October, 1934, however, the Commissar for the Judiciary informed a meeting of professors in political economy that "whoever wants to become a fighter in National Socialist Germany must unequivocally accept the entity of the National Socialist philosophy." "The war of theories," he said, "must give way to academic peace."

SOCIAL PROTECTION SECURE

Intelligent, well-supported social measures for the people's wholesome economic life and protection against life's hazards are not new to Germany. They date from the time of Bismarck. That statesman saw the necessity of meeting with good works the challenge of a rising Socialism. The progressive extension and application of that early legislation brought German provisions against sickness, accident, old age, and unemployment to a leading position in the world. Under the Republic, these were retained and supplemented, if rather bureaucratically administered. In housing conditions for the working class, there was great advance. The deluge of post-war unemployment made unforeseen financial demands upon the insurance system. Large special State grants were required to meet them, together with increased assessments laid upon the insured who were employed. On the whole, a creditable care has been taken of the workless millions. It lessened somewhat under the strains imposed on resources during the last year of the Republic.

A general observation is that the Nazis, during their first year, under the spur of their own fresh promises and with a lessening number of the workless, improved service to the unemployed. They raised several hundred million marks by an inescapable system of private donations, and applied them ably and impartially. The transfer of many of the social benefit features of the deposed trade unions to the new German Labor Front necessarily operated against the smoothest administration. No sustained charges have been made of intention to impair the services. The Nazi program, on the contrary, proposes to extend them, notably in further provisions for old age and the care of mothers and children. In the state of German conviction and experience regarding social welfare, popular demand will prevent backward steps in any of these areas.

RELIGION AND "RACISM"

Number 24 of the Party Program declares that "the Party, as such, stands for positive Christianity." Whatever it means, the stand has not served to avert the rise of several problems for the Churches, both Protestant and Catholic. Some have come to be major issues; others raised little contention. Withdrawal of independent administrative authority from the numerous States left twenty-eight Protestant State Churches (*Landes Kirchen*) suspended in the air. This made necessary their merging without delay into a national Federation of Churches. It was a development that most churchmen had known for a long time should come. A development forcing it, therefore, aroused little heat, and the preliminary steps were taken without much opposing opinion.

The new church organization precipitated another question. What shall be the form of government— episcopal or democratic? About this the two church parties agreed quickly, though for different reasons. The National Socialist wing wished to follow the "leader" principle of the Party. The other, more concerned for the spiritual interests of the Church, believed that these would not be best served by trusting them to the fortunes of a parliamentary system that could be influenced politically by the great body of once confirmed but not now practicing Christians. Both sides then elected to have bishops. Thus far there was peace.

Two other issues, the direct offspring of Nazi doctrine and technique, set the two parties at odds. One is the implication of *Gleichschaltung;* the other, the creed of "racism." Induced by the Nazi campaigning propaganda, there came into existence a body calling themselves German Christians. They were the ordinary confirmed Lutherans full of Nazi yeast. The majority of them became ready to go the full distance in making the Church servant of the new State and order. They grew in numbers by the mil-

lion until they gained an actual voting majority of
Protestants.   In the test vote on the Reichsbishopric
they swamped the opposition.   They had the aid of
the monopolized Nazi press and broadcast.   The
Storm Troopers bullied many votes their way.   An
expression from Hitler favoring the German Christians' candidate did the rest.   (He is Müller by name,
a two-talented, East Prussian army chaplain who was
in the Chancellor's confidence.)

Müller immediately read content into his powers
that virtually set aside the Constitution of the
Church.   Dissenting pastors were dismissed.   New
regulations were attempted on no authority save his
own and that of a Council not recognized as legally
constituted.   Several thousands of the clergy instituted the Pastors' Emergency League to offer organized opposition to the Reichsbishop, and protection
to its members.   By the appointment of Commissars
for the Churches, the machinery of some of the States
has been used to discipline opponents.

The breach widened over the attempt to introduce
the Aryan racial doctrine into church administration.
The Aryan principle, applied to the Church, demanded the separation from the Christian ministry
of all pastors with so much non-Aryan blood as would
descend from one grandparent.   The ruling would
affect church lay officers also.   The opposition, con-
sisting of nearly all the better-known church bishops,
pastors, and scholars, denounced the decree as a violation of the laws of the Church and a fundamental
denial of the Gospel teachings concerning the universality and unity of believers.   Beyond denuncia-
tion, they rejected it in practice.   The president of
the German Christians, made Bishop of Prussia,
proved particularly offensive in trying to enforce the

rule and had to be recalled. This cost the German Christians much prestige. With other influences operating adversely, the German Christians disbanded as a body and reformed their lines.

Expounders of the Aryan doctrine elevate it to the place of racial science. While the crass manifestations of it are indistinguishable from race prejudice in ugly form and "Nordic superiority" raised to the nth degree, it does go beyond both of them in postulates. The proposition is that only by complete fidelity to the folk instincts, feelings, and ways of its racial forbears can a nation attain to the full flower of its capacities and powers, and so fulfil its own destiny and make its contribution to the whole of mankind.

First, then, a people who have let their racial springs become overlaid with time, must search back and farther back to the sources—on beyond history to folklore and mythology. "National Socialism," one authority explains, "is rooted in the recognition that only a people that has attained to an inner harmony as a result of racial factors is able to conduct the affairs of a powerful and vital state. It therefore imposes upon the State the supreme duty of preserving and improving the racial stock."

Logically, it must follow that this pure stream once uncovered and charted must be protected from the intake of other bloods and cultures. Without trying to give the doctrine the sanctions of a science, other races have practiced it vigorously—none more consistently than the race which now in Germany is its chief victim. With the upsurge of German nationalism, the Teutonic cults (not new among this people) are having their heyday. And by their extravagances as spokesmen for the German people, they make ridicu-

lous before the world their countrymen, most of
whom entertain no such delusions of grandeur.

Another onset came, when the Reichsbishop, acting under Party duress, made an agreement handing
over all the Protestant Youth organizations to the
Hitler Youth, for training two days each week and
two Sundays a month. This meant a practical monopoly of the children's leisure time to the corresponding exclusion of the parent societies. The right
to engage their members in any physical training or
sport was also surrendered, together with independent conduct of camps.

The differences became an open organized schism
by the late spring of 1934. The Synod of the Gospel
Confession established itself at Barmen in June of
that year. It separates itself and its adherents from
the authority of the Reichsbishop. The Administrative Council includes the Bishops of Bavaria and of
Württemberg and a list of other distinguished pastors, scholars, and laymen of the German churches.

Among them is Pastor Niemöller, vicar of the great
Dahlem congregation in Berlin. Dismissed by
Müller, he continues to preach. On the Sundays
when he serves in that church, the Underground
train with passengers from all over Berlin almost
empties at that station. The spirit of the congregation is one that no wise government will undertake
to subdue. When Niemöller received the order of
dismissal, he went straight to headquarters to tell
his superior that only once before had he disobeyed
orders. (As a "U" boat commander in 1918 he sank
his ship instead of turning it over to the conquerors.)
He must again refuse to recognize an order. It is
hard to pin on such a man the charge that he is not

a good German—one used often by the Nazis in withering the resistance of the weak.

In fairness, those of the German Christian persuasion may not all be dismissed as renegades. Many are earnest Christians who wished, as one expressed it, "to carry the Church, that is real Christianity, into the Revolution." He deplored that, instead, "the Revolution was taken into the Church." Others (and they are numerous) believe that the Church had withdrawn too much from common life and needed to have its scholasticism and formalism modernized and humanized.

Other credits may not be withheld. Religious education has been restored in all the schools. There has returned a wide and reasoned emphasis upon the sound old German love of song and story portraying honor, honesty, industry, civic integrity, discipline, obedience, family loyalties, the heroic virtues, love of country, and fidelity to the best of customs and culture.

The reformed German Christian Society is credited with fewer than 100,000 members. The "school" which advocated abolition of the Old Testament is a negligible faction, sharply rebuked by Müller himself and pronounced heretical. Pastors among them may number as many as 1,000 out of 18,000 in the Protestant Churches. Between them and the 6,000 members of the Pastors' Emergency League stand the nearly two-thirds uncommitted. The Chancellor has not cast in his influence and power finally on either side. The Reichscommissar for the Churches has intervened. He made matters worse and resigned. Hitler insists that the issues must be settled within the Church, but that they must be settled. There can be no peace while Müller remains. The leaders of the Confessional Synod and their immense following will not be beaten down. Attempts at suppression by force will only lead to fuller prison camps and more martyrdoms.

For the Catholics, the main issues are equally acute but less complicated. The Papal authority leaves no room for an inner division in that Church. The undivided power of the Church, therefore, is thrown against the racial doctrine. The highest German prelates have openly challenged it as pagan. The Pope has said "no good Catholic can be a National Socialist." The Concordat arranged between the Vatican and the Government early in the Nazi régime had gone far in defining satisfactory relations. Religious education by the Church was assured for all Catholic children. The Church would abstain from political action and in turn be guaranteed freedom from interference by the State both in its religious ministry and its administration.

One question was left for later settlement—the status of the Catholic Youth societies. Negotiations have failed to reach an agreement. Meanwhile, there have occurred many disturbing events, involving mistreatment of priests by Storm Troopers, and of Catholic Youth groups by young Hitlerites. One great assembly of Catholic journeymen had to be adjourned because of Nazi violence. Some arrests of Catholic churchmen for opposition to the State have taken place. In a few cases prison sentences followed. The fatalities of June 30, 1934, included Klausner, head of the German Catholic Action society. This event and the killing of the staunch Catholic Chancellor in Vienna by Austrian Nazis are said to have brought the unfinished Concordat negotiations to a state of suspension.

Nazi "racism" has been envisaged at its worst in dealing with the Jews. First, it must be asked whether the onslaught on this race in Germany is wholly unprovoked. Are the Jews themselves blameless? "What have you to answer for in Germany?" was put to some of them directly. The answers have come from those still able to be objective. The 600,000 Jews among the 60,000,000 of Germany are concentrated largely in the chief cities. This made them conspicuous. They had risen in the cities to be dominant in certain professions. They furnished fully one-half of the lawyers and doctors in Berlin. Court and hospital positions came to be filled with them. Denied officer status in the Imperial Army, they may have lost less than their share of talent in the war. In the ranks, they had their full quota and sustained proportionate losses. Among those who stayed at home were flagrant cases of war profiteering, but Jews by no means monopolized that odious rôle.

Jewish foreign money flowed in during the inflation to buy up German homes, apartment houses and industries. There were Jews officially prominent and responsible in the Government's inflation policy that worked devastation throughout the middle class of Germans. The author of the hated Marxism had been a Jew. Jewish leadership in the leading Marxist Party was considerable, in the Communist Party almost exclusive. Several of the worst post-war graft scandals involved Jews. In the economic crises, through sheer ability and industry, or by artifice, they often managed to fare better than their neighbors. The unwise (and they were numerous) flaunted their rising prosperity and power before the offended Germans. Easy immigration laws under the Republic permitted an influx of the least attractive

Semites from Poland and Galicia. These prospered by hook and crook, shamed the cultured Jews, and got on the Teuton nerves generally.

Preëminence in press, stage, cinema, and literature was won by Jews. In his *Preface to Morals*, Walter Lippmann wrote about "the acids of modernity eating at the foundations of the old cultures." They were eating in Germany—at the State, at the Church, at the Synagogue, at the family, at other old German ideals that on the whole are not a bad lot. Conspicuous among the acid generators were groups of brilliant Jews. They made shining marks for an indiscriminate, blasting propaganda.

The charges had some basis in fact, but they were magnified and distorted out of semblance to reality. The punishments as well have been yet more out of proportion to the offenses at their worst. They have been unintelligent and costly for Germany inside and out. Here the Nazis manifested that German blind spot remarked so often during the war—an ineptness for estimating what international reactions will be to their national conduct, and what the consequences to themselves.

Beyond being stupid, the physical mistreatment of the Jews must be rated cowardly. Of all elements in Germany, the Jews were least able to defend themselves. On the whole, brute force simply took vengeance on a 1 per cent minority. Hitler as Chancellor forbade it, and shortly succeeded in arresting it. But the *Führer* and his collaborators must be assessed as responsible for inciting a spirit of contempt and hate in the agitational period that was certain to result directly in terrorism. This included beatings and murder. When "Perish the Jew" is an imprecation sown far and wide by speeches, songs, and print in a revolutionary campaign for power, dead men is the harvest to be expected.

The extent of the brutality has been exaggerated in sections of the foreign press. Jews in Germany so placed as to be best informed testify to this. On the other hand, there were more instances of it than most Germans not directly implicated became aware of. One foreign consulate handled the cases of seventy molested Jewish citizens within his jurisdiction up to the close of the stormiest period, including the day of universal boycott. Some of them had invited it by presuming on their citizenship to give them protection in places and situations in which they had no business to be found. That shameless and cruel treatment overtook hundreds is beyond question. Scores were killed. When the violent and authoritative character of the agitation are taken into account, the surprising thing is that the assault did not result in more victims, and that it so soon ran its course.

In other directions, the anti-Jewish policy has gone on to extreme objectives. These include the exclusion of members of that race from all Government posts, from lowest to highest throughout the Reich. All teaching and court positions are embraced in the order. Jewish students in universities and Gymnasia are limited to the racial percentage in the population. Jews generally will not have the elective franchise. Party and Government pressures are forcing Jewish heads out of business houses. The State sets the example for commercial discrimination by refusing to buy supplies and services from Jewish firms. No Jewish editors remain. Jews are banished from the cinema and the stage. In the first instance, toleration of Jews in the learned professions was fixed at 1 per cent—the ratio of their people to the total population. This severe rule has been greatly modified to provide tenure for all who fought in the German Army, or who otherwise merit special consideration. Half the Berlin lawyers first debarred were soon reinstated.

Strong influences are at work for further moderation. Many German business enterprises, hard hit by the withdrawal of foreign customers, press for relief. Resistance in other quarters to the sweeping repressions is being offered on the highest ethical and spiritual grounds. This cannot fail to have remedial effect in time. The sense of justice is not dead in Germany, though for a time confused. From authentic sources, knowledge comes that the existing situation is recognized to be untenable permanently and that steps are being considered to improve it. Time will be required for such a tidal anti-Semitic movement to subside. Senseless extremists in the Party manage to thwart remedial action. ·On the other hand, many of the counter-offensives of the Jews outside are no more intelligent than those of the Nazi fanatics. They tend to further rancor and to prolong the strife. It is an open question whether the whole situation had not progressed better if left with the Jewish leaders within Germany. Very many eminent Jews within and outside Germany so believe.

Although most of the small shopkeepers carry on and are patronized, Jewish economic life is tragically dislocated. Of this, the leaders complain less than about the spiritual oppression. Notwithstanding claims to the contrary, very many of them love Germany. It is the land of their loyalty. The majority of them, given the opportunity, would choose not to leave. This makes what is being visited on them hurt most. They say: "We did not expect it from Germany." They ask, "How can the generations of our youth be reared in such an atmosphere of social suffocation?" Emigration on a large scale is seen as the only escape if the oppression persists. And whither? A few thousands of intellectuals may find hospitality in other lands by special arrangement. But what about the six hundred thousand? The Polish frontier is open to them, but few cross it to join the 9 per cent of Jewish population already there, hundreds of thousands of whom live in the direst poverty. Palestine, at the most, can absorb only about ten thousand a year for ten years.

The spirit of one young Jew in his twenties, let it be hoped, will find in time a meeting point of reconciliation with his present oppressors. He said: "I will be the last of my race to leave Germany. My family has been German 250 years. I was a child during the war, but my two brothers went to the front. One was killed; the health of the other broken. The fortune gained through generations was lost in the inflation. The small going business I have reëstablished prospers still. It may be crippled or even closed, but I can find some way to live. The intimate streets I have played in will be left, and the memory of every happy event of twenty years. Berlin is beautiful and beauty surrounds it. My dead are buried there. I can at least die there."

WHY GERMANY REARMS

Next to Anti-Semitism, the aspect of this current German Revolution which has most engrossed outside attention is what has passed for militarism. Disquiet, alarm, even panic seized Europe. Whatever substance there is to the fears has been amplified and broadcasted for certain international political ends. At Geneva, it served well for a time the purposes of those nations determined in the name of security to maintain their armaments for defense of the European *status quo,* with all its dangers to peace. For the press and lobby of the munition makers, it was a gift of the gods.

Despite the uproar, militarism as such appears well down the line in the Nazi program if the present temper and utterances of the individual leaders and members, from Hitler down, are entitled to weight. It is still less in evidence among the people. Much mingling among them leaves one with the impression that they believe the ends sought can and should be gained without resort to war. The most encouraging experiences are met with in finding young Nazis in uniform saying, "If we could sit down with the young Frenchmen and Poles, we believe ways through can be found without our having to go out to kill one another." Away from the newspaper barrages and scares, the long-time observer arrives where William Telling does. He writes in the *London Times:*

"That they have warlike tendencies, either these working men or even the middle-class officials now at the head of affairs, I am loth to believe. The young aristocrats who are with them realize that the wish is for some kind of Socialism and that pre-war fighting is almost impossible. The main preoccupation would seem to' be the reorganization of the country after several years of uncertainty."

There is a mood, nevertheless, which is dangerous. Its presence is unmistakable and must be faced. It

can and may easily provoke deeds that will again
start the guns roaring. The causes and cure are
legitimate concerns of civilization. To understand
it, we must go back to Versailles, with its clause
about "sole war-guilt," and what was built on the
foundation of that convenient fiction.

There were three possible settlements of the issues
left by the Armistice of November 11, 1918. One
was a German peace. If the Central Powers had won,
the peace would have been dictated by Germany. It
would have been a bitter peace—no less so than the
one imposed by the conquerors at Versailles. If any
one doubts this, the treaty forced on the Russians at
Brest-Litovsk will supply the needed corrective.

Or, a peace of reconciliation was conceivable. To
seek such a peace, the President of the United States
took his reputation, and, as it proved, his life in his
hands to go in person to Versailles. But Wilson
took there a purpose that had precedence over the
precise terms of the settlement—a League of Nations
to be a permanent instrument for adjusting all national quarrels of past, present, and future origin.
This the crafty Clemenceau discerned. As one cynic
has observed, he gave Wilson the Covenant of the
League to serve for an "all-day candy sucker," and
himself took about everything else on the table. The
result is a political structure set up in Europe that
can be maintained only by a vastly superior armament on the part of France, Poland, Czechoslovakia,
Jugoslavia, and Roumania. It was a victors' peace.
It determined by force rather than equity a whole
portfolio of issues over which the Continental wars
had been fought for centuries.

The Covenant in the Treaty made provision for
the dissatisfied and aggrieved among the nations to

bring their troubles to the League for adjustment. This was devised in part to make possible rectification of settlements in the Treaty of the sort that most informed persons not bound by nationalistic interest recognized from the beginning would have to be made some time. Now just where have the defeated nations and some of the disappointed victors got in their representations to the League? Exactly nowhere. League Council meetings and special conferences that might take cognizance are more likely to be premised on the condition that the issues be not taken up. And why the impasse? Because in Europe a nation around a council table, without enough military power to be a threat to its neighbors, habitually receives too scant consideration to justify the time and expense of sitting there.

Wilson, with the representatives of the British Dominions and Latin-American States, backed morally by the smaller Continental nations, undertook to redress the balance by terms that would reduce the victors' armaments to the level enforced on Germany and the other defeated powers. They got no farther than to have written into the Treaty a statement of "intention" so to disarm. Germany (with her allies) was reduced to helplessness. When the job was completed and certified by the Disarmament Commission, the Reich was admitted to the League and given a seat on its Council. Whatever the "intention" on the part of the armed victors to disarm meant at Versailles, it has had no objective result. Rather, they have increased on the whole the weight of the encircling armaments. Poland, Czechoslovakia, Belgium, and France have had Germany ringed about for a decade with enough military air-craft to wipe out the industries of the country in any given forty-eight hours. Under the Treaty terms, the means for defence from attack in the air were prohibited.

Meanwhile Reparations, the Ruhr occupation, the lost colonies, the gerrymander of the Upper Silesia plebiscite, the Corridor thorn in the flesh, the galling humiliation of Germany's position and the clear purpose to perpetuate it made a nationalistic fanatic and a German dictator out of Adolf Hitler. He has led Germany out of the Disarmament Conference. Exit from the League of Nations will follow unless there is abandonment of the "victors" versus the "vanquished" policy. The Germans are done with any collaboration that does not rest on the right and the reality of equality status. Germany is proceeding to arm up to the defensive level. The marks set are published in the British White Paper on the three-cornered correspondence on the subject between Downing Street, Quai d'Orsay and Wilhelmstrasse. They are reasonable. A Government that would not take similar steps in such a Europe as exists would be unworthy of a people's confidence. This new German policy is backed by the conviction of the overwhelming body of the population.

FOOTLESS DIPLOMACY

The world has a changed Germany on its hands from the one dealt with in Locarno. The bowed figure has become erect. The confidence of the people in themselves is revived. What has taken place they call "deliverance from slave psychology." They consider the new spirit justified already by bringing about the final rationalizing of reparations by the Allies in their hope of checking the Nazi rise to power. If nationalistic ambitions that were better abandoned have not found encouragement in the fervid utterances of this Revolutionary oratory, they would be dead indeed. Certainly some embers of the old German militarism glow afresh. They are not reflected in the prevailing spirit of the people. Military display is less in evidence than in a half-dozen other States of Continental Europe.

One international German grievance concerns the Colonies. The fifth of President Wilson's "Fourteen Points," which conditioned the Armistice, stipulated that all colonial claims would be examined without prejudice and dealt with impartially. When Germany's representatives were called to Versailles to sign on the dotted line what they had had no part in discussing with the victors, all her colonies had been swept into the already swollen empires of the Allies. If these were returned, half the emotional state of the German people would be relieved.

God must know where the German-Polish frontier ought to be fixed. No human beings do, least of all the two peoples most concerned. For centuries, Germans and Slavs have crowded each other back and forth from the Elbe to the Vistula and beyond. Historically and ethnographically, the Poles appear to have the better claim to the Corridor territory. The name of the province has been Polish immemorially—Pomerz (by the sea). Both Polish and German maps and figures show a large consistent Polish majority in the population. When within the Empire before the war, the inhabitants uniformly seated Polish delegates in the Reichstag.

Germany has ruled it since Frederick the Great joined Austria and Russia in the spoliation and division of Poland in the eighteenth century. That made the Corridor German land prior to the independence of the American Colonies. It suggests an imperfect analogy. In a later war, England and the United States might be on opposing sides. If the former conquered, British peacemakers may be imagined coming to the settlement demanding for Canada a better access to the Atlantic seaboard. The Americans would be reminded that the port of New York was formerly British, that all New York State was once within the Empire. Accordingly, the state and city are carved out and made Canadian. New England is left like East Prussia, a bleeding arm cloven from the trunk. Perhaps some one versed in astronomical figures will calculate how long it would take for an American-British reconciliation!

Nevertheless, Hitler as head of the German Government swallowed what he said as agitator and states publicly that the Corridor is not worth fighting for. A Berlin University professor of history believes that 90 per cent of the Germans agree with him. Certain it is that Polish-German relations and understandings have improved under the Nazi régime up to the point of a ten-year pact of non-aggression. (Incidentally, it was agreed that the two sets of text books should be expunged of teachings tending to cause ill will.) This is going far for the Government of a nation whose people generally regard the Poles as culturally inferior, and who in times past have justified appropriation of their territory on the ground of the German superiority. It is an augury for peace better than an Eastern Locarno if the old Teutonic *Drang nach Osten* (Pressure to the East) is on the way to abandonment.

Looking toward France, one sees less to encourage the peacefully minded. On neither side of the Rhine is there much of that "moral disarmament" of which Premier Zaleski of Poland spoke at Geneva as essential to progress away from war. The Franco-German feud is centuries old. France acts under the impulsion of "four invasions by German armies in a hundred years." Two of the invasions came when the Germans drove Napoleon home out of their territory. The third took place in the war of 1871-72, declared foolishly by the Emperor of France, who fell into Bismarck's trap. The French position is not difficult to understand, particularly when a man is supreme at Berlin who on his way to power wrote: [17]

"So long as the eternal conflict between Germany and France consists merely of defence against French aggression, it will never come to a decision, but century after century Germany will be driven from one position after another. Not until this is fully understood in Germany, so that the German nation's will to live is no longer wasted in passive defence, but is gathered together for a final settlement with France, shall we be able to bring the eternal and fruitless struggle with that country to a decision."

Responsibility and realities have carried the author of that bitter language far, when in no less moving appeal, he asks the French people for peace, on the ground that no cause for strife remains between them territorially if once the Saar Valley is restored to the Reich.

The French Government knows France can no longer stand alone against the German strength, and so seeks to perpetuate German military helplessness. The deadlock between these two Powers is the shadow over Europe and the world. The Prime Minister of Great Britain was not having a case of

[17] Hitler, *My Battle*, p. 291.

"nerves" simply when, in trying to be the third savior
of the Disarmament Conference, he solemnly warned
the members that "the joints of civilization were
creaking" about their ears.

If danger from German aggression increases, security against it does not lie in lengthening the
years of international "strafing" that are more basi-
cally responsible for the strained condition than are
all other provocations put together. The need is for
mediation on behalf of human society. For this the
British and American people bear weighty responsibility, as the people farthest removed from immediate self-interest. They need to accept this responsibility even though Hitler and his colleagues, in their
present position of isolation, prove hard to ne-
gotiate with.

With one of the best cases in the world for a winning international policy, the Nazis have managed
to bungle just about everything. Hitler had an excellent germ idea. Over against the colonial and
naval policies of the last Kaiser, which antagonized
England and brought all of British resources into
the hostile alignment for the Great War, he advanced
as alternative the policy of effecting a Pan-German
solidarity throughout Central Europe. With Germany's overseas ambitions abandoned, he believed
that British fears could be turned in the direction of
an alliance. Certainly such a bloc could blanket all
of Europe to the east and south with its commerce.
With Italy in league, France would be separated
from her Slav allies and Communist Russia be held
at bay.

Wisdom would have dictated a peaceful, commercial, and cultural penetration through the substantial German elements in the post-war territories of

Denmark, Belgium, France, Switzerland, Austria, Czechoslovakia, Poland, and Lithuania. With her resources in manufactured goods and her markets for raw materials and food in return, and with her sciences and arts, Germany could forget frontiers for a season, even permanently, and go out on exchanges of trade and culture in the spirit of give and take to mutual profit.

Instead, on coming to power, the Nazis thrust out ignorant, blustering missioners to proclaim and organize narrow nationalism, absurd racial superiority, and political disloyalty within the neighbor boundaries. The inevitable followed. Danish good business relations became clouded. Belgium voted more money for defence. Without a chance in the world of the Nazis winning a handful of German Swiss away from loyalty to their staunch and free Republic, they provoke fear on the part of another goods-buying nation, and a larger army ranged along a frontier where other than good-will need never exist.

The Poles took the bull by the horns. They presented the alternatives of accepting a non-aggression pact or an invading army. The Reich of necessity chose the former on terms that any Government under the Republic would have found humiliating. The Germans of Czechoslovakia, who have need for solidarity to preserve their minority rights, were split three ways: Nazi, Marxian Socialist, and Christian Socialist (Catholic). The last two turned against the first one before the Czech Government suppressed it.

The climax of this ill-advised policy came with the footless meddling in Austria. Regarding relations between the two German peoples Hitler has held a guiding conviction, central in his thinking from childhood, as he confesses in *My Battle*. This passionate passage appears on its very first page:

"German Austria will have to return to the great German Motherland, but not for economic reasons. . . . Even if reunion, looked at from that point of view, were a matter of indifference, nay, even if it were actually injurious, it would still have to come. Common blood should belong to a common Reich. The German people have no right to dabble in a colonial policy as long as they are unable to gather their own sons into a common State. Not till the confines of the Reich include every single German and are certain of being able to nourish him can there be a moral right for Germany to acquire territory abroad whilst her people are in need."

In the post-war but pre-Nazi period, the majority of Austrians might have been won to union with Germany on terms of their administrative autonomy within a federation. Although union may be recognized as the only normal way out economically for Austria, as constituted by the post-war settlements, the Treaties forbid it. France, Italy, and other powers stand ready to enforce the prohibition, thus far at the price of financing this weakest member of the Succession States and guarding it with armies. The Nazi onslaught has put the desirable end farther away by turning a 60 per cent majority of Austrians against absorption into their system. The present Government in Vienna rests on a 20 per cent political base of Christian Socialists and the semi-private Heimwehr Army of Prince Stahremberg. Without the moral support of all the Allies' and Italian arms poised across the frontier, it would be overthrown either by the 40 per cent Nazi following or the equally numerous Marxian Socialists, whom the Dollfuss Government murderously shot up early in 1934. All of this has rendered the Austrian State still more unstable and made the Treaty watchdogs more alert and aggressive.

The killing of the Austrian Chancellor-Dictator, by some of his own subjects as the culmination of Nazi intrigue, has cost the new German régime the last consistent national support it had in Europe or elsewhere. On account of it, Mussolini has broken with Hitler.

No informed opinion credits the head of the German Reich with setting up the assassination plot or of having knowledge of it. Nevertheless, the assassination was a bloody harvest not to be unexpected from the seed that had been sown. The Reich from which the Nazi Chancellor had asked and received full authority and responsibility harbored along its Bavarian frontier a large armed force of Austrian Nazis banished from their home-land for revolutionary designs and acts which they had in no wise abandoned or concealed. They were barracked in Germany, fed, clothed, and armed by thousands. Trafficking between them and their comrades who remained under cover in Austria was constant. Their spokesman, the exiled Habicht, had enough contact with the conspiracy to broadcast in Munich "the outbreak of revolution and the Vienna Government's fall" the hour Dollfuss was shot.

Granted that the German Chancellor had no knowledge of the plot, it was his business as Dictator and *Führer* to know about it and to stop it. Failure at this point has proved costly. The Italian press, which speaks so clearly only when it is told to speak, charges flatly that the continued toleration of this threat to the independence of Austria, resident on German soil, marked Hitler as a ruler who failed to make good his solemn promise (presumably given to the *Duce* at the meeting of the two men near Venice a few weeks before the tragic event).   The death of Mussolini's friend has been followed by a reversal of Italian policy no less complete than modifying a demand for revision of the conqueror's peace and willingness to bargain with France to join in upholding the terms of Versailles.   A more disastrous *faux pas* on the German's part is difficult to imagine in the circumstances.   He has managed to close the one open space in the ring of European powers opposing his country's escape from Versailles. And England was never further from a German alliance than today.

PART IV

NEW DEAL AMERICA

POCKETBOOK REVOLT

WHATEVER of fundamental change is taking place in the political, economic, and social life of the United States at the hands of Government has rather eluded definition and label. "Calling it names" was simpler, though scarcely intelligent.

In the United States, unlike Russia, Italy, and Germany, there is no party with an explicit philosophy and body of dogma to account for the policies and procedures of the Federal Administration. Only by inference and some imagination can there be found in the statement of positions and purposes framed by the Democrats at Chicago in 1932 more than intimations of the uses since made of the mandate given them in the national election that followed. The campaign utterances of Mr. Roosevelt, read now, yield revealing flashes of light on the course he and his advisors had in mind. The language was vague and general enough to admit of almost anything being done under the terms used. The new ventures entered upon have been admittedly experimental. No single voice of a Stalin, Mussolini, or Hitler speaks out with finality. Rather more continues to be done than said.

Nothing about the mighty overturn of authority voted in November, 1932, was surprising, except perhaps the completeness of it. Even that was predictable. "Economic determinism" had the field. There was no old Autocracy or young Democracy to throw down; no upsurge of demand for a freedom long denied; no revolutionary parties to be crushed; no racial minority to be pilloried and suppressed; no international grievances to arouse a flaming nationalism. Then why the popular, if peaceful, uprising? The fourth-year pressure of a devastating economic slump on the exposed pocketbook nerve of the population is the answer.

The national income had been cut down nearly one-half. For something like one-fourth of the people earned income had vanished altogether. Their 12,000,000 or more breadwinners were workless. Bank closings and failures had brought untold hardships to the depositors of $5,000,000,000. Stock market wealth, on which men and women had lived and borrowed as though it were real, had passed through the wringer. From September, 1929, to May, 1932, the quoted market values of listings on the New York Stock Exchange shrank from $97,000,000,000 to $14,000,000,000, leaving a multitude ruined and disillusioned.

The debts remained. Urban real estate carried a mortgage load of $35,000,000,000. The farmers were under a debt structure of $12,000,000,000. Instead of receiving 20% of the national income, to which they were accustomed before the war, their earnings had fallen to 10%. Their sense of injury had changed to anger. The interest and servicing of debts ate up about one-fifth of the shrivelled income of the city, town, and country population. According to the President, if the federal, state, and other public debts were added to the private obligations, the total of liabilities exceeded the assets. Multiple taxation on the boom levels either consumed further the substance of the people's living, or went unpaid to mount still higher with penalties. The actual and prospective loss of homes, farms, and businesses was terrifying. The freezing of credits progressively weakened the foundations of financial institutions until no end of the disintegration could be seen.

The prevailing public mood mingled fear, pain, and patience until the 1932 national election gave voters the chance to do something on their own account. Then the floodgates of popular feeling opened. Circumstances, both objective and subjective, conspired against the Hoover Administration. The unparalleled depression struck it the first year and stubbornly persisted. No man could have been in the White House more poignantly sensitive to the sufferings entailed, or more devoted to their relief and to the removal of the causes. His ways of going about it squared with his most unselfish and deep convictions, but not with those of the nation's opinion makers. His own party was not ably led in either House of Congress. It was disunited and otherwise enfeebled.

The opposition, by obstructive tactics, gave a characteristic exhibition of present-day parliamentary sinfulness. They "played politics with misery," as the baffled President said. The phrase stung but deserved to stick. The conscientious Quaker refused to violate the dignity of the presidential office and of his own nature by plying the politician's and showman's craft to make the public more conscious of his leadership. By resisting measures in favor of special groups at the expense of the national welfare, he alienated large voting constituencies. The combination of dissatisfaction, distress, fear, and enmity reacted at the polls with a vehemence to leave no doubt about the national will for change.

The President-elect read large content into the mandate he received at the hands of nearly two-thirds of the voting electorate. He had much warrant for so doing, and more accrued in the months between the November election and the ensuing March 4. There was a long stretch of uncertainty between the two acclamations, "The King is dead" and "Long live the King." It served to set back such movements of recovery as had set in during 1932. These recessions increased public fears and in turn fed on the fears. No inaugural address since that of Lincoln in 1861 expressed so forcibly the sense of mission and the assurance of a man "called." In the conviction that "the people of this country demand action," he gave notice of the purpose to secure and use extraordinary executive powers commensurate with the emergency.

The master objectives of the Administration have become clear. There are two. They can first be discerned along the trail of Mr. Roosevelt's active pre-convention candidacy. They are further traceable in the major campaign speeches. In his dealings with the Congress which elected him, they have become explicit. They run parallel. They can be summed up in the limits of a single sentence—to induce economic recovery and insure its stability; and, in the process, to set up permanent social controls over the American economic system, designed to effect a more equitable distribution of the national income in favor of "the forgotten man." These twin objectives will be seen in more detail along the way under the light of the Administration's official program, the enabling legislation, the implementing of the Acts, and the personalities who inspire and execute them.

A SECTIONAL AND SOCIAL COALITION

Nothing has happened in the American political order like the demolition worked by the Communists, Fascists, and Nazis on the systems of State they found in power. The old Russian régime was sunk without trace. The Italian throne still stands with real prerogatives—a lonely landmark left in that sea of Fascist authority. The very liberal Constitution of the post-war German Republic has been transformed into the instrument of a Dictator. A new one in the making will seal the fate of democracy and parliamentarianism. There remain no President to check or remove the Chancellor, no independence in the constituent States. The voice of parliament, when heard at all, simply echoes what the *Führer* wants.

In contrast, the New Deal has been launched without any Administration proposal for setting aside, or even amending, the Constitution of the United States. Several attacks on the constitutionality of certain legislative provisions are pending before the Supreme Court. The principles upon which decisions seem likely to turn were laid down in the five to four majority opinion read by the Chief Justice in sustaining the Minnesota Mortgage Moratorium Law. The decision recognized "a growing appreciation of public needs"; "the necessity of finding ground for a rational compromise between individual rights and public welfare"; "use of the organization of society in order to protect the very bases of individual opportunity"; and "of reasonable means to safeguard the economic structure upon which the good of all depends." These read like familiar shibboleths of the President and his colleagues.

Nearly all Soviet, Italian, and German legislation is by edict of the Cabinet. The All-Union Soviet Congress sits a few days to listen to the Executives tell what they have done or will do, and then vote ratification of everything by acclamation. The Deputies in Rome, after a speech by one of the Party veterans and another by Mussolini, with like unanimity, passed the sweeping "Law of the Corporations" without debate. Since the German Reichstag voted away its deliberative character, that body has been assembled rarely, and then at the call of the Government whistle. No one of the sittings consumed over a few hours. The features each time were a speech by the Chancellor and the passage *viva voce* of a single short resolution.

The nearest approach to abdication by the Congress in Washington has been suggested in the extraordinary powers lodged temporarily with the Executive in respect to National Recovery, Agricultural Adjustment, Currency, Tariffs, and the like. Nevertheless, that branch of the Government continues to take itself seriously. The sessions have run the standard length of several months. The debate on measures goes on normally and long enough, if the dispatch of business has any valid claims. The House organization has shown a disposition to hedge in debate. The Senators talk as much and sonorously as ever. Hearings by Committees proceed as usual. Some proved sufficiently animated to raise indignation, clenched fists, and intervention by neutrals to

preserve peace and decorum.   The main point is that
an opposition exists.   It is heard by the country and
it votes.

The most arresting design in each of the revolutionary patterns overseas is that of Party. In each case
a new one was fashioned, waxed strong in conflicts,
often violent, and by force or the equivalent of it
seized the power for itself alone.   Not content with
that, the Communist, Fascist, and Nazi parties proceeded to outlaw all others in their respective countries.   The one new phenomenon in the domestic
party situation was the rising of the Democrats from
the grave dug in three terrible campaign beatings,
and burying the long-regnant Republican Party to a
like abysmal depth.   (The 1934 elections gave no
promise of a return to life.)

Even so, the display was not that of party strength
alone.   The Democratic strategists masterfully seized
upon a ripe political situation.   Mr. Roosevelt and
his fat Congressional majority were placed where
they are by the shift of Republican voters of long
standing.   The result is not a party fusion, but rather
a coalition of sectional economic interests.   There is
material here for the building of a permanently
powerful political régime based on Agriculture,
Labor, the less favored masses of the metropolitan
centers, and the rapidly growing body of liberal intellectuals.

Several strains on the combination exist.   There
is a wide spread in the economic theory and allegiance of the old core of northern and southern Democratic leadership and that of the Progressives in the
two old parties.   Through several administrations
these latter have acted together in Congress.   Many
of them want to go farther left than the New Deal

has yet gone.   They are heavily reënforced by influential makers of matured and more permanent public opinion, found notably in the fields of higher education, of social welfare and of religious education
(Catholic, Protestant, Jewish, and Liberal).   In May,
1934, two hundred of these petitioned the President
to go farther and faster in action against "the forces
of inertia, rapacity, reaction, and selfish policy" which
they saw threatening his program.

The real tests of the coalition will come when the
Administration proposes measures for casting the
several emergency policies into permanent molds.
The intellectual leadership which has the President's
ear and surrounds him in office believes that the present economic order has operated to inflict upon
masses of the people enduring social wrongs of the
first magnitude.   It holds further that the defects of
the system have involved the country in its present
miseries.   On this platform, a large permanent following for the Administration is being built up from
among the millions who have been losers and sufferers.

The President clearly reflects this view in speak-
ing to Congress in January, 1934, about "a mandate
of the whole people . . . to build on the ruins of
the past a new structure designed better to meet the
problems of modern civilization."   Such a view has
become the settled conviction of a very large voting
body that constitutes the more reasoned support behind the New Deal.   It is neither an unintelligent
nor a passing phase—this rapidly spreading recognition that either grave defects or abuses, or both, reside in a system that, in the sight of plenty, has
plunged a population into the unhappy economic ex-

periences of the past four years with their heavy social penalties.

The strength of the régime in Washington, then, is in a situation underlaid with a cause. The commission given is to a man rather than to a party. The bestowal was by free will, not by coercion, and so remains. His supporters can vote him out of power. They will do so if he fails them. They trust him, not the Congress. They approved the latter, giving him immense authority. If this procedure is a sign of weakness in American Democracy and away from the democratic ideal, there is saving sense in the Democracy bestowing the power instead of letting it be seized by an armed minority, and being unable to take it back. As Harold Callender remarked in the *New York Times* (May 6, 1934), it still has advantages over government by castor oil and concentration camps.

A number of circumstances point toward the timeliness and the desirability of some major political realignments. The Republican Party is so divided right and left that no issue in sight offers the prospect of reconciling the differences. The Party in power, under the surface, has disagreements no less deep, though better concealed for the time by adroit political management and the rewards of victory. The Socialists, always on the frontal attack, exert an influence to keep one of the major parties at least liberally left in order to hold in line its pinkish followers. Labor threatens now and again to take the road of separate party organization unless its demands are more nearly met by the existing parties. A Huey Long in Louisiana and an Upton Sinclair on the Pacific Coast reveal the presence of tangential political forces that can be released.

The road might be cleared for real progress if the old parties could be broken up and re-formed into one first-rate, self-acknowledged, unified party of con servatism opposed by another solidly strong party frankly forward-looking and not less militant than the advanced progressives now scattered among several camps. Two such parties should serve better to bring to focus the pressing issues of the time and sooner bring the electorate to informed decisions. An important by-product could well be the passing of the old party machines in the process.

Neither of the senior party organizations gives evidence of any bid for regeneration—least of all the one now flushed with victory. Parallel with "high thinking by the best minds," the Democratic machine busily entrenches itself. Critics have to go back to the period of Andrew Jackson for a comparable case of national avidity for the spoils. Even for Democrats, it is said only those are favored for appointments who hold the F.R.B.C. degree (For Roosevelt before the Convention). New alphabetic bureaus set up by the Administration, exempted brazenly from Civil Service classification, have woven much velvet for party men. The number of non-classified civil service employes of the Federal Government increased by 69,000 between March 4, 1933, and July 1, 1934. The highly efficient Department of Commerce personnel has been singled out and riddled by reorganization and dismissals. In the absence of any rational ground for the attack, an act of vengeance on Mr. Hoover's pride and joy may be safely, if wickedly, presumed. For months before and after the 1932 election, confirmation of his appointments was withheld as a policy to leave berths open in anticipation of the turnover in power. The

unprecedented billions expended for relief and public works have afforded "pork barrel" opportunities
beyond the fondest dreams of political avarice.

The capitalization of beneficences in the 1934
political campaigns was shameless. Governors and
Senators seeking reëlection related to their constituents the number of dollars that the Administration
has bestowed upon the State for each dollar paid by
the State in Federal revenues. The Iowa Democratic Party Committee went into print on the subject. After calculating an inflow of not less than
a quarter of a billion dollars, one of its electioneering
leaflets declares these obvious truths: "Every Iowan
desires that the liberal attitude adopted by the national government in dealing with this State shall be
continued. Much of the Federal relief came down
to Iowa people through the friendly coöperation of
our Democratic state and national governments."

Commenting on the prospects of the "outs" making much headway in an election with such past, present, and future largess in mind, "Al" Smith is credited with this salty observation: "No one shoots Santa
Claus around Christmas." It is not to be implied
that the rival party's politicians are more high-
minded. The level on which most partisans make
appointments does not breed confidence that they
would perform differently if entrusted with large
operating responsibilities in the nation's economic
system. The enduring worth and honor of the present Administration is not best served through the
political traffic directed by a "two-in-one" National
Committee Chairman-Postmaster General. No truly
great ameliorating movement can travel far on such
feet of clay.

The Secretary of the Interior, a model of executive probity, has not escaped the toils of patronage. According to the Chief Engineer of the Reclamation Service in a letter (May 15, 1934) addressed to applicants, the Secretary required that "each recommendation submitted to him for appointment to a non-Civil Service position in the Bureau of Reclamation be supported by clearance from some appropriate official in the Democratic Party organization." And in the following month, the former Bull Moose Republican himself instructed the Commissioner of the General Land Office to use for newspaper advertising purposes Democratic organs only, unless legal restrictions provided otherwise.

The *United States News* has gone farther in charging that the New Deal smells disappointingly of "Old Deal" politics. In the issue of July 9, 1934, David Lawrence writes bluntly: "The way in which codes have been modified by political pressure or through the influence of heavy campaign contributors has been all too transparent. Privileges are still sold hereabouts to the highest bidder, and if you doubt it, look over the list of appointments to powerful and influential public offices. Look, too, at the close connection between the active political campaigners, the members of the national committee, and the most important posts in government itself." Rather more of political independence was to be expected in a President who first won his spurs fighting the ruthless Tammany machine. This same Tammany Engineer Farley has now made a wheel of his Federal Juggernaut.

THE ECONOMIC LABORATORY

The major changes ushered in by the New Deal, or waiting on the doorstep, have direct or indirect economic objectives. Such measures as involve political principles and affect human rights are invoked because of their bearing upon the flow of financial blessings. The real argument remains over profits and pay envelopes, taxes, and debts—in short, the distribution and uses of wealth. The New Dealers, like the makers of the three patterns already examined, intend to "do things" to the existing economic order.

Repeated declarations by the President make the general intention unmistakably clear. In 1930, he began discussing ways and means "for the reconstituting of our economic machinery." [1] In the same volume, he insists upon the necessity of turning from "basic economic errors," "revolutionary changes in the conditions of modern life" having made it certain that we can never "go back to the old order" with its "pattern of an outworn tradition." He sees "the almost complete collapse of the American economic system" calling for a "rebuilding from the ground up." In the distribution of national income, "the reward for a day's work will have to be greater, on the average, than it has been, and the reward to capital, especially capital which is speculative, less." Otherwise "our ailing economic order" cannot be made to endure for long.

The message to Congress on January 3, 1934, gave some particulars on what the Administration's "integrated program, national in scope," was designed to save and what to cast out:

[1] *On Our Way,* p. 84, The John Day Company, New York.

"Viewed in the large, it is designed to save from destruction and to keep for the future the genuinely important values created by modern society. The vicious and wasteful parts of that society we could not save if we wished; they have chosen the way of self-destruction. We would save useful mechanical invention, machine production, industrial efficiency, modern means of communication, broad education. We would save and encourage the slowly growing impulse among consumers to enter the industrial market place equipped with sufficient organization to insist upon fair prices and honest sales.

"But the unnecessary expansion of industrial plants, the waste of natural resources, the exploitation of the consumers of natural monopolies, the accumulation of stagnant surpluses, child labor, and the ruthless exploitation of all labor, the encouragement of speculation with other people's money, these were consumed in the fires that they themselves kindled: we must make sure that as we reconstruct our life there be no soil in which such weeds can grow again."

The men who have most often and consistently spoken for the program as a whole, or for their parts of it, have dealt in some specifics. The keynotes, one and all, are pitched around planning and control in the interest of a wider distribution of income and, with it, of the good things of life. Thus Richberg, one of the most highly placed officials of the Chief Executive's inner circle, presented to the Merchants' Association of New York the choice "between private and public election of the direction of industry." "Unless industry," he told that body, "is sufficiently socialized by its private owners and managers so that great essential industries are operated under public obligations appropriate to the public interest in them, the advance of political control over private industry is inevitable."

The gifted and agile Tugwell dissents from "the policeman doctrine of government." He is for the political unit having "positive responsibilities of its own" beyond the function of simply "holding a balance among other groups." It should be "equipped to fight and overcome the forces of economic disintegrity." The point nearest to Utopia which humans are ever likely to gain, he thinks, will be in "a nation of well-paid workers, consuming most of the goods it produces." He argues: [2]

"It is necessary to this result that too much income shall not go to profits; for if it does, this will either be spent for wasteful luxuries which have to be made in extravagant ways, or will, if it is not spent, be distributed by bankers to enterprises who will overexpand their productive facilities, forgetting that the worker's buying power is not sufficient to create a demand for them. On this ground alone, if there were no other, a powerful argument could be made for a substantial equality of incomes and for the limitation of personal surpluses."

The Secretary of Agriculture will seem to some to be laying his hands on the jugular vein and windpipe of business when he says that "the supreme function of business men is not to make a profit." And still more definitely, he adds, "It is exceedingly important that business men never can take as large a percentage of the national income for profits as they did in 1929."

Professor Berle, of Columbia University Law School

---

[2] Reprinted from Tugwell: *Industrial Discipline*, p. 183, by permission of Columbia University Press.

and the Brain Trust, seconds the motion with, "The business of today is not an affair of making profits. That is incidental to a service of supply by which a people live and develop. Failing in that it is bankrupt morally, and financial bankruptcy shortly follows."

The Secretary of the Interior puts the case less technically in discussing how to get a prosperity far better than that called prosperity in the past. Mr. Ickes predicts, "We can't have it, if we allow the priests of the Golden Calf to raise up their fallen idol in our midst again and set the fashion of political worship for the rest of us, as they did for three-quarters of a century before 1932." He recalls "the long years before, when, in the name of 'rugged individualism,' 2 per cent of the people were getting control, noisily or quietly, of 80 per cent of the wealth of the country." He would "like to believe that the country will never again countenance the ways of the jungle in its economic affairs." [3]

A single paragraph in a lengthy exposition of the New Deal's Labor policy by the Chairman of the National Mediation Board registers a note in common with that sounded by all those at the heart of the Administration: [4]

"Industry pays depreciation and obsolescence charges on working capital and it pays interest on idle capital equipment. But Labor also depreciates, wears out, and gets old; it is rendered obsolete by technical improvements, and it is unemployed when equipment is idle. For property we have provided a measure of security against these hazards by providing reserves that are charged to operating costs.

[3] *New York Times*, April 1, 1934.
[4] W. M. Leiserson, *United States News*, September 24, 1934.

Each individual worker can no more provide his old-age and unemployment insurance than each small business man can carry his own fire insurance or each bank its own burglary insurance. The New Deal proposes, therefore, to inaugurate a system of social insurance that will provide for the labor investment in industry at least the measure of security that is provided for the capital investment. Unemployment, obsolescence, depreciation, and superannuation of labor are costs of production every bit as much as the similar charges commonly made for the protection of the capital investment are production costs."

What has been done substantially toward giving content and effect to the foregoing theories can be comprehended under the following six generalizations. The State has measurably replaced the bankers in the confidence of investors and in directing the outlet for surplus funds. From this and other positions, the Government has sought to establish itself on guard at important passes to what Lenin once called "the strategic heights" of the economic system. Debtors have been favored at the expense of creditors. Labor's position has been strengthened in its working relations with ownership and management. The income of farmers has been raised appreciably toward a parity with their costs and fixed charges of an earlier period. Ways and means of bettering the conditions of life for the least favored of the population have been employed beyond the measures undertaken by any preceding Administration. Discussion of the aims and achievements under the last three brackets will be reserved for the chapters dealing with Labor, Agriculture, and Social Welfare and Protection.

Without going into the details of how and when it got that way, the Federal Government now presides over the uses to which any very large sums of money may be put. Government has become not only the chief borrower of capital; through the Act controlling the issue of new securities, it practically decides who besides itself may borrow. The banks themselves have little alternative to lending their glut of deposits to the Government. According to a statement of the United States Chamber of Commerce, issued September 15, 1934, the Federal issues were totalling $3,667,000,000 a year, compared with corporate issues of $224,000,000, or one-sixteenth of the former sum. This condition alone spells a form of supreme economic control. This is a part of the New Deal design—one of the requisites of a planned economy. The Government's rise to this position was made easy by popular reaction during the débâcle of the former commercial banking and credit system, which a Secretary of the Treasury [5] of the fateful period characterized as "unsound" to the degree of constituting "a fatal weakness."

The outreach of the Government from its new position in finance is enormous. The Reconstruction Finance Corporation's reports on advances and repayments show the wide range of the Government's entrance, through loans, into business relations with enterprises that give it a voice equivalent to such control as formerly was exercised by creditor banks. The amount of salary paid an official determines whether a loan to his concern shall be made or refused. The list of properties over which obligations are held is impressively extensive and varied—

[5] Ogden L. Mills to the Academy of Political Science in New York City, March 21, 1934.

banks and trust companies; railroads; insurance companies; mortgage, building and loan associations; States and their political subdivisions; farms, crops, livestock, homes. Ultimately, to the extent that the loans are unpaid, the Government must succeed to actual ownership in undertakings of every description.

The spread of the new direct Federal undertakings is equally wide. The Emergency Housing Corporation has been empowered to do everything conceivable in the whole range of real estate and building construction combined, along with the financing of them. Besides housing in the ordinary terms, the authority to construct embraces roads, parks, playgrounds, sewers, and bridges. These operations under the Act may extend into the fields of all the utilities—heat, steam, water, gas, electricity, telephone, and transportation. Such undertakings on foot are at once the result of frozen private enterprise and the cause of it not thawing out.

The Tennessee Valley Authority extends into six States and reaches down to the employment of an R.F.C. loan to finance the purchase of favorably priced electric ranges, refrigerators, and water heaters by housewives in its jurisdiction. In Omaha, the pastor of a leading congregation announced that a Government-financed physical director was available in the church gymnasium to lead the women folks in reducing exercises. The agency of the Civil Works Administration, according to the *Brooklyn Daily Eagle,* organized the catching of rats in that city. The experiment cost $70 a rat.

Over all of production and distribution soared the Blue Eagle of the National Industrial Recovery Administration (NRA). It had 24,000,000 persons working under "codes of fair competition" in 460 lines of industries. The codes were framed by the respective industries with benefit of counsel from Labor and Consumer advisors. Government representatives assisted to secure a result that would receive the necessary sanction of the President. Upon his approval, these codes had the force of law. In his statement outlining the policies to be followed under the Act, the President referred to it as "one of the most important laws that ever came from Congress." The task would have two stages—first the emergency job of getting the people back to work; then to plan for a better future for the longer pull.

For the pull at recovery out of the depths (short as it was supposed to be), the incursion of the State into a measure of control was not unwelcome. The captains of industry, commerce and finance proved scarcely less baffled than the rank and file about what to do. Their many prophecies of an upturn around the corner failed. They were ready for a savior, if only an experimenter, to give them a helping hand. The United States Chamber of Commerce exerted its influence for passage of the National Recovery Act. The public considered some major intervention by the Government overdue.

Patience endured on all sides for a season as expenditures mounted for relief and other emergency features. All agreed that the workless and their dependents had to be cared for, that it would be expensive, that a good deal of waste was to be expected, if not some graft. It was reasoned that the nation after all was resourceful and so able to take a lot of financial punishment of the sort.

By the time Big Business began to pull up snugly

into the NRA collar and other pieces of alphabetic harness, the latter were found to be galling at several friction points. The *Chicago News* published a front-page editorial in the autumn of 1933 inquiring whether the country knew the year before that it was voting for Revolution. It suggested something not intended by the nation was being put over on the country. The *Tribune* of the same city on December 10 following laid down a barrage of statements by "brain trusters" to show that revolutionary changes were definitely and deliberately in the program. The purpose of the President "to plan for a better future" appeared quite clearly to mean holding "the strategic heights" (yielded during the crisis by general consent) and from them to carry the New Deal on to its permanent objectives.

Remonstrance and resistance to features of the legislation increased with time. The difficulties of enforcing the codes led early to the withdrawal of their application to communities under 2,500 population in size, and later to the entire suspension of them in several industries. Before resigning as Administrator, General Johnson declared himself in favor of reducing the number of codes to 250, or by more than one-half.

Charges were made that the set-up lent itself to the advantage of the larger units of an industry, and that the conditional suspension of the anti-trust laws restored conditions of monopoly. Certainly, some lines profited greatly from price-fixing privileges and requirements. Prices generally advanced the cost of living beyond the point necessary to recover the advanced outlay for wages. Of this Labor complained bitterly. It objected, too, that the close-up authority for administering the codes left Labor unrepresented.

Industry countered with "Labor is always right" at Washington.

Enforcement rested back finally on the Government. This irked the industries, less because of hardships imposed than of fears that the rôle of the State would be expanded. The air was filled with outcries and grumbling over the messing in of theorists with impracticable proposals. Executives bemoaned the time and money involved in code-making and operation. Hundreds of highly paid officials worked at little else.

Fear fed on recognition of the President's power to change a code at will. The output of Executive orders in the first year and a half reached nearly six times the number issued from 1862 to 1900. Protests became loud against orders under the NRA and AAA being beyond court review—"final if in accordance with the law." The fearsome licensing authority given the President under the Recovery Act was never employed, and was permitted to lapse in the new legislative Act of 1934. The Agricultural Administration used freely its corresponding power and has retained it.

The credits of the NRA bulk largest in its byproducts. These outweigh in value the contributions made to recovery. They are acknowledged and acclaimed by all save hopeless reactionaries. The codes fixed maximum work hours and minimum wages at a decent living level in principle. They forbade child labor and compelled collective bargaining. Under them, with variable application in the several industries, such cut-throat trade usages have been outlawed as secret discounts, premiums, gifts, "loss leaders," and price cutting. Only by common action and the presence of Government with authority could these large social gains have been realized.

A spiritual credit withal can be accorded to the Administration. Faith has been kept with the country in respect to the experimental nature of the NRA. Much patience has been shown toward honest criticism and constructive suggestions. In the revisions now on foot, there appears sincere, painstaking effort to meet the sober mind and will of the nation, though it means retirement of the Administration from certain positions previously taken. Of the central purpose to serve the interests of the greatest number, there can be no doubt. And that purpose will not be surrendered.

The program for the redistribution of wealth and income has proceeded in several directions. The minimum-wage provision of the NRA aims that way; the dealings with debts likewise. Some one early predicted that this would be a debtors' Government. In respect to loan relief, high finance can make no valid complaint. The big fellows in distress have been treated no less liberally than the little ones faced with the loss of their farms, homes, and businesses. Changing the money standard to the lower level, in so far as it has raised domestic prices, has written down the value of every loan and of every other holding represented by cash, bank deposit, insurance policy, bond, pension, annuity, other savings and fixed income of every form, including wages and salaries not raised to correspond. Pressures for a much larger measure of debt paying by inflation have been resisted thus far by the Administration, but the end of the pressure has not been reached.

Increased taxation of high incomes and inheritances constitutes another drive on wealth. The rate of death duties has been raised to 60 per cent for estates above $10,000,000. Mounting debts of the Federal Government become a standing threat of further attacks on large accumulations either through capital levies, or vast issues of paper currency, or out-right repudiation. There are elements in Congress and on the outer left fringe of the New Dealers whose freedom in borrowing and spending may have as explanation the contemplation of these simple ways of liquidation. Moderate laws passed by the last Congress provide procedures for the scaling down of debts and interest rates by agreements be-tween overburdened corporations and local govern-ments and three-fourths of their creditors which will be binding on all the respective creditors. There can be no serious objection in principle to creditors sustaining losses of capital and income proportionate to those undergone by farmers, wage-earners, salaried people, businesses, and stockholders. It should not be overlooked, however, that losses taken on bonds and mortgages affect millions of small holders of securities and life insurance policies.

Of all the epithets applied to the economics of the New Deal, that of "Communistic" is the most far-fetched. The two programs bear resemblance in no essential particular beyond both using the term "planned economy." The realities there and here are poles apart. The NRA, if raised to the nth power, would never be recognized by Com-munists as theirs. In the first place, the Communist Party would be its author. It would have a base on fixed Party dogma instead of being thrown together by the Brain Trust for a Congress to vote mostly blindfolded. There would be no nervous property owners around to be quieted. The Soviet State

owns everything involved since 1917. No employers,
jealous for their powers, need be reckoned with.
That State is the only employer in sight. No other
remains to give a job if a worker doesn't like the
one given him, for the State operates as well as owns
all industry. The trade unions would make no protest at anything. The Party has had them sewed up
tight for years. As for the consumers, one and all
buy their goods and services of the State at the State's
prices. The entire income of the whole population
is in the same almighty, exclusive hands for division,
the State thus far taking for itself the lion's share.

It is nearly as far a cry to Socialism, which adheres
to democratic procedure, as does the New Deal. No
group repudiate it as their scheme of things more
heartily than the Socialists. Their presidential candidate and party leader rarely misses opportunity for
attack upon New Deal fundamentals in his column
in the *New Leader,* an aggressive Socialist weekly.
In one issue he calls the Tennessee Valley project
"the one socialistic agency of the New Deal"—"a
flower in a garden of weeds, and great corporations
water the weeds." In an earlier number, the case
was stated with more doctrinal precision:

". . . no healthy society can live by trying to re-
distribute its own stored-up fat. A political government which has its finger in every kind of pie without real responsibility is a government which invites
bureaucracy and corruption. A government which
employs millions of unemployed workers at made-
work sets up a thoroughly unhealthy situation between government and the citizen. We do not want
a government which owns preferred stock in capitalist banks where some Jesse Jones can stick his
finger in the pie; we want socialized banking. We

do not want an indefinite continuance of CWA; we want social ownership and planned administration of industries operated for use, not profit, under boards of directors representing the workers in the industry and the consumers. Which is another way of saying that we want Socialism and not subsidies." [6]

If confined strictly to economics, some mild comparisons of the New Deal with Fascist policies in Italy and those of the Nazis in Germany are possible. All three adhere to the institution of private property. They are alike in requiring its uses to be adapted to the national welfare in contrast to that of the owning class primarily. They do not deny the principle of profit but seek to limit its sway. Through capital advances each Government exercises varying powers over industry and commerce. A planned national economy is the goal. Room remains for the competitive game. The codes of the NRA and the hand of the State in their framing and operation are suggestive of the "Corporation" pattern in Italy and that of the "Chamber" in Germany. To venture on a generalization—in each of the three countries the effort is directed toward making a capitalistic system better serve the great body of the population than any has yet done.

LABOR STRATEGY

Labor and employer relations presented the hardest nut for the New Deal to crack in its first two years. This nut in particular has a multi-plated shell of many interests at once strong and diverse. Moreover, to mix a metaphor, it is packed full of

[6] Norman Thomas in the *New Leader*, February 2, 1934.

political dynamite—an article with which this Administration deals gingerly.

The very genius of the New Deal calls for Labor to be powerfully organized up to the point of ability to deal with employers on terms of equality, at least. Otherwise, it cannot hope to bargain collectively with enough success to bring to Labor that larger share of the common income proposed by the New Deal. Under this official favoring attitude of the Administration and corresponding legislation, the organizing of workers into standard unions has moved forward. Between the peak of its numerical strength in 1920 and 1933 paid-up members in affiliation with the American Federation of Labor declined from 4,078,740 to 2,126,796. On September 1, 1934, there were 2,608,011. If members whose dues are not paid up because of inadequate employment be included the total organized strength was reckoned at 5,650,-000. The goal is set for 15,000,000 in three years.

Of more strategic importance is the extensive penetration of organization into territory hitherto little unionized. Until this period, such great employing interests as those of steel, automobiles, oil, rubber, and textiles (South) have stood out conspicuously against the recognition of independent unions. Their refusal to bargain with union representatives as such was persistent. Clause 7a of the National Industrial Recovery Act enjoined the collective bargaining principle upon every coded industry. Acceptance of it was the price of securing Administrative recognition of the code and other valuable considerations. The clause, called "Labor's Charter" by the President, reads:

"That employees shall have the right to organize and bargain collectively through representatives of

their own choosing, and shall be free from the interference, restraint, or coercion of employers of labor,
or their agents, in the designation of such representatives or in self-organization or in other con-
certed activities for the purpose of collective bargaining or other mutual aid or protection; that no
employee and no one seeking employment shall be
required as a condition of employment to join any
company union or to refrain from joining, organizing, or assisting a labor organization of his own
choosing."

The language of the Act left open an issue vital
to both sides, which they prepared to meet. The
standard unions rushed in to organize the contesting
industries. The employers showed zeal and haste in
furthering company unions in order not to concede
to the others the sole bargaining right for their employes. The standard unions came back with the
contention that company unions do not come within
the terms of the Act, as not being "free from interference, restraint, or coercion of employers."

The President [7] of the American Federation of
Labor has made this reasoned statement of the position: "In America, a citizen makes his own decisions,
or delegates that power to some one he selects for
that purpose. He may employ counsel for legal
matters and advisors in personal and business matters. Upon matters which concern him as a member
of a community, he votes for a representative to act
for him. The basic principle of the representative
system is majority rule—that is, whoever receives the
majority of votes from those concerned assumes responsibility for managing the affairs of the group.
No other basis would provide that responsibility

[7] William Green, *American Federationist*, May, 1934, pp. 465-67.

which makes possible orderly planning and execution. Definite location of responsibility is a fundamental rule of work—whether industrial or political. These are established principles in American life—so completely accepted as to need no justification. . . ."

Mr. Green then charges these unfriendly employers with determination to maintain control over the returns from joint work for the protection of their one-sidedly selfish interests. It is for "fighting Labor's rights" under the NRA that industries have increased their activities in setting up company unions, realizing "that their employees if left to their own inclinations would join unions affiliate to the American Federation of Labor." He continues:

"When the company union has failed to stop workers from joining a standard labor union and demanding the right to collective bargaining, executives are trying to divide the workers' forces by devising proportional representation schemes. They say that majority rule is unfair to the minority group and therefore every group must be represented proportionately in the bargaining process. Any such procedure would of course either hopelessly divide the bargaining group so as to defeat their purpose or result in differing work standards for various groups—an impossible administrative situation. The unions ask for majority rule, the right to establish representation free from coercion—that is, under government supervision—and the acceptance of representatives freely chosen for joint negotiations conducted in good faith."

This issue was forced to a crisis and decision in the automobile industry in the spring of 1934. A compromise resulted. The Federal Labor Union of

Automobile Workers lost the point of its exclusive
bargaining claim on the principle of majority rule,
but gained, along with that industry's acceptance of
collective bargaining, security from discrimination
against employes on account of standard union affiliation.   The most significant declaration in the five-
point agreement was the Government's first clear
statement of its own position as between types of
labor organization.   This declared "that it favors no
particular union or particular form of employee organization or representation."

.   With this interpretation, the industry won Point
Two of the agreement, which reads: "If there be
more than one group, each bargaining committee
shall have total membership pro rata to the number
of men each member represents."   With Government
neutral on this contested point, there remained to
organized Labor the sole recourse of having it out,
cheek and jowl, with employers who are hostile to
dealing with other than company unions.

Defeated in negotiation, Labor goes back to organize more completely for ultimate conquest of
workers' unitary representation.   This is a pivotal
point in Labor policy.   The Labor leaders point
with suspicion to the hundreds of employers who
sprinted to set up company unions in the early
months of the NRA period.   In refuting the claim
that the company union meets the conditions for true
collective bargaining, the *American Federationist* [8]
of March, 1934, paraphrases these numerous accusations from a report of the Federal Coördinator of
Transportation:

"Managements have participated in or supervised
or retained a measure of control over the constitu-

[8] P. 276.

tions, by-laws, and other governing rules of company
unions. Managements have supervised the rules
governing nominations and elections of the employees' representatives and officers, and have participated in election processes—at times taking charge
of the count of ballots. Managements have contributed financial support to company unions, and
have paid the salaries or expenses of the officers or
representatives of company unions when exclusively
engaged in the business of these unions. Managements have participated in the collection of dues,
fees, and assessments of company unions. Managements have extended special privileges, such as group
insurance, relief funds, and the like exclusively to
members of company unions. Managements have
encouraged or advised employees to join or not to
join particular organizations and have attempted to
prevent an exercise of free choice in such matters.
Managements have assessed demerits, made reductions in pay, discharged, or otherwise victimized
employees for failure to remain members of company unions or for soliciting membership in standard unions. Managements have kept lists of employees who are members of a labor organization
and have used these lists in administering discipline
or otherwise coercing employees with respect to
membership in labor organizations. Managements
have denied customary benefits, privileges, or opportunities to members in a standard labor organization."

The Labor forces under Federation generalship
move forward to other well-planned objectives with
standpat employers on the defensive. There is demand for effective representation on each NRA
Code Authority. It is maintained that "nine-tenths

of every law is its administration." The contention
is for Joint Industrial Relations Boards (each to
cover an entire major industry) "to adjust contro-
versies over problems that arise in connection with
provisions of the code." Labor moves to have these
Boards agencies of the Federal Administration rather
than of the Code Authorities. Such a Board would
be composed of an equal number of employers and
employes, appointed by the NRA Administrator.
The Board members would elect an impartial chairman. The new Board of three members set up by
the President in the Textile industry as part of the
1934 Strike settlement almost exactly meets these
specifications.

A third major Labor plank asks for a thirty-hour,
five-day week without reduction of the weekly wage.
The San Francisco Convention of the Federation,
late in 1934, gave prominence to the demand. Favoring opinion regarding it appears largely confined to
Labor circles and partisans. The measure is brought
forward as the way to take up unemployment—by
letting all do the work now performed by a part.
Opponents point out that its adoption would mean
acceptance of the present lowered standard of consumption for the population as a whole. And, further, that the sharp increase in cost of production
would put goods still farther beyond the reach of
the people at large. Thus demand would be again
lowered and the resulting unemployment begin over
again. And then, say the opponents, will it be a
twenty-hour week, another boost in prices and so the
expediting of us all around the vicious circle?

Meanwhile, what about the multitude of consumers victimized by every industrial struggle between Labor and its employers? They have been

coming slowly to consciousness. It is high time if
they expect to survive. The New Deal has recognized their existence and interests through a national
Consumers' Board, advisory in character. The consumers greatly outnumber either of the contesting
groups. Once organized and ably led, they could be
more formidable in politics than both. Unorganized
even, then can and will sweep any party from power
when they find themselves in distress as they did in
1932.

Developments are bringing Government nearer
and nearer to the stage of dilemma. It is difficult
to see how the Administration can miss being im-
paled on one of the horns. Neither contender in
the worker-employer conflict wants the State to have
the power of forcing his hand. Both expect to keep
intervention from that quarter limited to conciliation. When conciliation breaks down, Government
is expected to withdraw from the field and to be
concerned only with confining the struggle to economic tactics, thus preventing physical casualties.

Federal legislation does not yet go beyond that line.
But no Government can stop there if it is committed
to a planned economy that is to stay planned. A
paralyzing deadlock in any one of the major industries can bring down to ruin the best of "Plans."
Certain New Dealers of influence might not shrink
from putting employers under the screws, but the
political steersmen of the Administration will never
risk doing so at the cost of forcing and antagonizing
Labor. Here, then, is a power built up in good faith
as part of the New Deal which politically is in position to defeat a New Deal major policy—economic
planning.

This problem arises for any government the day

social control at its hands is introduced into the national economic system.   The Washington Administration cannot be charged solely with creating the
situation in which it finds itself.   Beyond a doubt,
the electorate unconsciously gave a mandate for
Government to move in the general directions the
New Deal has taken.   They meant to have it intervene in the situation in ways certain to precipitate
acutely just the kind of issues that have appeared
in this field of industrial relations.   They did it, to
be sure, without any intelligent idea of what was
involved for themselves in the way of compulsion.
They were thinking about having the other fellows
compelled.   A good look around over the world's
examples of planned economy should have been convincing enough that collectivism in society as now
motivated involves force and lots of it for everybody.

Planned economy can be had for a price.   Soviet
Russia has it and pays what that pattern of it costs.
Both employers and workers paid, by being taken
completely into camp and confined there.

In Mussolini's Corporative State, although the employers and employes, white collar and all, face each
other at every stage of their working relations, it is
in the presence of the Government, whose vote is
always final.   No vestige of right to block proceedings or operations by strike or lockout remains.
When they cannot agree, they continue performing
their economic functions while Government mediation goes on.   If conciliation fails, a system of courts
hands down a decision that binds everybody.   All
of this control and compulsion is put on the ground
that the interests of the whole nation come before
those of any part.   In short, it comes to this: that
Government tells all of them what the nation's in-

terests are and what each is to do about it. Agreements, court decisions, government decrees alike have the full force of law.

The Nazis' system cannot be seen as yet in orderly operation. Their economic situation is *in extremis*. An economic dictator commands owners and managers this way and that day by day. The big fellows squirm with slight effect. Some of them helped liberally to finance the Revolution without return on the investment to date. Regimented Labor has a voice of its own, but has no distinct power to make it effective if it spoke. These workers also may not strike nor be locked out by employers. The State through Labor Trustees and Honor Courts has the last word. In effect, the State determines wages, hours, conditions, prices, everything. State control in the name of the Nation has arrived for employers, workers, and consumers.

We, in the United States, continue in the era of industrial warfare in the name of liberty of action for employers and workers. They refuse peace enforced by Government. The Administration fears the political consequences of a move to enforce peace. Accordingly, struggles rage across the map between the contenders for superior bargaining power and the attending economic advantages. Labor presses feverishly for organization independent of the employers. The latter in the most powerful quarters counter with company unions, determined not to be displaced from the sole control so long exercised. Both are meeting with enough success to forecast an ultimate industrial struggle of huge dimensions and corresponding losses for the contestants and the public. The troubled President asks for a period of truce. For six months, while storing up munitions, the warriors may be content to rest on their arms.

In casting up the balance for and against the non-revolutionary wing of organized Labor with which the Administration marches much of the way, several criticisms are on the record. Employers generally consider that it does not accept or discharge responsibility commensurate with its demands. They are demands that, if met, involve contractual obligations, which may not be shirked by the leaders' inability or failure to exact fulfilment. So long as outlaw strikes, racketeering, and sabotage are practiced, the charge stands that Labor has not become of age. It is contended that many bodies of employes prefer an inside company form of organization; and that in some standard unions the members in large numbers are dissatisfied with their leaders.

The Communists, in their turn, curse the capitalistic ideology of American trade unionism for denying class-war theory and tactics. Socialists, likewise, condemn it as a bulwark of the present economic order, seeking only for the workers a comfortable pecuniary berth. Some members of the Administration hold the same view. They would have Labor drop the bargaining policy for one to overhaul industrial relations thoroughly in the direction of full democracy. The American Federation of Labor, patiently on the whole, continues on its course and bets on the sheer force of numbers, if once organized and free of State control, to win ultimately all of Labor's just right, rewards, and security.

Under the New Deal, honors have gone that way, with credit to the Administration, and to the moderates among both Labor leaders and employers. The notable gains are the outlawing of child labor and of sweatshops, firm establishment of the collective bargaining principle, and recognition that an industry to operate must provide the employes a decent living level. At the end of the day, these all must prove good to all groups directly and indirectly concerned, including the public.

FARMER GUIDANCE OR REGIMENTATION?

The New Deal found agriculture afflicted with compounded maladies. The strain of debts contracted when dollars were cheap in terms of what the farmers sold racked the whole structure. Prices of farm products had so far fallen that the gross farm income in relation to these debts had shifted from twice their volume to one-half of it. Land values during the war had been boosted fabulously under the stimulus of wheat at $2.00 a bushel and beef at $20 a hundred. Loans contracted on that level fell due when wheat brought twenty-five to fifty cents gross to the grower and beef sold for $4.00 a hundred at the packing-houses. The shrinkage in values wiped out all equities of owners in millions of mortgaged farms, closed thousands of banks with the devalued and frozen paper, and promised to make the great insurance companies unwilling holders of ruined farms not by acres but by townships. A majority of one-time owners faced tenantry.

Farmers with no mortgage obligations were headed into debt. Little that they sold met the costs of production. The goods they needed had to be bought, if at all, with produce that went less than two-thirds of the way in payment compared with the pre-war parity. States, counties, and school districts had joined the borrowing and spending boom when money was easy. The resulting load of taxation, after deflation had done its work on farm incomes, could not be carried. The land that mortgages might have spared was reverting to the States for taxes. The lost buying power of the farmers closed town and city factories. Tax delinquencies emptied township and county treasuries. In spite of Federal aid, 2,000 rural schools so recently as 1933-34 could not open in the absence of funds.

Emotionally, the farmer's mind frayed out with his clothes and credit. Post-war deflation began with him in 1919. The prosperous industrial years that followed brought him no relief. And when they failed, he sank to the depths amid his debts and taxes made bigger and higher by the attending bottomless market for his produce. The good purposes of the preceding Administration, expressed in the Farm Board scheme for buying surpluses, went wrong. Surpluses rose and farm prices took their final dive. The resulting measure of wrath and disgust can be gauged by the unanimity with which the northern agricultural States marched out of their hereditary Republican homeland over into the camp of political aliens.

Compared with the work of getting anything like united action on the part of some millions of farmers, the wheeling of four or five hundred industries into code formations was play. Our famous rural independence, it would appear, had been flattened down substantially by the economic pressures to which it had been subjected. Also, as an influence, there are now tens of thousands of young farm men and women, products of the agricultural colleges, with minds turned measurably toward thinking of their calling in terms of business—with capital, susceptibility to cost accounting processes, returns due for their labor, marketing strategy, parity with other divisions of the national economy, and reactions even to the play of international forces and situations. But, at the best, their organization had not passed much beyond an embryonic stage, or rather that of numerous embryos. No body existed to speak, nationally, much less to act, for any one of the great divisions of agriculture, such as Commerce and a dozen leading industries of the nation constantly command.

The job of winning farmer coöperation on a large scale had the highly favoring circumstance of very able men being placed in the Department of Agriculture. Their diagnosis of conditions and causes, if not perfect, was intelligible. Their proposed correctives, admittedly experimental, were appealing. They had the courage and initiative to act. Their skill in presenting the case to their constituency and to the public at large outclassed the near ballyhoo and bludgeoning of the NRA. With less authority, the AAA has advanced farther towards its goals, and held better the ground gained.

The root problem of agriculture was located in the low state of farm income in relation to farm debts, taxes, and other costs of operation. The objective set was to raise income substantially, and, by doing so, get the farmers onto a sufficiently paying basis to enable them to live and to save their properties.

Some very necessary by-products would attend this process. The money of the creditors would be recovered. The heavily involved insurance companies would be relieved from dangerous strain. Depositors

in banks frozen with farm mortgages might see some
of their funds thaw out.   With purchasing power
increased, the revival of goods buying by farm families would put men and women to work in the industries.

While Soviet Russia, Italy, and Germany battled
against too little agricultural production, the struggle
here was pitched against too much.   The falling off
of demand from several directions had resulted in
piled-up, unwieldy surpluses.   The abnormal war-
time export to Europe ended with the return of the
Continental countries to their normal production
and more.   For a time, the foreign markets were
kept open by loans from this country to the buying
nations at the rate of $500,000,000 a year.   Then
credit was withdrawn and selling slackened.   Old
customers found ways to feed themselves.   Germany,
France, and Italy raised their import tariff on wheat
higher than the selling price in the Chicago Pit.
Domestic cereal consumption had been decreasing
sharply before the depression.   The unemployed
state of millions lowered all lines of food consumption.   Parallel with under-purchasing and under-
consumption ran mounting production.   The accumulated carry-over of cotton became enough to
meet export demand for two years.   The wheat surplus in 1932 became three and a half times normal.

Neither economists nor business men have ever
devised ways to lift real prices for commodities that
no one is buying.   The Brazilians tried to do it with
unwanted coffee, and the Farm Board with wheat
and cotton.   They failed.   The Agricultural Adjustment Administration began at the production instead
of the selling end.   They proposed raising less, and
valiantly set about curtailments.   They brought

about the plowing up of 10,500,000 acres of growing cotton in 1933, and the planting of one-fourth less acreage in 1934. Some influence or influences doubled the price of cotton.

Wheat growing went its own way in 1933, rose speculatively for some months, then settled back to a level about 50% higher than that of the disastrous year before. Looking to the 1934 harvests, what the Secretary of Agriculture calls "a campaign of reason" among 1,200,000 wheat growers secured the coöperation of about one-half of them in reducing sowings 15%. Those complying represented tillers of four-fifths of the wheat acreage. Whether sowing 7,500,-000 fewer acres or the withering drought in the growing season of 1934 had more to do with dollar wheat in the United States may be long disputed by the pros and antis of a controlled economy. Credits aside, the lowered production has increased farm income—the result desired.

In the case of cotton and wheat, and later of corn, tobacco, and other products, cash subsidies bought the initial coöperation that reduced planting. The estimated outlay of the Government for the purpose is being collected from the processors, who pass the expense on to the consumers in increased prices for bread, meat, clothing, and smokes. Mr. and Mrs. Average Citizen may not be complacent about this going on indefinitely. Then either compulsion must be applied if the limiting of farm production shall be continued, or the same result be won by appeal to the intelligence of the farmers. Otherwise, the old surpluses will reappear under the higher price stimulation, to be followed by prices again slumping in a glutted market.

The AAA authorities have not been unwilling to

lay necessity upon a minority, pending an opportunity to build up a rule of intelligence. Amend-
ments to the original enabling Act which they asked
of Congress provided for power to enforce compliance on all growers of a given product, if two-thirds
of them elected to go in for an allotment plan to
limit planting. The penalty for a farmer marketing
a product above his allotment would be a tax high
enough to be discouraging if not prohibitive. The
Bankhead law enacted to control cotton illustrates
the device. It fixed the penalty tax at 50% of the
price received.

Thus far the approach to the farmers has been
preëminently democratic, as the only practical way.
The charge of "regimenting" them has slight validity
to date. Mr. Wallace has quite effectively disposed
of that stigma which some critics sought to attach
to the program. Addressing a body of Nebraskans
in April, 1934, he said:

"Society has always had rules and doubtless always
will have. The real issue is, first, whether we want
to change any of the rules, and, second, who is to do
the changing. In a civilized state, in order to obtain
the maximum of freedom, we must by common
agreement set certain boundaries to the free play of
our selfishness. When a majority finally imposes its
will upon a minority, the minority is thus regimented. That is democracy. This is what we have
always had in matters of large importance. It is
what I hope we shall always have in the future."

Application of the Bankhead law does not become
effective until under its provisions two-thirds of the
cotton growers so elect. In 1934, the growers of corn
and hogs who entered voluntarily into the allotment
plan numbered 1,100,000. The program for the

ensuing years will be determined by a poll of those same corn-hog contractors on two questions as follows:

Do you favor an adjustment program dealing with corn and hogs in 1935?

Do you favor a one-contract-per-farm adjustment program dealing with grains and livestock to become effective in 1936?

No law exists to compel a minority, but, if a favorable vote results, compulsory legislation may be asked for on the Bankhead law model. In the absence of an affirmative majority procedure no doubt will be along 1934 lines.

Southern growers have proved more responsive to persuasion than the farmers of the North and West. The Midwesterners went along as far as they did the first year because they saw real money in hand at once and more promised. Many took it without enthusiasm over the project as the way out permanently. On the whole, North and South, they have accepted the good faith and purposes of the Administration.

They should. Beyond the $1,000,000,000 of payments for less planting, loans on crops, and other benefits during 1934, the advance in farm prices has added an additional billion to farm incomes. The moratorium brought about to arrest foreclosures saved millions of farms to their owners for the time. Refinancing through Federal loans and guarantees have reduced principal sums and interest charges about 25%. The Farm Credit Administration has come to own directly or indirectly one-fourth of the total farm indebtedness in the United States. During the fifteen months, ending September 1, 1934,

FCA loans to 1,057,000 farmers amounted to $1,800,-
000,000. These beneficences should go far in serving to retain existing private ownership, although
further lifting of the price levels is being forecast as
necessary to that end.

The contrast is polar between these practices and
the savage economic bludgeoning into line which
the Russian peasants have received at the hands of
the Communist Party. Our problem differs radically
from that in Fascist Italy. Here leadership is being
given in correcting a surplus production. There it
is given to remedying a general state of deficit in
agriculture. Both here and there, treatment has
more the nature of guidance than of compulsion.
Farm indebtedness, so much the concern of the German Government and of our own, does not menace
small private land holdings in Italy.

Nazi Germany, too, strives to become more nearly
self-sufficient in those staple lines that the land is
capable of producing. To this end, Government
directs the volume of agricultural production and
monopolizes distribution of the products. There is
economic safety for that Government as buyer because the population must have all the food raised
to maintain existence. No huge surplus awaits demand for domestic consumption or export such as
swamped the Farm Board of the Hoover Administration. As with us, a moratorium has been established for farm debts while measures for the reduction of principal and interest are given effect. These
include refinancing on a large scale, with the Reich
Government assuming heavy obligations toward the
original creditors.

EDUCATION—A PRIMARY NEED

Education will be the forerunner of any marked changes in the pattern of American life, if they are to be effected consciously, peacefully, and permanently. Education for the New Deal, therefore, remains in larger part to be done.

The New Deal's democratic approach makes its educational task distinctive in both range and spirit. There exists here no such large illiterate population to be given elementary instruction as the Soviet Union inherited. Practically all formal education is in other hands than that of our Federal Government. Normally, it calls for little in the way of national attention or assistance to reach the objectives the American people set for the public school and higher educational systems. Imagination can scarcely be stretched to the length of foreseeing in the Government of the United States a national ministry of education dominating the field. Much less could public opinion here anticipate having all school and college text books and lectures revamped to teach revolutionary theories of human life, society, and the State advanced by a ruling minority Party, after the manner of the Communists, Fascists, and Nazis in their respective domains.

Nor is the controlling hand of this Government laid upon organs of expression through which the opinions and purposes of the people are formed. At every stage since March 4, 1933, there has been present an opposition vocal against all the New Deal measures. Not in the U.S.S.R., Italy, or Germany could a newspaper or magazine approach the *New York Herald Tribune,* the *Chicago Daily News* and the *Saturday Evening Post* in criticism of the Government's policies, and continue in circulation. The editors would be in exile, concentration camps, or under "protective arrest." And this right of battle is not enjoyed by the great metropolitan organs only. Toward most of the new issues presented, from one-third to two-thirds of the press of the land has been ranged in opposition. The *United States News* of June 4, 1934, reported 65 per cent of the nation's papers to hold varying degrees of hostility to the NRA—then the "holy of holies" of the New Deal.

During the early months of the Administration, most editors acted charitably. Giving the President a chance to cope with the crisis in his own way appealed to sportsmanship. Public opinion generally enjoined that attitude. A year later forbearance ceased. The enemy batteries went into action. The New Deal Administrator, and even his Chief, exhibited temper under the provocation. They first countered on a level none too high. "Tories" and "chiselers" were epithets directed at the critics. In contrast, no language could breathe urbanity more disarming than that of Tugwell, smiling target of the other side's sharpshooters. No friend of free journalism could disagree with that bland young man's penetrating address to the American Society of Newspaper Editors, meeting in Washington in April, 1934. The spirit and reasoning of these lines from the opening paragraphs marked the entire message:

"The President's program can be attained only in the presence of full comment, of interpretation, and of criticism from the newspapers and magazines of this country. It is human, I suppose, to prefer praise to blame and to desire sympathy rather than

hostility to the great national movement of free
social coöperation which we are now in; but I realize
that the science of human nature which we describe
as politics becomes cheap and tawdry chicanery if its
practitioners are debarred, even by the unorganized
coercion of mass emotions, from the right to oppose
and criticize. And since there is no major point of
the President's policy where it is necessary to shrink
from criticism or to conceal the facts, I desire to con-
gratulate you on the recent evidences in your respective publications of an awakened public interest in
the discussion of our public affairs. I only wish that
the more analytical phase of this interest and critical
discussion had begun earlier, at the time when the
main features of the New Deal were being hammered
out in Congress and throughout the Administration.
At that time there was almost too easy an acceptance
of any and every measure which was proposed.
Today, my only regret is that you did not earlier
realize that coöperation with the efforts for national
recovery did not imply the absence of interpretation
and criticism."

There was a considerable fluttering in the dove-
cote over the presidential reluctance to have em-
bodied in the Newspaper Code a clause to insure
against any administrative curb of press freedom.
The President thought the first amendment to the
Constitution gave full protection. The *Daily News*
of Chicago displayed no little agitation in serving
editorial notice that it would "utterly decline to sign
any agreement which subjects this newspaper to
coercion of any sort exercised by anybody which
tends in the slightest particular to impair its right
to speak freely and without restraint on any question under the sun."

Some of the Chief Executive's subordinates later caused outcry among correspondents by rules within bureaus and departments for giving out official information, which some of the newshawks thought meant suppression. During the uproar the President made some observations on the amplitude of newspaper discussion in a letter read before the National Editorial Association in May, 1934: "Freedom of the press means freedom of expression, both in news columns and editorial columns. There has been no attempt in Washington to 'gag' newspaper men or stifle editorial comment. There will be no such attempt." And here a deft touch of ironic humor: "Judging by both these columns in papers in every part of the country, this freedom is freer than it has ever been in our history."

At the same time, the Administration has advantages in the publicity game. Any Government has them. What issues from its spokesmen has national import, and gets a national hearing. Not since the days and methods of floating Liberty bonds has a Federal program had the high-pressure promotional techniques employed in its behalf that launched the NRA. Beyond priceless newspaper space given it as news, millions were spent for paid advertising, radio broadcasts, picture films, parades, posters, bulletins, and labels. Bombardment of the public mind bore resemblance to the smashing propaganda drives put on by the Bolshevik and Nazi machines. But it lacked their fighting spirit. Comparatively, the response was feeble. The effort to create a crusading mentality failed. The dollar and cents objectives called forth neither sacrifice nor heroism.

The greatest asset of the whole New Deal combination is the gift of the President for reassuring address to the people over the radio networks. But this personal access and power contrasts flatly with exclusive radio systems owned, monopolized, and manipulated by dictatorial governments. There is the difference between having the right to be informed and to choose between courses of action, and the necessity of enduring total ignorance of what alternatives to the officially prescribed course might be. Notably beyond the measure of any former Administration, this one is expending money and talent for publicity respecting its program and the results.

The makers of revolution by compulsion parallel their monopoly of adult education with equally rigid forms for molding the mind of the young. For making a whole new generation to order, the ruling parties in Soviet Russia, Italy, and Germany go beyond employing the schools. In the three countries, the program of official indoctrination extends over into the sphere of the home, the Church, and those other institutions that in a democratic society by common consent supplement the State in an enriching ministry to the culture of childhood and youth.

Communist organizations for the young throughout the Soviet Union are set to drive in a wedge between children and all independently minded parents. They succeed in a large measure. No other societies for the young of any age may exist. The Church is forbidden to conduct any class or school for ages under eighteen. The Italian *Ballila, Avanguardisti* and Young Fascist formations almost monopolize legality of existence for youth societies of both the sexes.

The Hitler Youth Movement bids for the exclusive enrolment of all the young of German blood. The Party exerts relentless pressures in that direc-

tion. The Protestant youth organizations have not
been dissolved, although, by order of the Reichsbishop, the time of the boys and girls has become so
absorbed in Hitler Youth activities that there remains to them the possibility to function only feebly
in their own right. The Catholic authorities and
the Government continue in deadlock since the Nazis
came to power over the status to be granted the youth
societies of that Communion. Confirmation classes
remain untouched and religious instruction is given
in the schools.

The corresponding societies here at home—Boy
Scouts, Young Men's and Young Women's Christian
Associations, and Hebrew counterparts, Catholic Action, Epworth League, and Christian Endeavor—
have no reason to know there is a New Deal so far
as organizational status and freedom of program go.
This fact lays upon them and upon the multitude
of other cultural bodies in the United States heavy
responsibilities for educational service to their members on the social issues surging in the national life.
The New Deal did not create the issues. The New
Deal wrestles with them. They cannot be safely
shirked. An eternity does not remain in which to
do the teaching and the learning if violent attempts
at the reordering of our life are to be avoided.

There is no part of the American population without need to be taught. All believers in Capitalism
need to know that the institution cannot go on un-
changed. Its old forms are not good enough. On
this the majority mind of this nation, and of most
other nations, is made up. The "gluttons for punishment" who want to invite the return of 1929 and
its aftermath are few in these United States. The
highest intelligence resident in capitalistic circles

must be aware of impending and actually ongoing
changes. Let those possessing the awareness teach
their less far-sighted fellows. There is reason for
encouragement when the United States Chamber of
Commerce platform is hospitable to talk like this:

"Whether our present economic miseries turn out
to be a vantage point in the evolution of human
society, depends upon the American business leader.
Upon his attitude depends whether industry will
accept with sufficient promptness the new human and
economic creed which in our time is being written
in the hearts and consciences of men; namely, that
capital must receive less and laborers and consumers
more; that bonuses have an unparalleled value in
goodwill only when they are shared by executives
with workers; that unemployment reserves and sickness and old-age benefits must be universal; that it
is the well-being of the millions which makes a
country great, and permits a highly developed business system to function and be profitable; that in a
land of plenty it is the duty of economic organization to bring about a fair distribution of the huge
supplies of goods produced by modern mechaniza-
tion and science and engineering; and that the only
justification for any economic and social order is
that it promotes the welfare of human beings." [9]

The clamant enemies of capitalistic society who
are for throwing down the whole structure, and at
once, have as much to learn. They are dealing with
a people a large part of whom are owners. Most
of the others want to be possessors on their own account. At its best, the system across the world advanced living conditions for the masses more rapidly and generally than they had experienced in cen-

[9] Frederick M. Davenport, Washington, May 3, 1934.

turies preceding. Its most marked achievement has taken place on this continent. "Our industry supports a larger population, furnishes it more generously with goods, and requires the expenditure of less effort than was ever true at any other time or in any other place." [10] It is not in the temper of this people to proceed with wholesale destruction of the means by which the large majority of them even in 1934 live in comparative peace and comfort.

Certain apostles of "liberty" have self-restraint to learn. They appear overwrought. Much of the crying out about regimentation sounds like fear of what may be done. In comparison with the restrictions thrown around the plain Soviet, Italian, or German citizen, the American who thinks himself most circumscribed ranges over a paradise of freedom.

But this middle-class America has before it lessons to learn and take to heart if the ministry of freedom is to be preserved. Lip service will not do. No slovenly loyalty to its principles and practices will save it from the fate met in Russia, Italy, and Germany at the hands of hard-driving men who want results, and have been shown how to get them. At this point, the President of the University of Wisconsin has spoken prophetically: "Neither an irrational radicalism nor an irrational reaction is tolerable under such circumstances. We shall escape the phase of social disruption, through which so much of mankind has lately passed, only through the exercise of a cool and constructive intelligence that refuses to let its approach to reality be obscured either by the traditions of reaction or by the tentative theorizings of radicalism."

10 *Industrial Discipline*, p. 136.

Finally, will there be learned in time the wisdom of sacrifice by us all? In the past twenty-five years, the American human fiber has softened. A high-school boy in a home of high principle and decent living was asked to write out the program his generation would lay down for society. The pages contained only demands for rights and benefits—no single word about duties and services to be performed in return or even to gain the ends prescribed. His paper reflects a prevailing attitude to life. This is the most vulnerable point at which Communism and Fascism attack the bourgeois social order.

The issues focus down to something like this: Whether the sober fair-minded body of this people will accept self-discipline and responsibility for the common good they idealize, or wait for a party of violence on horseback to browbeat us into an enforced coöperation. In *America Must Choose,* the author[11] luminously imparts a vision the multitude will acclaim with little notion of paying the price he faithfully names:

"Only those really close to science can know the abundance that could be ours with even-handed justice and a generous distribution between groups. Our grinding efforts to subsist, in the mass, on the farm and in great cities alike, the world over, would drop into the far background in the light of the attainments we could command. We can stand as free men in the sun. But we cannot dream our way into that future. We must be ready to make sacrifices to a known end. As we wrestle with all the infinite complexities which now beset us, the temptation is to give way to false and easy hopes and to easy ways

[11] Henry A. Wallace, Secretary of Agriculture.

of thinking. But we cannot afford to dream again
until we have taken hold of things as they are."

What a challenge to the agencies of education that
in their varied capacities reach and mold the nation's mind and will—the schools and colleges, the
churches and their auxiliary societies, the network
of men's and women's clubs, the trade unions and
chambers of commerce, the press, moving picture,
radio and stage, and last but best—the home! If
these be but spurred by the challenges of the New
Dealers to perform their teaching function right-
eously and adequately, the lasting results will amply
repay the costs of all the experiments and mistakes
and will stand as the crowning service to their
country.

GOVERNMENT AND THE HOME

Viewed as revolution, the New Deal occupies itself
with other objectives than changing the institution
of the family and the status of its members. In its
program of relief and reconstruction, the policies
toward family life have been consistently enlightened
and generous. Large outlays of money have been
used in favoring forms of assistance that lent themselves to keeping families intact. It has been an
expensive course, but, in the long run, less so than
having more households dissolved. In such a crisis,
the strains upon domestic security are severe enough
under the best administrative treatment possible.
The provision of goods or cash relief to families
largely displaced the old soup-kitchen with its far
more blasting consequences to dignity and self-
respect. In other wise ways, the Government and its

agents in the far-flung field of relief have acted to
protect the imperilled values of countless homes.
Withal, the haunting fear grows with the spread and
duration of relief that resort to public care is going
to leave some millions of the population so demor-
alized by long-continued unemployment as to be permanently unemployable.   The succeeding chapter
on social welfare deals with programs to better conditions permanently for normal family life.

The Administration's appointments have given a
recognition to women beyond that accorded them
by any of its predecessors.   Three of them were in-
novations in American political life—the naming of
one woman to a place in the National Cabinet,
another to head a foreign legation, and a third to be
Director of the Mint.   This course sharply contrasts
with Mussolini's bent to continue the Italian frown
on women in politics.   The short shrift Hitler made
of the German women who had attained political
consciousness and expression also looks in the opposite direction.   In Soviet Russia, where much felici-
tation goes on about "the emancipation of woman,"
no woman has reached the distinction of becoming a
People's Commissar, an office corresponding to one
of our Federal Cabinet portfolios.

Significant things are afoot on behalf of youth.
None of them have revolutionary intent.   The advancing of Federal funds in a considerable volume
serves to keep open thousands of schools, conspicuously in the South.   This is a New Deal departure—
one of many in the direction of entering into certain
responsibilities formerly borne exclusively by the
States.   The implications are political rather than
educational or social.   Until now, such intervention
always met fierce southern resistance.   Half of the

new school-building construction in the country goes
on with funds of the Public Works Administration.
In September, 1934, over $200,000,000 were being so
employed. In part, the pressure on school housing
facilities is a New Deal credit due to the release of
children under the code provisions excluding their
labor. The provision of partial scholarships to college students marks another innovation. It keeps
about 75,000 of them at study and off the labor
market.

The Civilian Conservation Camps perform perhaps the most useful new ministry to young men
under twenty-five. Since their inception, early in
the Administration, more than 850,000 men (includ-
cluding some war veterans) have been assembled as
volunteers in work camps across the country, each for
a standard period of six months. Five-sixths of the
$1.00 a day wage paid goes to the family whose mem-
ber is thus engaged. The small balance becomes his
spending money. The work assigned has been forestry as a major. Five million acres have been added
to the national preserves and improved, thus advancing the forestry program several years.

Supervision by the army has kept the political
spoilsmen at bay. The degree of discipline imposed
has been moderate and beneficial. Outdoor life and
work yield their inevitable happy fruit of health and
vigor. In tens of thousands of cases the results
amount to physical transformation. The institution
has worked toward absorbing the wandering hosts
of youth, who had been breaking away from their
homes and taking to the open road. It has kept
many others from entering those endangered ranks.
The appropriations applied to this project for the
first eighteen months amounted to $443,000,000. Of

this sum, $113,000,000 went in remittances to families on relief from which the campers were selected. It is doubtful if other expenditures upon emergency undertakings have brought an equally satisfactory economic and social return.

A considerable, yet rather desultory, attack has been made upon the workless army found in the more intellectual ranks of the young. These number literally millions. The Federal Bureau of Education drew attention to the dimensions of the problem in a call to school and social agencies for a conference in May, 1934, to study and deal with the condition:

"There are in America today about 20,000,000 young people between sixteen and twenty-five years of age. Of this number, about 2,000,000 are in high schools, 1,000,000 are in colleges, a few are in other schools, and 250,000 are temporarily in Civilian Conservation Corps camps. This leaves 16,500,000. While no accurate statistics of employment are available, you are aware of how distressingly few of these young people are employed."

The constructive treatment for getting down to cases must rest with the local agencies. Federal funds, available for quite wide supplementary educational programs in the cities, make possible courses of study without cost to the unemployed. They enrol many of the otherwise idle young. Colleges and high schools are holding students for graduate work in unusual numbers. This Administration, as did the preceding one on the launching of community financial efforts for relief and welfare causes, has laid stress upon the vital importance of maintaining the character-building agencies in unimpaired strength.

The stake is one of extreme gravity. Outside the

farm contingent in this age group, the usefulness
of multitudes of the young may be lost permanently to society. A Dartmouth College senior in
one of these fateful years began his valedictory to
the graduating class to this effect, chilling as it was
accurate: "We go out into a world that has no use
for us." The condition is ominous for any social
order when hundreds of thousands of young men
and women with the best-trained minds emerge from
their preparation for life justified in coming to the
same conclusion. As the years without opportunity
lengthen, this best of raw material for revolution
increases. Post-war Germany's accumulation of workless university graduates in engineering, law, medicine, the sciences, and education kindled into the
most flaming followers of a Hitler crusading against
the régime that called itself their government.

And why not? Let the question be asked realistically. It is hardly to the credit of the more ma-
ture, educated generation among us now in or just
out of college that they accept their plight with so
much complacency. More of them might well be
challenging fundamentally the integrity of a system
that can get so palpably out of gear. The standpat
and reactionary leadership of the country, bewailing
the rise and prevalence of radicalism in the seats of
learning, with more discernment, would give thanks
that there is not more, and be using the time of grace
to improve the social and economic order before
these they fear take the lead and move to destroy it.

The great revolutions of the twentieth century
have revealed what classes actually fight for their
cause when convinced they have no other recourse.
The bourgeoisie and the elders have conspicuously
avoided risking their skins. Workingmen led by

intellectuals made up the winning combination in violent revolutionary Russia. Mussolini bloomed out of a blacksmith's family into a rampant, realistic intellectual protesting against conformity. Youth furnished him the fighters he led to power in Italy. The son of a humble civil servant of another country battered the way to Nazi rule in Germany with a few hundred thousands of workless younger men from shops, mills, and schools, whom he roused out of idleness to action by bold and sincere promises of deliverance.

The really moderate Brain Trusters of 1932-36, right or wrong in practical governance, may prove blessings in disguise if they succeed in directing the intelligence of America to the defects and evils of our society, and arouse the will to remove them in patient yet purposeful democratic fashion. Of a certainty, they serve better their day and generation than the great body of intellectuals, old and young, who wait with naïve simplicity for some impersonal tidal force to return a prosperity and refloat them into snug financial harbors from off the mud flats of this continuing economic depression.

CATCHING UP IN SOCIAL MEASURES

Organized social protection in the United States by the initiative and direction of government, whether local, state or national, has been of slow and irregular growth. The Federal power in the past remained unconcerned about it. Some of the States cautiously approached insurance against industrial accidents and occupational diseases. Others committed themselves to old-age and mothers' pensions.

One ventured timidly against unemployment. The country as a whole, in respect to these social measures, lagged a generation behind Germany and New Zealand. Later Great Britain forged ahead of us, and yet more recently Soviet Russia.

Varied reasons account for this backwardness. A certain economic abundance in the new land reached down sufficiently into the ranks of workers to prevent an oppressive sense of need for such protection from arising. The lower and needier categories of workers have not been in control of Labor's interests. Prosperous industrial employers in America, the most generous private givers in the world, measurably met individual cases of misfortune among employes through the charities they supported. Religious organizations, the Red Cross, tax-supported and private hospitals, orphanages, and institutions for the indigent poor went far to mitigate misery. Some private industrial enterprises had successful company systems of protection which employers and employes maintained jointly.

Then Socialism found its voice here later than in the lands just named. Whether the socialist proposals are workable or not, the pressures exerted on society by Socialists so work upon conscience and fear as to secure more consideration of the claims of the under-privileged. Benefits of this character flow directly from socialistic influences in proportion to the numerical organized strength of the agitators in advance of any basic modification of the industrial-economic order prevailing. Rapid industrialization taking place in the United States in the new century heightened greatly need for protection against the attending hazards. With it grew demand for action from organized Labor, Socialists, the social-welfare professional fraternity, churchmen, and the ranks of liberal writers and intellectuals in general.

Whereas the established Federal policy had been to remain within its immediate sphere of pensioning war veterans and civil servants, and extending its patronage over the National Red Cross, the New Deal Administration moved out positively to give direction and support to plans for a comprehensive system of social insurance. Official spokesmen early announced in this direction vigorous Federal intervention in what they regard a long-neglected situation. The catastrophic prevalence of present-day social maladjustment and of attendant suffering has so impressed public opinion that highly favorable legislation can hardly fail of enactment. Those in the inner circles of Government most likely to determine the lines of action are on record for a nationwide system of protection against all of the major social adversities that overtake people—sickness, accident, old age, widowhood, orphanhood, and unemployment.

In a broadcast of August 13, 1934, the Secretary of Labor made an impressive statement of the facts which impel the Administration to go to Congress and the country for substantial protective measures. She reports that expenditures for relief already have been far in excess of those made in the countries having unemployment insurance. Following are some of the misfortunes and tragedies of common life that she asks be borne by the whole of society instead of being left to rest either upon the immediate sufferers, their families, or already overburdened charities.

In industry under full operation, 25,000 workers are killed each year; 150,000 receive permanent injuries; nearly 3,000,000 are disabled temporarily. Accidents outside industries cause three times as many deaths and injuries. Two per cent of the population are subjected to sickness at any given time—many for long and costly periods. Most of the 6,500,000 men and women in the country over sixty-five years of age are financially dependent. They constitute a large section of those on relief, while 40 per cent of the total number on relief rolls are under sixteen years of age—many in families with no living breadwinner.

Equally ambitious and more spectacular are several huge projects on foot or proposed, looking to the permanent bettering of conditions of life for millions of people now living at or below the margins of decent existence. One of these relates to housing. The President's message to Congress on the subject on May 14, 1934, asked for legislation (which was granted) to correct a condition of which this is his description: "Many of our homes are in decadent condition and not fit for human habitation. They need repairing and modernizing to bring them up to the standard of the times. Many new homes now are needed to replace those not worth repairing. The protection of the health and safety of the people demands that this renovating and building be done speedily."

Previously, $123,000,000 were set apart for a beginning at slum clearance and model housing development in congested cities. Units in this program are actually under construction. The new legislation was asked for "to return many of the unemployed to useful and gainful occupation" and "to produce tangible, useful wealth in a form for which there is great social and economic need." Federal participation in these projects, while new ventures for this Government, place it in line with the Communist, Fascist, and Nazi régimes (British also) which have engaged themselves more or less extensively in providing low-cost healthful housing space. More arresting is Uncle Sam's entrance into the actual construction of homes by thousands and the later assumption of landlordship. The outlook is for yet larger adventure in this direction in 1935.

Another undertaking of real social vision aims at the creation and settlement of what are termed subsistence homesteads. These are designed so to locate families and equip them that part-time industrial employment and part farm work on the small tract of land they will own will serve to afford superior surroundings, a better level of living, and more economic security than the crowded cities of this machine age. They are being instituted, too, near industries where changing conditions of operation and marketing have brought the living of workers down to or below marginal borders, as in given coal mining territories. Enterprises of this description have been set up from coast to coast, north and south. In most of them applicants for the places exceed the number available. The director of the Section states that present requests for this form of service worthy of attention would absorb the use of $750,000,000. The units are conveyed to the new owners at cost with terms of a slow amortization. A typical tract will include two to five acres to cost, with buildings, $2,000 to $3,000. The communities thus formed are being laid out and constructed on lines that afford convenience, pleasing architecture, and hygienic

living.   Private industrial corporations are taking
favorable note of this method of relieving the con-
gested housing of their workers.

The responsiveness of families to this outlet from
their plight and the enlisted interest of industrialists
have fed the Administration's ambition for the
scheme.   The President calls it one of his "own pet
children."   In September, 1934, there were 22,000
applications for the 5,000 homesteads ready or
planned and 300,000 inquirers on the list.   The Congressional session of 1935 promises to be presented
with large plans for subsistence homesteads as a
major in the program for permanent relief to an
estimated 3,000,000 in the population who seemed
doomed otherwise to a life of worklessness and to
being a standing charge on charity.

Implicit in the movement is a recognition that the
flood-tide into the great industrial and commercial
centers is due to ebb.   Both Mussolini and Hitler
have put on corresponding programs to redress the
overbalance in urban living.   In 1932, the installa-
tion of a domestic passport system in Soviet Russia
forced several millions of people, not industrially
useful, out of the overcrowded centers.   The Government neglected to find them space in which to
establish themselves.

No less ambitious are designs for the resettlement
of other millions now stranded or living precariously
on land ill suited to its present uses.   Voluntary migration is contemplated from worn-out farms in the
east, the sandy cut-off timber lands of Michigan,
Wisconsin, and Minnesota, and the semi-arid areas
on the eastern border of the Rocky Mountain pla-
teau where year by year the settlers battle for exist-

ence with hot winds, drought, or grasshoppers, or all three combined.

More than 2,500,000 acres of land in thirty States were included in active buying-up projects up to the autumn of 1934. The Chief of the Land Policy Section estimated the number of families needing deliverance at between 750,000 and 1,000,000. The families thus disadvantaged have become recurring or permanent objects of relief. It is proposed to transfer them to areas of fertility, watered plentifully by irrigation or nature, and now sparsely settled. The first appropriation made to the object was $25,000,000. The Relief Administrator announced purchase of the first 1,000,000 acres by early October, 1934, for around $5.00 an acre. For his first $25,000,-000, he expected to pick up between four and five million acres to be turned into parks, forests, and game preserves. Some will revert to Indian reservations. A presidential allocation of $12,500,000 from the drought relief fund helps to finance the transfer and rehabilitation of the migrating families.

The shifts of population in Italy and Germany from city to country are marked by little, if any, option to the people most concerned. The German industries have been required on quite a scale to dismiss young unmarried workers in favor of older ones with families. The youth are despatched to farms to work for their subsistence. The labor service camps of Germany are recruited by both voluntary enlistment and pressure.

One measure offered that borders on the fantastic proposes redemption of a consistently semi-arid belt extending from the Canadian border to the Texas Panhandle. It is advanced that a 100-mile wide belt of planted forest across the Dakotas, Nebraska, Kansas, and Oklahoma will so alter the climate as to render the territory economically habitable. Granting the premises, the settlers from 1870 for three decades, who planted and nurtured thousands of acres of trees of every variety then known, only to see them die after a few years of fitful and scrubby growth, will wish the new plantings well, while advising that enough artesian wells be bored to keep the new growths watered and alive until the climate and soils hostile to tree culture have surrendered.

The single master project of all in the series for bettering human life goes forward under what is known as the Tennesee Valley Authority. It alone embraces as much territory as all the reclamation undertakings the Fascists have going to make better places for Italians to work, live, and multiply. All England is only one-third larger. The plans comprehend every normal activity of the population. The vision is admirable. The President believes a lasting contribution will be made to American life "by controlling every river, creek, and rivulet . . . and by planning for a highly civilized use of the land by the population of the whole area." There will be included "a multitude of human activities and physical developments." He has expressed the opinion that here will be worked out experimentally demonstrations to be applied progressively to the other great water systems of the land.

The Chairman of the TVA [12] analyzes the far-reaching experiment into its parts—a land-use survey; plans for forestry and for soil protection; the development of coöperatives and business-counseling service; the generation, transmission and sale of electric current and the building of rural transmission

12 Arthur E. Morgan, *New York Times*, March 25, 1934.

lines; the building of dams and power-plants; the development of new and cheaper fertilizers; a program for balancing agriculture and industry; vocational training for redistributing the population; rural health work; and studies of local government, of regional police service, and in other fields.

The corporation is "clothed with the powers of government, but possessed of the flexibility and initiative of a private enterprise." Present activities extend from the construction of a dam to impound 3,100,000 acre-feet of water to selling electricity with which housewives "will bake their pone, clean their rugs, refrigerate the babies' milk, wash their clothes, and read their evening paper." Here is something challenging to good-will. It may be paternalism. Norman Thomas owns it as the only item in the New Deal worthy to be called Socialism. It deserves to succeed.

QUIET ON THE RELIGIOUS FRONT

Religion is more comfortable in the New Deal berth than in any reserved for it under the three Dictatorships. The Communist system has no place for it whatever. The policy is to kill it off, if possible, by denying nutrition and feeding slow poison. Mussolini recognizes the uses of religion within the limits of moral guidance, religious instruction, worship, and other-worldliness. To serve those ends, the Italian churches have initiative, encouragement, and assigned obligations. For them to proceed outside these recognized spheres is to trespass upon the holy ground of State and Party. The Church of Rome has accepted the confining compartments, but

with much protest. Although the German *Führer*
speaks about the same language as the *Duce* on matters religious, his followers enter the domain officially reserved to the churches to interfere both with
teaching and administration. Among the first results
have been a wide, deep Protestant schism, and what
looks like head-on collision with the Vatican.

In their religious orientation, the four Heads of
Government stand far apart. Stalin's mother (Russian Orthodox) induced him to study for the priesthood. He reacted strongly from this and now is in
the Marxist camp of aggressive, revolutionary atheists. The *Duce* gets near to religious confession in
My Autobiography. He refers to himself as "deeply
Catholic." Emphasis should be placed on "deeply";
outwardly he is not churchly. He necessarily broke
that mooring in youth to become a left-wing Socialist
when membership in that Party was proscribed by
the Church. He takes no pains to give outward evidence of a return to anchorage. Entering on a period
of greater responsibilities, he "asked the assistance of
God," and "invoked the memory of the dead." He
has instilled into Fascist faith a sense of the presence
of those fallen in the cause. He writes "the God
of just men will guide all the fallen to eternal light
and will reward the souls of all who lived nobly, and
who wrote in blood the goodness and ardor of their
faith."

The traceable lines of Hitler's present personal
church connections are equally sketchy. Also of
Catholic parentage, he has never strayed so far afield
as to join a Marxian Party. His utterances reflect
profession of belief in Deity and of responsibility
toward Him. Churchmen having serious contact
with him find there only slender discernment of the

realities either in individual experience or in church
polity. The President of the United States is a ves-
tryman in the Protestant Episcopal Church in a long
family line of lay officials in that Communion. Under normal conditions, his attendance on worship is
consistent. On ships of the Navy, he has conducted
Divine Service.

In Soviet Russia, the Church threw its influence
against Communism coming to power, and anathematized the new Government for its affront to religion
and morality. Officially, the Catholic Church held
aloof while the Fascists stormed their way up to
"The March on Rome." At that time, a formal
note to the Party Quadrumvirate inquired what the
Church was to expect at their hands. The answer
appeared to be reassuring. The triumph over the
anti-religious Socialists and Communists doubtless
met with satisfaction in that quarter.

Although many young German Catholics went
Nazi, the hierarchy from the beginning has been dis-
trustfully cold toward that Party. A series of strong
pronouncements against Nazi doctrines and practices
that conflict with Catholic teaching and order have
come from the highest of the clergy. Several of the
pastoral utterances have been printed for wide circulation. A large section of the Protestant laity
helped the National Socialists battle the way to
power. They continue loyal and militant in the
Party. By the assertion of their Nazi principles
within the Churches, they have driven great sections
of the Lutheran Communion into revolt against the
ecclesiastical administration they voted into office.

Strong religious influences worked for the election
of Mr. Roosevelt on the merits of his social record,
outlook, and proposals. This support came from

Catholics, Protestants, and Jews proportionately. The candidate made an open bid for this vote in his campaign speech at Detroit. He stated there that he stood substantially on the social, economic, and industrial programs of the Federal Council of the Churches of Christ in America, of the National Catholic Welfare Council, and of the American Conference of Jewish Rabbis. No recurrence appeared of the unworthy religious issue injected into the canvass four years earlier. There was no candidacy to provoke it. The Republican Party's wavering about Prohibition took most of the fight for its ticket out of the Protestant forces that had counted so heavily in 1928. Officially, all of the churches remained aloof as between men and parties. The stalwarts among the churchmen voted "regular"; the independent, liberal, and younger elements voted for the New Deal. The spirit of some went so far as to be expressed picturesquely by one who "welcomed the chance to vote for the Kingdom of God." Mention should not be omitted of an appreciable and probably growing religious contingent that votes Socialist consistently.

This body of support from the religious forces continues with the Administration. In fact, it has had accessions with the Eighteenth Amendment no longer an issue. The President and members of the Cabinet, some of whom are active in their Communions, appear before representative religious gatherings to further interest and coöperation in the affairs of common concern.

No doctrinal, educational, or administrative issues of domestic import exist between the Government and the Churches. An equal solidarity does not obtain in respect to international policies. The bigger navy program of the Administration does not have approval from the strong religious forces that are actively at work for the reduction of armament. They are no more happy over one more Administration that does not take up cudgels with the Senate to secure a favorable vote on this country's entrance to the International Court of Justice at The Hague. Likewise, they would choose to have more courage displayed in squaring the immigration laws for Orientals with those affecting other races. The outstanding fact remains, however, that, in the entire field of Government-Church relations here, religious activity meets no single hampering or unfriendly condition at the hands of the State. This freedom the churches cherish and will defend.

RETREAT TO NATIONALISM

Nationalism did not father the New Deal as it did the Fascist and Nazi revolutions. Strong nationalistic influences, though, are being exercised over the Government's policies. In several respects, the Administration has gone the way of the world in its crisis, with each nation taking up the cry of an army in rout: "Save himself who can."

The courses of action have led far from Wilsonian internationalism. No adventures have been entered upon internationally to which a price has been attached. The awkward rôle played in the Economic Conference in London (1933) furnished an example likely to become historic. Under high light before a world audience, with a suddenness and emphasis that astonished recent confrères who thought they knew the President's mind, the assembled represent-

atives of sixty-six nations were informed that the
United States would set its currency house in order
alone. The rest of the world could wait for stabilization. The Conference never recovered from the
blow. It adjourned with economic nationalism the
confirmed policy of more governments than before,
and with no negligible anti-American animus.

Continuing the timid approach of former administrations to the war debts and the thorny issues tan-
gled therein, marks again the rule of nationalism—
and this time of unintelligence. One of those domestic situations exists which Sir Arthur Salter exposed in addressing the Academy of Political Science
on international aspects of recovery. The former Director of the Economic and Financial Section of the
League of Nations reported his learning at Geneva
that the chief obstacle to composing economic conflicts was not true national interest but "a calcula-
tion of political pressures from sectional interests in
their respective parliaments."

This states precisely why we get nowhere either
in war debt payments or adjustments. All informed
persons recognize that these accounts will never be
paid on anything like the present level of figures.
The leaders of both our major political parties know
that a proposal to reduce them materially, made by
one party, would be followed by the other opposing
it. They know that this would bring the party taking the initiative to defeat no less disastrous than
the one suffered by the party which tried to take this
country into the League of Nations. A major impasse affecting world recovery remains. An ignorant
nationalism and politicians who follow instead of
lead thus expose democracy to one of its defects.

The hybrid economic and political nationalism

supporting the Administration forced an unseemly, if not unethical, pace in legislation that put independence for the Philippines more nearly on skids than rails. The primary motive was to remove Filipino free imports from the American market. With independent status for the Islands established, tariffs could be invoked to keep out the present inflow of sugar, fats, and fibers. The veto of Hoover and a remonstrance by Roosevelt were not equal to staying the hand of the agricultural bloc, reënforced by the Democratic element opposed on principle to an expansionist policy for the United States.

The President himself gives leadership in a stay-at-home policy toward the neighboring nations to the south. The withdrawal of marines from Nicaragua continued the movement begun by his predecessor. The accomplished American retirement from administration in Haiti, also, had been initiated earlier. The hands-off attitude toward revolutionary Cuba (at least violent hands) indicated a change in policy. This has been confirmed by repeal of the paternal "Platt Amendment." Accepted by the Island Republic at the time of its liberation from Spanish power, this had validated armed intervention by the United States whenever given conditions arose which threatened the stability of the young State.

Outcroppings of nationalism appear prominently in talk and action about foreign trade relations. Insistence upon priority of attention to domestic affairs appears to reduce those interests at times to an immediate concern, and exclusive of considerations that enter into longer views. "Frankly, the interest of our own citizens must, in each instance, come first," is the principle bluntly laid down by the President in a discussion of freer trade between the nations of North, Central, and South America.[13]   Having yet wider application is this statement in the inaugural address:

"Our international trade relations, though vastly important, are in point of time and necessity secondary to the establishment of a sound national economy.   I favor as a practical policy the putting of first things first.   I shall spare no effort to restore world trade by international economic readjustment, but the emergency at home can not wait on that accomplishment."

Reversion to the big-navy ideas and program further reveals the nationalistic slant of this Government.   Peaceful words and manifestos to other nations have little meaning and no good effect among realistic Europeans and Orientals when pronounced by the spokesmen of a nation that in two years adds $414,000,000 to its armament expenditures, already the largest in the world.   Lining up in the Disarmament Conference with the opposition to monstrous tanks and cannon and other "offensive" weapons is equally unconvincing so long as no reticence is shown in giving our naval and military forces the most aggressive enginery for war at sea and in the air.   We could devise nothing our neighbors would fear more.   Neither battleships nor bombing planes are so constituted that remaining at home is enforced upon them.   This Administration builds both at a rate that promises to increase rather than decrease the man and money power taken from production. Meanwhile the State Department was reduced (1933-4) to less than $12,500,000 a year.

When the Vinson bill to authorize new naval construction up to treaty limits was pending, the people

[13] *On Our Way*, p. 112.

and organizations opposed to more arming on our
part protested to official Washington against its passage. They were told the authorizations were being
made as "a statement of policy" only. The measure
carried no appropriation. The action of future Con-
gresses would determine whether the policy would
be carried out. The pressures to build have not been
withstood. Access to the PWA roll could be gained
without benefit of Congress. It had been done before, in 1933, for the tidy sum of $247,000,000 for
new fighting ships and planes. The Secretary of the
Navy in July, 1934, announced a new beneficence
of $40,700,000 for fourteen destroyers and six sub-
marines—toward the one billion the Vinson specifications foot up to—a mere trifle of forty millions, yet
a token. The new construction ordered and building will bring up the naval strength to exceed that
of Great Britain in number of ships and in tonnage.
The President, during his 1934 cruise in the Pacific,
pledged the crew of the *Houston* a navy built to full
treaty strength in three or four years.

This New Deal nationalism bears no relationship
to the rampant passions aroused by either Fascists
or Nazis. Nor is American life being afflicted by the
real or faked prophecies of imminent wars that trouble the mind of Russians. We do not drill our city
populations in fleeing to dugouts from practice air
raids. We have not begun training the children of
tender years in soldiery. But militariwise, the "Deal"
is really not new. It is "dictated by an inward-look-
ing nationalism." Our people have not yet renounced
resort to war in the nation's interest with any such
degree of finality as they call upon the Communists to
renounce it as a method to gain class ends. The

timely and earnest probe of the Senate Committee into the ways of armament makers, while it stirs us to indignation, at best promises to lead no farther in results than a legislative effort to prevent profits being made out of what passes for patriotism.

This is not the school of political thinking that inspirited the last Democratic administration. It is akin to the movement of post-war economic nationalism which Walter Lippmann says "has driven out the Wilson principles of international coöperation." Raymond Fosdick likewise ranges the two systems in conflict. "The whole philosophy upon which the League of Nations movement rests," he says, "is now being challenged in high places and the next few years are bound to see a struggle for survival between the spirit of the internationalism, represented in the Covenant of the League of Nations, and the older form of nationalism now appearing in a new guise."

PLAYING SAFE ABROAD

The foreign policies of the Administration reflect generally its realistic nationalism. They can be called revolutionary in no respect. They have veered this way and that from the courses pursued by former administrations. Zigzagging is habitually a feature of the United States Government's dealings with other nations. Shifts take place, and not only with a change of parties in Washington. Neither party has a clear line of its own to follow in the conduct of international affairs. This fact constitutes a very considerable hindrance in the way of maintaining satisfactory working relations with powers that have more sense of direction about where they are going.

They do not know where American diplomacy will be heading after today.

Both post-war and pre-war periods of American diplomacy have been marked by these contradictions. The Latin-American countries are treated by turn to reciprocity, intervention, hands off, and All-Western teamwork in a single generation. This Administration is playing the team game with them. The President made this point of policy articulate in a speech before the Woodrow Wilson Foundation in December, 1933. A few days earlier, the Secretary of State at the Pan-American Conference in Montevideo had spoken and voted for embodiment of the principle in treaties binding the respective governments to its observance. This passage occurs in Mr. Roosevelt's address.[14] Nothing could be more palatable to our Latin cousins:

"The maintenance of law and the orderly processes of government in this hemisphere are the concern of each individual nation within its own borders first of all. It is only if and when the failure of orderly processes affects the other nations of the continent that it becomes their concern; and the point to stress is that in such event it becomes the joint concern of a whole continent in which we are all neighbors."

Woodrow Wilson's name in association with foreign affairs calls up the premier spectacle the world saw here of a great situation sacrificed to high politics. Whether the decision by the United States not to enter the League of Nations was wise or not, the contradiction between two branches of the Government was costly to the United States in loss of prestige. The smashing defeat administered to the Democratic Party for that far adventure into internation-

14 The *New York Times*, December 28, 1933.

alism served to dissuade the Party from resuming the
journey.   Of all its first-line figures, Newton D.
Baker has been the only one to keep full faith with
the man who died for the Covenant he inspired and
defended.   The Party's present leader as Chief Executive thus states the policy he pursues League-
wise:

"We are giving coöperation . . . in every matter
which is not primarily political and in every matter
which obviously represents the views and the good
of the peoples of the world as distinguished from
the views and the good of political leaders, of privi-
leged classes, or of imperialistic aims." Judged by
the absence of any known pressure to get the Senate
to act in the matter, entrance to the World Court on
the part of his country does not meet the specifications above.   Or are his energies consumed on objectives nearer home?

The President's personal contribution to international confusion came at the 1933 London Economic
Conference.   As partial preparation for the Conference, distinguished representatives of the British,
French, German, and Italian Governments, on invi-
tation from the White House, came to confer on the
major issues of common interest.   In a radio talk on
May 7, the President named third in the subjects covered "the setting up of a stabilization of currencies
in order to restart the flow of exchange of crops and
goods among nations."   That same month he declared with more urgency: "The Conference must
establish order in place of the present chaos by a stabilization of currencies. . . ."   The following month,
the assembled Conference went on the rocks on being
informed from the same source that the United States

would be unable for the time to participate in any united plan for currency stabilization.

It was a blow from which the practice of conferring internationally for the solution of world problems will be long recovering. The *London Express* cartooned the futile gathering under the caption, "Hiawatha in London." In the reception room of Hotel Economic Conference hung the framed order, "All tomahawks to be left in the coat room." Followed the parody:

> "Came the Ohbewares and Bigtalks,
> Came the Chinwags and the Greatminds,
> Came the Sunshines and the Coldfeet,
> Came the Mournees and Optimahas,
> Came the Wisemen and the Wisecracks,
> Came the Concords and Wontgiveways,
> All the warriors drawn together
> By the signal of the peace pipe."

The big issues which no Administration can ignore have to do with trade, debts, and armaments. About the first, there has been much talk but few agreements. The Yankee trader, it may be suspected, has not yet surrendered sufficiently the notion that there can be selling without buying. The status of the debts is worse than ever. Even token payments have been stopped by the working of a law forbidding loans to nations in default—an Act conceived more in spite than in reason. Devaluation of the dollar reduced them 40 per cent—a gift out of hand in effect.

The course taken toward general disarmament has presented a correct front with little to show in results. The offers made on behalf of the United States in the Disarmament Conference have gone beyond any previously made. They included readi-

ness to join in any measures of reduction to be shared
by all; to submit to inspection to insure compliance
with promises made; to join in consultation with
other powers concerned when the peace was threatened; and, if the United States concurs in the judgment taken to determine the violator of peace, to
refrain from any effort that will thwart action taken
by other nations against an aggressor.

The President further addressed to the nations an
appeal for common action in behalf of peace in terms
that would have real significance if adopted. These
included eliminating over a short period of years, and
by progressive steps, every weapon of offence each
nation possessed, and forbearance from creating any
new ones. Further, the pledge would be taken by
each nation that its armed forces would not be permitted to cross its borders into the territory of another nation. In the present cynical and agitated
state of the European and the Far-Eastern minds, the
proposals went into the international wastebaskets
along with Soviet Russia's bid for all to join in complete disarmament on land, on the sea, and in the
air. Parallel with the presidential offerings goes on
the building of the sea and aircraft of the United
States on a scale to win praise from the Navy League
—always a dubious compliment in the eyes of the
friends of peaceful international ways.

The recognition of Soviet Russia registers another
reversal of a United States Government policy resulting from a change of administrations. Also it may
be called the one single case of political boldness exhibited in the handling of our foreign affairs since
March 4, 1932. Aligned in opposition were the Roman Catholic Church, the American Federation of
Labor, and the American Legion.

The action itself was due. Recognition had become an overrated issue both by those actively for and against it. The fear of red revolution being turned loose never had validity. The company of nations not paying the debts attributed to them had become so large that the Soviet Union of Republics could not be consistently kept out of the house longer on the ground of repudiation. There were evidences, too, of that Government desiring to play the part of a better neighbor.

The positive grounds for recognition most publicized were a bit specious. Litvinoff had dangled before the London Economic Conference an alleged buying market of $1,000,000,000. The ardent pros claimed half of this for the United States. Idle factories would be opened and workmen employed. This was for the consumption of Labor. Nothing has happened to bring orders. The volume has declined almost to invisibility. New trade plans are deadlocked by the combination of Soviet need for credit and the legislation prohibiting loans to non-paying debtors—but Moscow and Washington have hopes.

The "victory" for religious liberty proclaimed in the press as coming out of the negotiations was pure illusion. No concessions were made. Americans in Soviet Russia are subject still to the same limitations thrown around religious observances that they were before. Like the Russian churches, they can conduct the Divine Service, and do precisely nothing else. The other usual activities of the Western churches are denied to them, including the instruction of children outside the home.

If recognition has brought a positive result beyond that of establishing practicable open working relations between two great powers and the resulting

better feeling between their peoples, it is in the direction of possibly checking Japanese aggression in
the Soviet Far East, assuming the Island Empire to
have covetous territorial ambitions toward Siberia.

The whole sums up about to this. The New Deal
for things international is the Old Deal—rather
nearer to George Washington's cautions than to
Woodrow Wilson's visions. The plain man (for
whom Will Rogers speaks, and whom this Administration heeds) probably wants it that way. There
is much to be said for his view. Embarrassment or
worse has overtaken Uncle Sam on most occasions
when he has stepped out of the home circle. Again
and again, he has been caught out—confused about
where he really wanted to go. The "war to end
war" he got into appears after the fact to have been
sadly misnamed. The peace that followed looks more
like a prolific breeder of wars, little and big. The
lending spree abroad exchanged a lot of his easy
war profits into stacks of bad paper.

But no one tells him how he can stay at home with
the huge surpluses of farm products his farmers can
and want to raise. It was export of those crops and
of his manufactures that helped induce his high-
powered prosperity with its long payrolls and high
wages. Can he be contented self-contained a second
century, as he was in 1800? The internationally
minded wise men of the time unanimously say
"No." And the same answer, they think, goes for
all the world. In any case, the New Deal is playing
the foreign game "safe." It has no world revolution
up its sleeve. It is satisfied with its space on the map.

SELECTED BIBLIOGRAPHY
(Presenting Varied Points of View)

PART I—COMMUNIST U.S.S.R.

Chamberlin, William H. *Russia's Iron Age*. Boston. Little, Brown and Company. 1934. $4.00.

Colton, Ethan. *The XYZ of Communism*. New York. The Macmillan Company. 1931. $3.00.

Counts, George S., and Lodge, Nucia. *New Russia's Primer*. Boston. Houghton Mifflin Company. 1931. $1.75.

Hindus, Maurice. *The Great Offensive*. New York. Harrison Smith and Robert Haas. 1933. $3.00.

Lenin, V. I. *The State and Revolution*. New York. International Publishers Company. 1932. $1.50 (paper 30 cents).

Robinson, G. T. *Rural Russia Under the Old Régime*. New York. Longmans, Green and Company. 1932. $4.00.

Stalin, Joseph. *Leninism*. New York. International Publishers Company. 1928-1933. Vols. 1 and 2. $2.50 each.

State Planning Commission. *Summary of the Fulfilment of the First Five Year Plan*. Moscow. 1933. $1.00.

Woody, Thomas. *New Minds: New Men*. New York. The Macmillan Company. 1932. $4.00.

PART II—FASCIST ITALY

Barnes, James S. *Universal Aspects of Fascism*. London. Williams and Norgate, Ltd. 1929. 10s. 6d.

Currey, Muriel. *Italian Foreign Policy, 1918-1932*. London. Nicholson and Watson, Ltd. 1932. 18s.

Dutt, R. Palme. *Fascism and Social Revolution*. New

York. International Publishers Company. 1934. $2.25.

Haider, Carmen. *Capital and Labor under Fascism.* New York. Columbia University Press. 1930. $4.50.

Munro, Ion S. *Through Fascism to World Power.* London. Alexander Maclehose and Company. 1933. 12s. 6d.

Mussolini, Benito. *Political and Social Doctrines of Fascism.* London. The Hogarth Press. 1933. 1s.

Pitigliani, Fausto. *The Italian Corporative State.* New York. The Macmillan Company. 1934. $2.50.

Salvemini, Gaetano. *Fascist Dictatorship in Italy.* New York. Henry Holt. 1927. $3.00.

Silani, Tommaso, Editor. *What Is Fascism and Why?* New York. The Macmillan Company. 1931. $5.00.

Strachey, Evelyn John St. Loe. *The Menace of Fascism.* New York. Covici, Friede, Inc. 1933. $2.25.

PART III–NAZI GERMANY

Anonymous. *Germany: Twilight or New Dawn?* New York. McGraw-Hill Book Company. 1933. $2.00.

Dawson, W. H. *Germany Under the Treaty.* New York. Longmans, Green and Company. 1933. $3.00.

Henri, Ernst. *Hitler Over Europe.* New York. Simon and Schuster. 1934. $1.90.

Hitler, Adolph. *My Battle.* Boston. Houghton Mifflin Company. 1933. $3.00.

Hoover, Calvin B. *Germany Enters the Third Reich.* New York. The Macmillan Company. 1933. $2.50.

MacFarland, Charles S. *The New Church and the New Germany.* New York. The Macmillan Company. 1934. $2.25.

Mowrer, Edgar A. *Germany Puts the Clock Back.* New York. William Morrow and Company. 1933. $2.50.

Schmidt, Richard, and Grabovsky, Adolph, Editors. *Disarmament and Equal Rights.* Berlin. Carl Heymans Verlag. 1934.

Shuster, George N. *Strong Man Rules.* New York. Appleton-Century Company. 1934. $2.00.

PART IV—NEW DEAL AMERICA

Dearing, Charles L., and others. *The ABC of the New Deal.* Washington, D. C. The Brookings Institution. 1934. $1.50.

Landis, Benson Y. *Must the Nation Plan?* New York. Association Press. 1934. $2.00.

McDonald, William. *The Menace of Recovery.* New York. The Macmillan Company. 1934. $2.50.

Ogburn, William F., Editor. *Social Change and the New Deal.* Chicago. University of Chicago Press. 1934. $1.00.

Robey, Ralph. *Roosevelt Versus Recovery.* New York. Harper and Brothers. 1934. $2.00.

Roosevelt, Franklin D. *On Our Way.* New York. The John Day Company. 1934. $2.50.

Thomas, Norman. *The Choice Before Us.* New York. The Macmillan Company. 1934. $2.50.

Tugwell, Rexford Guy. *The Industrial Discipline.* New York. Columbia University Press. 1933. $2.50.

Unofficial Observer. *The New Dealers.* New York. Simon and Schuster. 1934. $2.75.

Wallace, Schuyler C. *The New Deal in Action.* New York. Harper and Brothers. 1934. $2.00.

RELATED WORKS

Beard, Charles A. *The Open Door at Home.* New York. The Macmillan Company. 1934. $3.00.

Chase, Stuart. *The Economy of Abundance.* New York. The Macmillan Company. 1934. $3.00.

Columbia University Commission. *Economic Reconstruction.* 1934. $3.00.

Dean, Vera Micheles, and others. *New Governments in Europe.* New York. Thomas Nelson and Sons. 1934. $2.50.

Hoover, Herbert. *The Challenge to Liberty.* New York. Charles Scribner's Sons. 1934. $1.75.

Johnson, F. Ernest, and others. *Economics and the Good*

Life. New York. Association Press. 1934. $1.50 (paper $1.00).

Leven, M., and others. *America's Capacity to Consume.* Washington, D. C. The Brookings Institution. 1934. $3.00.

Lippmann, Walter. *The Method of Freedom.* New York. The Macmillan Company. 1934. $1.50.

Nourse, Edwin G., and others. *America's Capacity to Produce.* Washington, D. C. The Brookings Institution. 1934. $3.50.

Salter, Sir Arthur. *The Framework of an Ordered Society.* New York. The Macmillan Company. 1933. 75 cents.

Soule, George. *The Coming American Revolution.* New York. The Macmillan Company. 1934. $2.50.

The President's Committee. *Recent Social Trends.* Vols. 1 and 2. New York. McGraw-Hill Book Company. 1933. $10.00 (to schools and colleges, $5.00).

INDEX

Agriculture: 31, 113, 150, 183, 224, 259
Agricultural Adjustment Administration: 228, 244, 261
Alexander, King of Jugoslavia: 145, 147
American Federation of Labor: 249, 258
Anschluss: 145
Armament: 74, 78, 146, 157, 210, 213, 296, 301
Armies: 71, 93
Aryan Clause: 198, 201
Austria: 145, 146, 219
Avanguardisti: 119, 121

Baker, Newton D.: 300
Balilla: 119, 121
Berle, A. A.: 237
Bolsheviks: 2
Bulgaria: 146
Brüning: 186

Capitalism: 23, 28, 39, 76, 78, 105, 133, 168, 171, 230, 272, 273
Chamber of Commerce, of the U. S.: 240, 242, 273
Chamberlin, W. H.: 29, 34, 36, 55
Chambers (*Staende*): 168
Civilian Conservation Corps: 278
Class War, theory and practice of: 5
Clemenceau, Georges: 142, 212
Collective bargaining: 110, 249
Communist Party:
  and backward peoples, 70
  and education, 44
  and labor, 22
  and morals, 65
  and national self-determination, 68
  and New Deal, 246
  and religion, 58
  and world revolution, 74

Communist Party (Cont.):
  Central Committee of, 9
  civil organizations of, 10
  class-war theory, 4
  "Cleanings" of, 9, 37
  Commission of Control, 13
  Congress of, 9
  Functions of, 11
  in Germany, 162, 164
  membership of, 9
  official name of, 4
  Political Bureau of, 9
  political sections of, 12
  power of, 11
  rôle of, 21
  theory of the State, 6
Communist Youth, League of: 11
Company Unions: 250
Constitution, of the United States: 227
Consumers: 254
Controlled economy: 13, 20, 27, 96, 100, 105, 116, 118, 170, 183, 186, 226, 240, 244, 255, 262, 288
Corbino, Senator: 127
Corporative State: 256
  basic claim for, 111
  confederations of, 98
  corporations of, 99
  Ministry of Corporations in, 102
  National Council of Corporations, 101
  National Federations of, 98, 114
  Occupational Associations, 96, 113
  Provincial Unions, 98
Council of People's Commissars, commission of Soviet Control of the, 12
Currency: 228, 245, 300
Czechoslovakia: 146

309

Wages: 19, 27, 49, 110, 174, 179, 244
Wallace, Henry A.: 237, 264, 275
"War Guilt": 149
Wilson, Woodrow: 142, 151, 212, 215, 293, 298, 299, 304
Women: 48, 73, 131, 175, 195, 277

Work hours: 19, 24, 110, 129, 179, 244, 254
World revolution: 75

Yaroslavsky, Emil: 59
Youth: 52, 125, 196, 275, 277, 284

Zinoviev, Gregory: 75